ANYTHING GOES

The Death of Honesty

THEODORE DALRYMPLE

Monday Books

A CIP catalogue record for this title is available
from the British Library

ISBN: 978-1-906308-09-4

Typeset by Andrew Searle
Printed and bound by CPI Group (UK) Ltd, Croydon, CR0 4YY

www.mondaybooks.com
http://mondaybooks.wordpress.com/
info@mondaybooks.com

Contents

Foreword

We live in curious times (though it is possible that all times are curious in one way or another). To a degree that is not within my living memory, we now feel obliged to avoid saying what we think and to say what we do not think. The self-censorship is therefore both negative and positive: there are things that we cannot say, and things that we must say. The latter is probably worse in its effects than the former, since a degree of negative self-censorship has always been a necessary part of social existence.

What is the reason for this increased self-censorship? We do not yet live under a regime of open terror, in which we fear the midnight knock on the door. Even if every telephone call is recorded and available to the government whenever it deems it necessary to listen in to us, we do not live in fear of the government unless we suffer from outright paranoia. If the government is oppressive, it is so in a very muted and discreet way by comparison with dictatorships of the past.

Nevertheless (and if I may be allowed a slightly fanciful metaphor), we live in a Kafka-esque mental and cultural atmosphere, in which we fear to be accused of having entertained dangerous or unorthodox thoughts. The atmosphere is Kafka-esque because the orthodoxy to which we must subscribe is not laid out clearly, it may even be self-contradictory, but it is felt to exist, and to oppose it is to lay oneself open to the charge of heresy.

Like mist or smoke, this atmosphere is able to penetrate even where one would not have expected it to, for example into committees in hospitals. There I have listened to obvious untruths pronounced by ambitious nonentities without myself protesting. I too have partaken of the pusillanimity of the age, so I recognise it when I see it.

Perhaps our fundamental problem is our overestimation of power as the only thing worth having, an overestimation particularly dangerous when it is combined with the demagogic insistence that power must be equally distributed in the population: an insistence on an impossibility that, of course, works to the advantage of the demagogues, whose demagoguery gives them a great deal of power, explicit and implicit.

5

Be that as it may, I should like to adapt slightly the supposed dictum of Edmund Burke that all that it necessary for evil to triumph is for good men to do nothing. All that is necessary for untruth to become orthodoxy is for men to be afraid to utter what they think is the truth. Unfortunately, reality is that which will not be mocked; it always has its revenge.

Theodore Dalrymple, September 2011

I TOLD YOU SO

TO SAY I TOLD YOU SO is psychologically gratifying but morally wrong and no doubt rather unattractive; nevertheless, I should have been less than human if I had not many times felt a strong temptation to say it in the wake of the riots that shook England in August 2011 like a tree laden with rotten fruit.

For almost twenty years I had been adverting in the press to the unpleasant and criminal nature of a substantial portion of the young British population, and to the degraded nature of the life lived in large parts of our cities. In so far as anyone took any notice of what I wrote, it was almost always to accuse me of cynicism, misanthropy, class prejudice, snobbery, exaggeration, anecdotalism or outright fabrication. I was asked more than once whether I made up the stories I relayed from the general hospital and prison in which I worked as a doctor, these stories being apparently beyond the capacity of those who asked the question to conceive of as being true, though survey after survey showed that the phenomena I was describing were widespread and were evident to anyone with the most minimal powers of observation. Indeed, it seemed to me to require extraordinary willpower, manifested by voluntary blindness, *not* to see them. Of course, it is true that I did alter details, for obvious reasons, and tried to give some literary polish to the stories; but in essence, they were true and if anything underplayed the violence and depravity that I heard about and witnessed day after day, year after year. I once attempted to keep a diary of all that I saw and heard, taken down without any attempt at literary refashioning, in the most literal possible way; but I soon realised that it would have been impossible to read, so appalling was what I had to record. The diary depressed me terribly, and I had to stop keeping it after about four days; I realised then that my literary refashioning of the stories I heard was necessary for me as well as for the reader, because I needed to distance myself from the raw, terrible reality.

It is true that my sample of English life was a selected one, but it was not small; in all, I heard about the lives of five per cent of the inhabitants of the city, itself a large one, and my hospital was one of only four that served a similar population. There was no reason to suppose that the stories I would have heard in any of the other hospitals had I worked in them would have been substantially different, either in nature or number. In other words, my anecdotes, amusing as I hoped them to be, were indicative of something of the greatest national importance, much more important indeed than a lot of what passed for important news.

Well, the riots illuminated as if by lightning flash the social landscape that I had been trying, with very limited success, to describe for my fellow citizens who seemed determined not to see it. Suddenly they could not avert their gaze from reality, and it appalled them, as well it might. They were discomfited.

However, the work of psychic healing – that is to say, the restoration of wilful and comforting blindness – by means of intellectual and emotional dishonesty started at once. Many were those who spoke of the tragedy of the rioters having destroyed amenities in the very areas in which they themselves lived, such that the quality of their lives would be yet worsened by their own activities.

This is by now an old way by which intellectuals seek to demonstrate their compassion to the world, their superior comprehension of the predicament of others, and their own absence of unattractive condemnatory rigour.

A few years ago, for example, I was briefly interviewed on the BBC in the company of a junior minister, in the wake of some relatively minor riots in the poorer areas of some of our cities. The minister, with the intonation of constipated compassion that we have come to know so well, said that one of the tragedies of the riots was that the rioters rioted in their own areas, to which I retorted by asking her whether she thought it would be better if they came to riot in *her* area. (I was reminded of Afrikaner policemen during the years of apartheid who referred to black rioters in townships as having 'fouled their own nest.' The only difference between the Afrikaner policemen and the minister was that while the former approved, the latter disapproved.) My question she ignored, as if it were not the question of a gentleman, though in fact (in my opinion) it went straight to the heart of her patent dishonesty, exposing her opinion as insincere, untruthful and offered purely for rhetorical effect. It demonstrated that the riots, and the questions they raised, interested her not at all; what interested her was herself and her political standing with a large section of the population that was also predisposed to such dishonesty for fear of having to face unpleasant reality.

I was invited in the wake of the riots in 2011 on to a well-known foreign television station; my fellow guest on the programme was a man of liberal sympathies. Most of what he said was perfectly sensible, but when I suggested that one of the reasons for the riots was the violent and degraded nature of much of British culture and social life, for example the grotesque public drunkenness that is to be witnessed up and down the country every Friday and Saturday night, with virtually no attempt at control by anyone, thus demonstrating to all the impunity of bad behaviour, he clearly bridled. There was a difference, he said, between people getting 'pissed' (the word he used, thus demonstrating the vulgarisation not only of British life, but of British minds) on a Friday or Saturday night and burning down buildings in riots.

Now obviously this is quite right in a narrow sense. A drunk and an arsonist *are* different. But human life is lived in a context, psychological and social (or, in this case, antisocial). What my fellow guest wanted to imply by his rejection of my point was that, while there was something wrong with the social *milieu* from which the rioters came, it was a circumscribed problem: that the rioters were a kind of *lumpenproletariat*, to use a Marxist phrase, shall we say five per cent of the population isolated or 'excluded' from the rest of society, but that otherwise there was not much to worry about in Britain, that its liberal and permissive mores were perfectly fine.

This is not realistic, nor is it intended to be realistic: it is intended to be comforting. Among other things, it is intended to protect liberal intellectuals from the painful necessity of having to rethink their whole world-outlook, and from having to accept at least some of the blame for the deeply unpleasant nature of contemporary British society.

Let me here resort to anecdote to illustrate my point.

I live when in England in a small town in Shropshire (to whose surrounding countryside I respond emotionally as to no other in the world). By day, it is delightful; my house abuts a charming Elizabethan cottage near church grounds that look as if they materialised from an Anthony Trollope novel. By night, however, it is transformed, invaded by standard British youths who come to get drunk, scream, shout, and impose themselves upon the quiet streets, whose residents have simply to put up with it and suffer in silence the drunken vandalism to their property. The average age of the person on the street drops from 60 to 20, with few older people venturing out. Charm and delight vanish. Not long ago, my street awoke to the sound of a young man being kicked almost to death by other young men, all of whom had spilled forth from a pub at 2am. The driver of a local taxi service, who accepts only prearranged pick-ups, tells me that it is now normal (in the statistical sense) for young women to emerge from the bars and try to entice him to drive them home by baring their breasts, even pushing them against his windows if for some reason he has to stop in town. (I laughed when hearing this, but in essence it is not funny.)

To all this, the criminally-stupid Shropshire council had responded by extending the licensing hours of the pub where most of the aggressive, noisy and destructive young men and women gather until four in the morning, without the slightest consultation with the townspeople or reference to their interests.

Recently I stayed a couple of nights in the middle of the week in Manchester, in the Palace Hotel on the Oxford Road. On one of the nights I was woken at about one in the morning by the sound of drunken British revellers, a sound that to me has all the charm of a fascist rally. The drunken screaming and shouting continued until about four; the next morning, right outside the front door, there were police lines with the familiar tape saying 'do not cross', and a forensic tent within. A man had been beaten nearly to death there at about 1.30 in the morning, and was still in a coma in hospital. The event had not interrupted the drunkenness, however, which had continued unabated and, presumably, uninterrupted by any authority; in England, there is scant difference between the sound of people enjoying themselves and people being murdered.

My Shropshire taxi driver was talking not about an isolated transgression of customs but about a whole manner of cultural comportment. By no means coincidentally, the young British find themselves hated, feared, and despised throughout Europe, wherever they gather to have what they call 'a good time'. They turn entire Greek, Spanish, and Turkish resorts into B-movie Sodoms and Gomorrahs. They cover pavements with vomit, rape one another, and indulge in casual drunken violence. In one Greek resort, 12 young British women were arrested recently after indulging in 'an outdoor oral sex competition'.

Another anecdote comes to my mind, this time not about drunkenness, but about impunity – often in the context of drunken violence, however. I wrote to the Chief Constable of my city to complain that assaults in the hospital in which I worked were not dealt with properly by the police; that they neither arrested nor charged those responsible for them. Chief Constables in Britain having long since been turned into political eunuchs, much more concerned with the preservation of their favour with political overlords than with the preservation of the peace, the Chief Constable replied that what I said was not true, that the police always took such assaults seriously. Such a reply could only mean ignorance or deliberate untruth; be that as it may, within a short time notices appeared in the hospital to the effect that, from then on, anyone who committed an assault in the hospital would be arrested and charged. Not only was this a tacit admission that my complaint had been justified, but it seemed also a tacit admission that, in most circumstances and most places other than in the hospital, assault would be ignored.

The connection with drunkenness is obvious: for a large percentage of those who commit assault or are victims of assault are drunk. (The connection between drunkenness and violence is more complex than is often supposed and is not simply a pharmacological effect of alcohol. Behaviour while under the influence of alcohol depends upon personal disposition but also – perhaps more importantly – upon social context. As I am sure many readers know, it is perfectly possible to be drunk without becoming aggressive or violent.)

A society in which the above anecdotes are not only possible, but representative of its ethical, legal and administrative mores, should not be surprised if a section of its population, believing itself to have been deprived of its inalienable right to a high standard of living, full of grievance but also aware of its own radical worthlessness, with no ethical boundaries worth the name, and with a culture that celebrates the most degraded conduct, should from time to time exhibit the full beauty of its collective personality. But a great deal of the responsibility lies with those who not only have persistently and wilfully failed to notice that an education costing £50,000 per head has equipped these young people with no useful attainments, not even the ability to read, write or reckon; who have promoted every possible way to encourage family breakdown (or rather, the

13

non-formation of a family in the first place); but have also persuaded the objects of their social experimentation that they are endowed by their governments with certain inalienable rights, among these being a level of consumption equal to those who work hard, save money, display determination and have learnt difficult skills. 'We are fed up with being broke,' said one rioter, as if the quality of being flush with money were normal, natural and a human right.

The promotion of rights to tangible benefits leads eventually to a vile mentality, which oscillates between ingratitude at best − for why should they be grateful for the receipt of something that is a right? − and resentment at worst. Resentment, the only human emotion that can last a lifetime, provides infinite justification for one's own bad actions. He who stokes resentment stokes riots.

THE QUIVERING UPPER LIP

WHEN MY MOTHER ARRIVED in England as a refugee from Nazi Germany, shortly before the outbreak of World War II, she found the people admirable, though not without the defects that corresponded to their virtues. By the time she died, two-thirds of a century later, she found them rude, dishonest, and charmless. They did not seem to her, moreover, to have any virtues to compensate for their unpleasant qualities. I occasionally asked her to think of some, but she couldn't; and neither, frankly, could I.

It wasn't simply that she had been robbed twice during her last five years, having never been the victim of a crime before – experiences that, at so advanced an age, would surely change anyone's opinion of one's fellow citizens. Few things are more despicable, after all, or more indicative of moral nihilism, than a willingness to prey upon the old and frail. No, even before she was robbed she had noticed that a transvaluation of all values seemed to have taken place in her adopted land. The human qualities that people valued and inculcated when she arrived had become mocked, despised, and repudiated by the time she died. The past really was a foreign country; and they did do things differently there.

What, exactly, were the qualities that my mother had so admired? Above all, there was the people's manner. The British seemed to her self-contained, self-controlled, law-abiding yet tolerant of others no matter how eccentric, and with a deeply ironic view of life that encouraged them to laugh at themselves and to appreciate their own unimportance in the scheme of things. If Horace Walpole was right – that the world is a comedy to those who think and a tragedy to those who feel – the English were the most thoughtful people in the world. They were polite and considerate, not pushy or boastful; the self-confident took care not to humiliate the shy or timid; and even the most accomplished was aware that his achievements were a drop in the ocean of possibility, and might have been much greater if he had tried harder or been more talented.

Those characteristics had undoubted drawbacks. They could lead to complacency and philistinism, for if the world was a comedy, nothing was serious. They could easily slide into arrogance: the rest

15

of the world can teach us nothing. The literary archetype of such arrogance was Mr Podsnap in Dickens's *Our Mutual Friend*, a man convinced that all that was British was best, and who 'had even acquired a peculiar flourish of his right arm in often clearing the world of its most difficult problems, by sweeping them behind him.' Still, taken all in all, my mother found the British culture of the day possessed of a deep and seductive, if subtle and by no means transparent or obvious, charm.

My mother was not alone. André Maurois, the great French Anglophile, for example, wrote a classic text about British character, *Les silences du Colonel Bramble*. Maurois was a translator and liaison officer between the French and British armies during World War I and lived closely for many months with British officers and their men. *Les silences* was the fruit of his observations. Maurois found the British combination of social self-confidence and existential modesty attractive. It was then a common French opinion that the British were less intelligent than the French; and in the book, Maurois' fictional alter ego, Aurelle, discusses the matter with one of the British officers.

'Don't you yourself find,' said Major Parker, 'that intelligence is valued by you at more than its worth? We are like the young Persians of whom Herodotus speaks, and who, until the age of twenty, learnt only three things: how to ride, archery and not to lie.'

Aurelle spots the paradox. 'You despise the academic,' he replies, 'and you quote Herodotus. Even better, I caught you the other day *in flagrante*, reading Xenophon... Very few French, I assure you...'

Parker quickly disavows any intellectual virtue in his choice of citations or reading matter. 'That's very different,' he says. 'The Greeks and Romans interest us, not as an object of enquiry, but as our ancestors and as sportsmen. I like Xenophon – he is the perfect example of a British gentleman.'

Forty years later, in 1959, another French writer, Tony Mayer, in his short book *La vie anglaise*, noticed the reluctance of the English to draw attention to their accomplishments, to blow their own trumpets: 'Conversation still plays an important role in England. They speak a lot, but in general they say nothing. As it is bad form to mention personal or professional matters which could lead to discussion, they prefer to speak in generalities.' The Franco-Romanian playwright Eugène Ionesco brilliantly parodied this tendency in his *La cantatrice chauve* (*The Bald Soprano*), in which a respectable English couple has a long conversation at a dinner party. At the end, after many pages of utter banalities, they realise that they are actually married, and have been for a long time.

Appearances in Britain could deceive. The British, after all, despised intellectuals, but were long at the forefront of intellectual inquiry; they were philistines, yet created a way of life in the countryside as graceful as any that has ever existed; they had a state religion, but came to find religious enthusiasm bad form. Mayer comments:

> Even in the most ordinary places and circumstances, an accident happens. You hit by chance upon a subject that you have long studied; you go as far as allowing your interest in it to show. And suddenly you realise that your interlocutor – so reserved, so polite – not only knows a hundred times more about this subject than you, but about an infinite number of other subjects as well.

This attractive modesty mixed also with a mild perfidy (this is *la perfide Albion* we are talking of, after all): irony, understatement, and double meaning were everywhere, waiting to trap the unwary foreigner. The British lived as if they had taken to heart the lines of America's greatest poet (who, not coincidentally, lived her whole life in New England):

> Tell all the Truth but tell it slant Success in Circuit lies . . .

The habit of indirection in speech, combined with probity of action, gave English life its savour and its interest. Mayer provided a brief interpretive key for the unwary:

> I may be wrong – I am absolutely sure. I don't know much about – I am a specialist in. No trouble at all – What a burden! We must keep in touch – Goodbye forever. Must you go? – At last! Not too bad – Absolutely wonderful.

The orderliness and restraint of political life in Britain also struck my refugee mother. The British leaders were not giants among men but – much more important for someone fleeing Nazi Germany – they were

17

not brutes, either. They were civilised men; the nearest they came to the exercise of arbitrary power was a sense of *noblesse oblige*, and the human breast is capable of far worse sentiments. Politics was, to them and the voters, only part of life, and by no means the most important. Maurois' Dr O'Grady describes to Aurelle what he calls 'the safety-valve of parliament': 'From now on, elected champions have our riots and *coups d'état* for us in the chamber, which leaves the rest of the nation the leisure to play cricket.' Major Parker takes up the theme, also addressing Aurelle: 'What good has it done you French to change government eight times in a century? The riot for you has become a national institution. In England it would be impossible to make a revolution. If people gathered near Westminster shouting slogans, a policeman would tell them to go away and they would go.'

Many remarked upon the gentleness of British behaviour in public. Homicidal violence and street robberies were vanishingly rare. But it wasn't only in the absence of crime that the gentleness made itself felt. British pastimes were peaceful and reflective: gardening and the keeping of pigeons, for example. Vast sporting crowds would gather in such good order that sporting events resembled church meetings, as both George Orwell and anthropologist Geoffrey Gorer (writing in 1955) noted.

Newsreels of the time reinforce the point. The faces of people in sports crowds did not contort in hatred, snarling and screaming, but were peaceful and good-humoured, if a little pinched and obviously impoverished. The crowds were almost self-regulating; as late as the early sixties, the British read with incredulity reports that, on the Continent, wire barriers, police baton charges, and tear gas were often necessary to control crowds. Incidents of crowd misbehaviour in Britain were so unusual that when one did happen, it caused a sensation.

The English must have been the only people in the world for whom a typical response to someone who accidentally stepped on one's toes was to apologise oneself. British behaviour when ill or injured was stoic. Aurelle recounts in *Les silences du Colonel Bramble* seeing an officer he knew on a stretcher, obviously near death from a terrible abdominal injury. The officer says to him: 'Please say goodbye to the colonel for me and ask him to write home that I didn't suffer too much. I hope this is not too much trouble for you.

Thanks very much indeed.' Tony Mayer, too, says of the English that when they were ill they usually apologised: 'I'm sorry to bother you, Doctor.'

No culture changes suddenly, and the elderly often retained the attitudes of their youth. I remember working for a short time in a general practice in a small country town where an old man called me to his house. I found him very weak from chronic blood loss, unable to rise from his bed, and asked him why he had not called me earlier. 'I didn't like to disturb you, Doctor,' he said. 'I know you are a very busy man.'

From a rational point of view, this was absurd. What could I possibly need to do that was more important than attending to such an ill man? But I found his self-effacement deeply moving. It was not the product of a lack of self-esteem, that psychological notion used to justify rampant egotism; nor was it the result of having been downtrodden by a tyrannical government that accorded no worth to its citizens. It was instead an existential, almost religious, modesty, an awareness that he was far from being all-important.

I experienced other instances of this modesty. I used to pass the time of day with the husband of an elderly patient of mine who would accompany her to the hospital. One day, I found him so jaundiced that he was almost orange. At his age, it was overwhelmingly likely to mean one thing: inoperable cancer. He was dying. He knew it and I knew it; he knew that I knew it. I asked him how he was. 'Not very well,' he said. 'I'm very sorry to hear that,' I replied. 'Well,' he said quietly, and with a slight smile, 'we shall just have to do the best we can, won't we?' Two weeks later, he was dead.

I often remember the nobility of this quite ordinary man's conduct and words. He wanted an appropriate, but only an appropriate, degree of commiseration from me; in his view, which was that of his generation and culture, it was a moral requirement that emotion and sentiment should be expressed proportionately, and not in an exaggerated or self-absorbed way. My acquaintance with him was slight; therefore my regret, while genuine, should be slight. (Oddly enough, my regret has grown over the years, with the memory.) Further, he considered it important that he should not embarrass me with any displays of emotion that might discomfit me. A man has to think of others, even when he is dying.

My wife, also a doctor, worked solely among the old, and found them, as I did, considerate even when suffering, as well as humorous and lacking in self-importance. Her patients were largely working class – a refutation of the idea, commonly expressed, that the cultural ideal that I have described characterised only the upper echelons of society.

Gradually, but overwhelmingly, the culture and character of British restraint have changed into the exact opposite. Extravagance of gesture, vehemence of expression, vainglorious boastfulness, self-exposure, and absence of inhibition are what we tend to admire now – and the old modesty is scorned. It is as if the population became convinced of Blake's fatuous dictum that it is better to strangle a baby in the cradle than to let a desire remain unacted upon.

Certainly, many Britons under the age of 30 or even 40 now embrace a kind of sub-psychotherapeutic theory that desires, if not unleashed, will fester within and eventually manifest themselves in dangerous ways. To control oneself for the sake of the social order, let alone for dignity or decorum (a word that would either mean nothing to large numbers of the British these days, or provoke among them peals of laughter), is thus both personally and socially harmful.

I have spoken with young British people who regularly drink themselves into oblivion, passing first through a prolonged phase of public nuisance. To a man (and woman), they believe that by doing so they are getting rid of inhibitions that might otherwise do them psychological and even physical harm. The same belief seems universal among those who spend hours at soccer games screaming abuse and making threatening gestures (whose meaning many would put into practice, were those events not policed in military fashion).

Lack of self-control is just as character-forming as self-control: but it forms a different, and much worse and shallower, character. Further, once self-control becomes neither second nature nor a desired goal, but rather a vice to avoid at all costs, there is no plumbing the depths to which people will sink.

No person with the slightest apprehension of human psychology will be surprised to learn that as a consequence of the change in the character of the British, indictable crime has risen at least 900 per cent since 1950. In the same period, the homicide rate has doubled – and would have gone up ten times, had it not been for improvements in trauma surgery and resuscitation techniques. And all this despite the fact that the proportion of the population in the age group most likely to commit crimes has fallen considerably.

Two things are worth noting about this shift in national character: it is not the first such shift in British history; and the change is not entirely spontaneous or the result of impersonal social forces.

Before the English and British became known for self-restraint and an ironic detachment from life, they had a reputation for high emotionalism and an inability to control their passions. The German poet Heinrich Heine, among others, detested them as violent and vulgar. It was only during the reign of William IV – 'Silly Billy,' the king before Victoria – that they transformed into something approaching the restrained people whom I encountered as a child and sometimes as a doctor. The main difference between the vulgar people whom Heine detested and the people loathed and feared throughout Europe (and beyond) today is that the earlier Britons often possessed talent and genius, and in some sense stood in the forefront of human endeavour; we cannot say that of the British now.

But the second point is also important. The moralisation of the British in the first third of the nineteenth century – their transformation from a people lacking self-control into exemplars of restraint – was the product of intellectual and legislative activity. So, too, was the reverse movement.

Consider in this light public drunkenness. For 100 years or more in Britain, the popular view was that such drunkenness was reprehensible and the rightful object of repression. (My heart leaps with joy when I see in France a public notice underscoring the provisions of the law 'for the suppression of public drunkenness.') Several changes then came: officials halved the tax on alcohol; intellectuals attacked the idea of self-restraint, making it culturally unacceptable; universities unapologetically began to advertise themselves as places where students could get drunk often and regularly; and finally the government, noting that drunkenness was dramatically increasing, claimed that increasing the hours of availability of alcohol would encourage a more responsible, 'Mediterranean' drinking culture, in which people would sip slowly, rather than gulp fast. It is difficult not to suspect also the role of financial inducements to politicians in all this, for even they could hardly be so stupid.

Habits become character. Perhaps they shouldn't, but they do. Therefore, when I hear that some American states seek to lower the drinking age from 21 to 18, on the grounds that it is absurd that an 18-year-old can join the army and die for his country but not drink a beer in a public bar, I experience a strong reaction. It is a more important goal of government to uphold civilisation than to find a general principle that will iron out all the apparent inconsistencies of the current dispensation.

Not long ago, I attended the graduation of a friend's son at an upstate New York university. The night before, and the night after, I observed the students through the windows of their frat houses getting drunk. They were behaving in a silly way, but they were not causing a public nuisance because they did not dare to step out of their houses. If they did, the local police would arrest them; or, if not, the university authorities would catch them and suspend them. (This, incidentally, is powerful evidence that drunks do know what they are doing and that the law is absolutely right not to accept drunkenness as a negation of *mens rea*.)

No doubt the student drunkenness in the frat houses was unsatisfactory from an abstract point of view; but from the point of view of upholding civilisation, to say nothing of the quality of life of the townspeople, it was all highly satisfactory. In England, that town would have been a nightmare at night that no decent person would have wanted to be out in. So I say to Americans: if you want your young people to develop character, have the courage of your inconsistencies! Excoriate sin, especially in public places, but turn a blind eye to it when necessary – as it often is.

THE PAINS OF MEMORY

WE ARE ENJOINED, WHEN we suffer or feel unhappy (which are not necessarily quite the same thing, of course), to consider those who are yet worse off than ourselves. This is supposed to relieve and console us, but it rarely does. The most that it achieves is to make us feel guilty that we are so miserable over comparative trifles when others have so many worse travails than ours; and this in turn makes us feel more wretched than ever. Moreover, there is a curious moral asymmetry at work: while the thought that there are always people worse off than ourselves is supposed to be edifying, the thought that there are always people better off than ourselves is not. Indeed, it is the very reverse, a powerful stimulus to resentment, the longest-lived, most gratifying and most harmful of all emotions.

As children, many of us were told to finish what was on our plate because there were so many hungry people in the world who would have been grateful for what we left. I confess that, at a very early age, I was puzzled by this line of moral reasoning: I did not see how the hungry people of Africa would be helped if I stuffed food I really did not want down my protesting gullet. But a home is not a parliament, and I did, more or less, what I was told.

Youth, it is often said, is a generous age, fully of pity and compassion. I do not agree: I think it is mainly an age of self-pity, when one is inclined to imagine that the problems of growing up are the greatest problems in the world. 1968 in Paris, for example, was all about self-pity, not about making the world a better place. You can see from the photographs that the student rioters were spoilt and narcissistic children, posing carefully for the photographers.

In France, there has been a huge 40th anniversary outpouring of books devoted to the events of 1968, and one in particular caught my eye and angered me: a book of posters and caricatures by the student participants. I opened it, and there was a caricature of de Gaulle, his face revealed as a mask behind which was his real face, that of Hitler. I slammed the book shut in disgust. What whippersnappers the *soixante-huitards* were!

Shortly after then, I was taught physiology by a woman called Gerta Vrbova, later a professor. She was very distinguished in her field, neuro-muscular physiology, and world-famous in it: though, of course, you could go a very long way on an average street before you met anyone who knew anything of her subject, or even of its existence.

I regret to say that I was not a very good student, not being gifted in the right fashion and, to be honest, not very conscientious either. I wish now that I had been more attentive, but at the time I was only intellectually aware, not emotionally aware, that time's arrow flew in one direction only. I still thought my life was so long that there would be time for everything, and that no omission on my part would have lasting or irrecoverable consequences.

Everyone in the department knew that Dr Vrbova had suffered greatly in the war, but she never spoke of it. On the contrary, her work appeared far more important to her than her past; most of us were too young, too callow and too spoilt to appreciate the depth of the kind of suffering that she had endured. And so it was with great interest that I recently came across her memoir, *Trust and Deceit*, quite by chance. It starts with a moving explanation of why she wrote it (in 2006):

> I should like to explain why I now feel the need to extract from my memory people, places and events that have been buried there for half a century. After all, 'forgetting' them was what helped me to live a normal life, pursue my career as a scientist and bring up my children, with what I hope was minimal damage.
>
> Yet the burden of my past, the memories of my loving family who perished in the gas chambers of Nazi Germany and the story of my own survival are now haunting me and demanding that they be written down so that they should not be irretrievably lost.

Dr Vrbova was born in Slovakia of bourgeois Jewish parentage, speaking German at home and Slovak at school. Her father was a businessman who trusted to the fundamental goodness of his neighbours and fellow citizens, and in the protection of the law, refusing to emigrate despite all the signs of trouble to come, until it was too late. (One of his employees, whom he had always treated well, joyfully took over his business without a qualm when the opportunity arose as a result of anti-Semitic legislation, and of course ran it into the ground, just as the new African owners did when Idi Amin confiscated Indian-owned businesses in Uganda.)

Dr Vrbova's family fled to Budapest because of the comparatively mild regime there of Admiral Horthy; but Horthy was replaced by Hitler because he was not anti-Semitic enough, and the subsequent regime grew much more murderous. On the final occasion that Dr Vrbova saw her father, he said to her, 'You must forgive me that I have always made the wrong decisions, and brought you into danger. Your mother wanted us to emigrate, but I had too much trust in my fellow citizens...' With dignified poignancy, Dr Vrbova, who was 17 when this happened, writes, 'Somehow I knew that this was the last time I would see him.' And it was.

She and her mother were arrested by the Gestapo, but on the sixth day of her interrogation, Dr Vrbova managed to escape by jumping out of a window while the guard's back was turned. She wanted her mother to go with her, but her mother could not face the danger of escape and stayed behind; she did not really want to live any longer and was deported to Auschwitz where she was gassed.

Remaining at large, Dr Vrbova met up with some young men on the run. One of them fell in love with her and wanted her to sleep with him, but she was not attracted to him and refused. Neither of them had ever had sexual relations; he was killed the next day, and she felt deeply sad for the rest of her life that she had not agreed to give him his moment of ecstasy before he died.

To have made a distinguished career after such experiences (and many others that I have omitted), to have found life still to be worthwhile, to have been able to deal equably with spoilt young middle class students who had experienced nothing remotely comparable to all that she had suffered by the age of 17, and whose idea of conflict and suffering was not being allowed by their parents to stay out after ten o'clock at night, was admirable.

It was her forgetfulness – a very different thing from amnesia – that made it possible. By forgetfulness I mean the decision to put these terribly painful things to the back of her mind. She must have understood that dwelling on them was of no use if she were to live a tolerable life; that if she were not forgetful in that sense, she would never smile or enjoy anything again; but that now that she was approaching the end of her life, things were different:

I owe those who did not survive the Holocaust, as well as those who might benefit from my experience, an account of my observations of certain events that took place in Europe during those terrible years when a highly sophisticated society perpetrated the most horrible crimes in history.

It was not only because Dr Vrbova taught (or rather, tried to teach) me that I found her book so moving. My mother died in 2005 aged 85. She came to England from Nazi Germany in 1939. Her father was a doctor who evidently had also not seen the writing on the wall, just like Dr Vrbova's father had not. A major in the German army in the First World War, he was a German patriot who had won two Iron Crosses.

After my mother's death, I found a cache of letters from her father, some from Nazi Germany and the rest (after July 1939) from Shanghai, to where he managed to escape with his wife and older daughter. The language in which these letters were written changed abruptly from German to English on 4 September 1939.

The letters from Germany describe, without commentary, his journeys to all the embassies and consulates in search of a visa. It came as a surprise to me, for example, that Haiti maintained a consulate in Nazi Germany. No South American country would accept him; eventually, China did.

In 1942, from Shanghai, he wrote:

It is a beautiful spring day and the sun is shining brightly. But there is no sun bright enough to penetrate the dark clouds that are covering the whole earth.

My mother was 21 at the time.

In 1945, she received a letter from her sister asking her in what language she wanted the gravestones of her two parents: German or English?

There was another cache of letters, tied up still in red ribbon. It was of letters from her first fiancé, a fighter pilot in the Royal Air Force. Among them was the telegram from the War Office, telling her that he had gone missing in the defence of Malta, and another saying, after an interval of a few weeks, he must be presumed dead. There was also a love letter from Malta, written by him on the very day before he went missing; and a letter from his wing-commander giving an eye-witness account of the shooting down of his aircraft.

I discovered many other things from these letters: for example, that my mother had entered domestic service when she arrived in England in order to survive financially. There are other things too painful to disclose.

Now my mother spoke very little of her past, right up to her death. Her memories died with her. She would speak of her childhood up to 30th January 1933 – that of a bourgeois girl growing up – but there was a complete blank (except that she had seen Hitler in the stadium in the 1936 Olympics) until such time as she had found her feet in England. She gave every appearance of having enjoyed the war.

Most of my mother's suffering was unknown to me. Of course, there were people who suffered much worse than she: she never saw the inside of a concentration or extermination camp, for example. But yet, never to have seen her parents again, to have emigrated, friendless and penniless, to another country at the age of 17, and to have lost her fiancé killed in a war: that is enough for any human being.

She dealt with it by silence. When the Mayor of Berlin invited her back to Berlin towards the end of her life, she accepted, much to my surprise; and she pored over a map of the city, pointing out to me where she had lived and where she had gone to school. When she arrived the streets were there, but she recognised nothing; bombs had razed everything to the ground.

I offered to go with her, but she went on her own. It is an unfashionable truth in these times of psychobabble and emotional intelligence, but a trouble shared is often a trouble doubled. She wanted all that she had seen, and all that she suffered, to go with her to the grave, for she was of the pessimistic view that man never learns, at least from the experience of others. I do not entirely agree, and wish she had said more; but she had earned the right to silence.

INFLATION'S MORAL HAZARD

INFORMATION FROM THE MOST diverse sources sometimes coalesces and provokes reflection on a subject to which one has not previously given sufficient thought. This happened to me recently with regard to the effect of monetary inflation on human character. With many observers predicting a substantial rise in inflation as a result of various government spending programmes undertaken to reverse the current global downturn, the topic is anything but academic.

I was reading *The Innocence of Edith Thompson*, by Lewis Broad, a book written in the 1950s about a murder in 1920s London. Freddy Bywaters was a handsome young sailor, Edith Thompson an unsatisfactorily married woman. They had a torrid love affair, and Bywaters eventually stabbed Thompson's husband to death as he walked home one evening from the theatre with his wife. Thompson's love letters to Bywaters, prosecutors claimed, were an incitement to murder – such an incitement that they rendered her a murderess herself. She was found guilty and hanged.

Broad's book happens to mention Thompson's comparative prosperity. She managed a millinery shop and earned enough to put her in the middle class: 'six pounds per week', as the author puts it, 'or twelve pounds in our debased currency.' A doubling of prices in three decades called a debasement of the currency? What would Broad have written if he knew what was to come in the years ahead?

Then I began reading *Ursa Major*, a study of Doctor Johnson by C.E. Vulliamy. It was hostile to the great man; but from the point of view of inflation, what was interesting was Johnson's pension from the Crown. Worth £300 per year when granted in 1762, Vulliamy informs us, it would have been worth £800 at the time of *Ursa Major*'s publication in 1946.

But that £800, according to Broad's book, would have been worth only £400 as recently as 1921. If we put these two stories together, it means that £300 in 1762 was the equivalent of £400 in 1921; or that in a century and a half, prices rose in Britain by about 33%, an overall rate so slow as to have been almost imperceptible year to year. Such stability must have seemed more a fact of nature than a consequence of human behaviour or policy, and therefore something that would last forever.

I can attest to a prolonged era of price stability from evidence in my own lifetime. When I was born, it cost one and a half times as much to send a letter as it had 100 years earlier. In my childhood, during the 1950s, we still used the same coins, with the same denominations, that people had used during the Victorian era. Occasionally, indeed, we came across pre-Victorian coins and their continued use was not absurd: although prices had risen, they still bore some resemblance to what they had been in the earlier time.

I also remember the vast white £5 notes that my father kept in a roll in his pocket, only 100 or 200 of which would have been needed in those days to buy a decent house. And it was still possible for a boy like me to buy something with the smallest coin of the realm, a farthing, worth one-960th of a pound.

The regime of relative price stability soon collapsed. During the 1960s and 1970s, the sums of money of which everyone spoke increased, first by a little and then by a lot. All that had seemed solid, to paraphrase Marx, melted into air.

At the time, I gave no thought to the effects of this inflation, which tended to be discussed in purely economic terms. In a naive way, I assumed that since most people's income tended to rise with inflation, there was nothing to worry about. I did not suffer personally because of it, nor did most of the people I knew. If a product once cost y and now cost $10y$, what did it matter, so long as your income had gone up by ten times, too? Since people seemed better off, one could even assume that incomes had risen faster than inflation.

Yet this was a crude way of looking at things, as my father's fate should have instructed me. He sold his business in the 1960s, at the end of the period of price stability that had reigned throughout his life, for what then seemed a large amount of money. He was a man who held a deep contempt for financial speculation with the result that he did nothing as inflation inexorably eroded his savings. He grew poorer through the remaining 30 years of his life, and might have sunk into poverty had he not moved into a house that I owned.

For a while, I was angry about what seemed my father's improvidence. As the current financial crisis has conclusively demonstrated, however, not everyone is blessed with foresight, not even those whose livelihood depends on the claim of possessing it. My father was born of a generation that saw money as a store of value, a far from dishonourable notion. And as I reach the age when inflation might cause me some embarrassment, my sympathy with my father's plight has grown. I am no longer young enough to fight another day, economically speaking: the destruction of my wealth by inflation would be final.

Like my father, I am not particularly avaricious; on the other hand, I have no vocation for poverty and share the prejudice of most of mankind that a loss of capital and a sharp decline of income are much to be feared. In an era of price stability, a man of my disposition could judge with a degree of certainty how much money he would need for each year of his retirement. The calculation of how much principal he would require now, in order to yield that amount of money in interest each year in the future, was relatively simple and would yield financial tranquillity.

That kind of tranquillity about one's financial future is more difficult for most of us to achieve now. U.S. President Ronald Reagan and British Prime Minister Margaret Thatcher brought raging inflation under control during the 1980s, but they could not reverse the public's loss of confidence in money as a store of value. People must today try to foresee not only how long they will live but also the reigning economic conditions of the next 40 years. And this, to quote Doctor Johnson in another context, 'requires faculties which it has not pleased our Creator to give us.'

There seems to be no choice, then, but for everyone to have constant regard to his own pile, and to try to outwit the economic moth and rust that threaten to erode all but the largest fortunes: he must speculate, or risk losing nearly everything. The question of whether it is best to hold shares, or bonds, or property, or some combination of them, is constantly before him. Further, funds' managers and investors do not always have the same interests. A man trying to preserve a competence learns to trust neither himself nor others.

Many times I have received advice to borrow as much as I could so that I might buy the best and most expensive house possible. And for many years it seemed good advice, for what could be more advantageous than to buy an appreciating asset with depreciating currency? It was a painless way to become rich.

I did not take the advice. I remained sufficiently a child of the regime of constant prices that I found it difficult to imagine how a sum that seemed vast now would seem trifling in just a few years. Even so, I borrowed within what I thought to be my means, and thereby accumulated assets of a value that I could not have obtained by the steady build up of savings. The curious result has been that at no point in my career could I have afforded to buy the property that I now own, whose value greatly exceeds my cumulative income over the years. If my borrowing had been bolder, the value would exceed my earnings even more.

My situation is no different from that of millions of others. And since we are all richer than we should otherwise be, is there anything to complain about? The problem is that this 'richer' represents a curious kind of wealth. I must live somewhere, and everywhere else has appreciated in value, too. I don't live any better in my house than I did before simply because it is worth three times what I paid for it. Its increase in value is thus of no use to me, unless I want to sell it to live in a less valuable house and invest the difference.

But for many years people have treated rising property values as if they were the real thing, and the government has supported this belief by allowing extremely easy credit.

During those fat years, a man could sit at home watching television and imagine that he was growing richer thereby. I remember an eminent professor telling me that he was making nearly £600 per day merely by owning a very large house in a fashionable area. The government could not have been better pleased, for the majority of the population felt prosperous as never before and attributed their affluence to the government's wise economic guidance.

But asset inflation as the principal source of wealth corrodes the character of people. It not only undermines the traditional bourgeois virtues but makes them ridiculous and even reverses them. Prudence becomes imprudence, sobriety becomes mean-spiritedness, self-control becomes betrayal of the inner self, patience and steadiness becomes inflexibility. And circumstances force almost everyone to join in the dance.

Except in one circumstance: the possession of a salary and a pension that the government promises to index against inflation. This is the situation of public sector workers and is a pyramid scheme, too. But meantime, such employment will seem a safe haven, and the temptation will be for government to expand it, with the happy consequence – for itself – of increasing dependence. And dependence, too, undermines character.

It is no coincidence that the Western leader most worried about a new bout of inflation is German Chancellor Angela Merkel. If there is one thing that Germans agree about, it is the necessity of a sound currency. The hyperinflation of the 1920s brought about a German change in mentality as great as the one caused by the First World War, with what disastrous consequences 50 million dead might attest if they had voice. The solidity of the Deutschmark was the great German achievement of the second half of the twentieth century.

Inflation is not a bogey for everyone – not for those who wish to restructure society, for example. But for the rest of us, the consequences of its full-blown return are not likely to be good: for inflation is not an economic problem only, or even mainly, but one that afflicts the human soul.

FROM MELTING POT
TO STIR-FRY

WITHIN A FEW HUNDRED yards of my flat in London there are Chinese, Thai, Lebanese, Italian, French, Georgian, Persian, Greek, Spanish and Indian restaurants. I suspect that this is the kind of thing people have in mind when they talk of multiculturalism: a different cuisine every night.

Certainly, I am very far from decrying a wide choice of cuisines. We have become so accustomed to such a choice, in fact, that we now find a monotonous diet if not a torment exactly, at least a minor hardship. Some people, indeed, measure the sophistication of a person by the number of cuisines with which he is intimately familiar: and to be able to discourse knowledgeably about the food of a remote country to someone who is completely ignorant of it is to gain a moral ascendancy over him similar in nature to that of an art-lover who can discourse freely on the life of Luca Signorelli to someone in whom that name rings only the faintest of bells if any at all.

I don't exclude myself from these remarks, particularly with regard to the hardship of a monotonous diet. My wife and I were once stuck in a beautiful and unspoilt, because inaccessible, seventeenth-century town on the Rio Magdalena in Colombia, where there was at the time, to all intents and purposes, only one restaurant. And to this day, we can both easily conjure up in our mind's ear the sound of the proprietress reciting the invariant menu. 'Hay carne, hay pollo, hay pescado, hay bagre' (There's beef, there's chicken, there's fish, there's bagre - a kind of catfish whose flesh was muddier even than that of ordinary Rio Magdalena fish) is a kind of private joke between us when we are offered the same meal twice in succession. By the end of a couple of weeks of twice daily meals of the same things cooked the same way with the same accompaniments we would have welcomed even the kind of food that we would not normally have eaten, just for a change, and so long as it wasn't carne, pollo, pescado or bagre.

Not everyone likes variety, of course. I remember reading - how long ago it all seems now! - a textbook of psychology in which it was claimed that babies fell naturally into two great classes, those who were eager to eat what they had never tried before, and those who adamantly refused to do so. Pictures of two babies, one gurgling with delight as the spoon with the new food was pushed in the direction of its mouth, and the other turning away from it in angry disgust, illustrated the text. I have no idea whether this distinction still holds – or even whether it ever did – but I certainly know a child who, from a very early age, refused to eat anything other than a very restricted number of things, calling all else 'slime'. His parents tried to starve him into more catholic tastes, but it was they, rather than he, who gave way.

Naturally, even the most adventurous of eaters usually draws the line somewhere, and finds what others eat to be disgusting. Few of us would anticipate with delight eating the grubs so favoured by the Aborigines, or drinking the mixed blood and milk that is nectar to the Masai. But this does not alter the obvious fact that, in the last half-century, our culinary tastes have altered decisively in the direction of variety, thanks to the unprecedented intermingling of races, nations and cultures brought about by mass migrations and easy travel.

In Britain, for example, with its somewhat limited culinary tradition, the national dish has changed from fish and chips to chicken tikka masala, a dish that does not exist in India yet is clearly of Indian inspiration. There can scarcely be an English town or village with a population of more than 1000 that is without its Indian restaurant, and I have often had occasion to be grateful for this fact. And this fact was a consequence of mass migration.

The invention and acceptance in Britain of the chicken tikka masala is often used as an example of multiculturalism in beneficent action. Not long ago, indeed, I was at a conference in Britain on multiculturalism and - almost on cue as it were - the chicken tikka masala was trotted out and exhibited, much like a prize bull at a dairy show.

It would be easy to produce many other, more important instances of cultural cross-fertilisation. Without some assimilation of foreign elements, cultures are inclined to stagnate and grow stale. The European discovery of Japanese woodblock prints had an immense effect on European art; and the modern art of India, which in my opinion is more vibrant and aesthetically much more interesting and agreeable than our own, makes use of western techniques. The work of exiled and immigrant writers is now often more interesting than that of native metropolitans, and English above all is a language that has been enriched by its ready, indeed eager, assimilation of foreign words and concepts.

Yet no one who values human diversity would (presumably) wish for customs and traditions to be so interpenetrative that no distinct customs and traditions any longer existed. There is therefore something to be said for placing a value on our customs just because they are our customs and we are attached to them. Thai cuisine (of which I happen to be fond) would die out if there were no significant population that valued it above all other cuisines, merely because it happened by accident of birth to be theirs, and not because they had studied all cuisines and come to the conclusion, based upon philosophically indubitable principles, that theirs was the best cuisine in any objective sense.

Nor, of course, do we speak our own language because of its peculiar beauties, strengths and expressiveness, though it may in fact have all these qualities; we speak it because it is ours. When we live at home in our own country, we have no intention of giving up our own language, and to replace it by the languages of immigrants, however numerous the immigrants might be. We have no intention either of learning their languages. And since language is so important a part of culture, our determination, whether we articulate it or not, to continue to speak it by itself calls into doubt the sincerity - or perhaps merely the coherence - of adherents of multiculturalism. Whatever language people may speak in the home, English will remain the language of the public space. This is not chauvinism: it is the mere recognition of the obvious.

Moreover, it is also clear that the customary nature of customs does not and cannot justify all customs whatsoever. Supporters of multiculturalism have cuisine in mind precisely because a preference for one cuisine over another is not a moral or political choice, but a private aesthetic one. 'I like cuisine x because I grew up with it' does not offend us as an explanation; 'I think female circumcision is a good thing because it was the custom among the people with whom I grew up' strikes us as a totally inadequate reason for the continuation of the practice. Patriotism, Dr Johnson once remarked, is the last resort of the scoundrel; but it would be as true, or perhaps more true, to say that custom is the last resort of the scoundrel.

Not all customs or traditions are folklorically picturesque, mere matters of dancing round a village maypole in prettily-embroidered costumes. It hardly needs pointing out that the political traditions of many countries, which arise organically from their culture, are not such as we would wish to see transplanted into our own lands with immigrants from those countries, however delicious their cuisine. Indeed, it is highly likely that the desire to escape the consequences of those political traditions is one of the strongest (though not by any means the only) motive for migrating in the first place. No one would wish to see the Cambodian political experience reproduced elsewhere: for even before the arrival of the Khmer Rouge, it was far from admirable. There is no need for us to look to the Arabs for political guidance either, to put it mildly, though whether they should look to us for such guidance is another and much more difficult question. Our answer will depend upon how evangelical we feel about the liberal democracy that has grown out of our own traditions and historical experience, and how far we think it is of universal application. I confess that I am a sceptic, for two related reasons: first because politics by no means expresses all that is important or admirable about a country (if it did, then the countries with the best polities would be the best in all respects, which is far from being the case), and second because political forms cannot be successfully transplanted unless they are compatible with a country's culture and society.

The reason that India, for example, became and has remained a parliamentary democracy was not because such a democracy was imposed on it - very much to the contrary - but because it accorded with the wishes of its people, or at least a very important and determining section of its people, who saw much to admire in the British example. Had the British resisted independence with the ferocity of, say, the French in Algeria, India's historical experience would have been very different and its present democracy would not have emerged.

Whatever our foreign policy should be - whether we believe we ought to promote the welfare of others or merely to pursue our interests - there is no reason at all for us, indeed there is no real possibility for us, to be multiculturalists at home, if by multiculturalism is meant the granting of legal and social equality, recognition and protection to all the customs, traditions, beliefs and practices whatsoever of immigrants, as if multiculturalism were merely a kind of fusion cooking. Of course, we will spontaneously take from immigrants aspects of their traditions that we find congenial, but this will be an informal assimilation, not mediated by governmental decree. Multiculturalism as a doctrine is just another instance of the tendency of a portion of the intelligentsia to exhibit its virtue and generosity for all the world to see, as well as provide a minor if lucrative source of employment to cultural bureaucrats.

As anyone who has ever tried it knows, understanding another culture is a Herculean labour, even when that culture is comparatively close to one's own. My wife, who is French, speaks English perfectly, but it took her many years of residence to appreciate that the English used words according to context in very different ways, which range from the literal meaning to a meaning precisely the opposite of what they appear to mean. Even now, after a quarter of a century, it surprises her that 'It's been most enjoyable, we must meet again soon,' actually often means 'Under no circumstances do I wish to see you again, and if I did, I would be most put out and embarrassed.' A native would understand this instantly.

If it is not easy for the British and French to understand one another, though they are separated by only twenty miles of water and have been studying and reacting to each other for hundreds of years, and when their cultures are in many respects so similar, what chance is there for people to understand, in any but the most superficial way, the hundreds of extremely diverse cultures from which immigrants now come to our shores? To understand Amharic culture in any detail is the work of a lifetime for a highly intelligent person of American or European background who is determined and motivated to do so; for one person to understand Bengali, Somali, Yemeni and Vietnamese cultures as well (and these are only a handful) is impossible.

It follows from this that it is for immigrants who do us the honour of coming to our country to understand us, not for us to understand them – which is impossible in any case. It is for them to make the mental, intellectual and cultural adjustments, not us. It is a simple as that.

In special circumstances, it is well that certain people should try to learn something of the culture of immigrants. But it is humanity that should demand it, not bureaucratic multiculturalism. As a doctor in an area with many immigrants, I found the fact that I had visited many of the countries from which they came to be a great advantage, for it created a rapport that would not have been easy to create otherwise. It takes little effort of the imagination to understand the relief of a Congolese in a large British city to meet a doctor who had travelled through the Congo (and loved it). And it was very necessary in my work that I should understand the situation of Muslim girls brought up in Britain and forced into unwanted, indeed repellent, marriages to a first cousin in a village in Pakistan. But understanding and sympathy cannot be decreed; besides, the ultimate answer to the problems of the multicultural society is the melting pot, not the solution preferred by bureaucrats and their intellectual allies, the salad bowl (which perhaps one day in Europe at any rate will turn itself into the stir-fry).

In case I should be accused of insensitivity towards immigrants, I should like to point out that I am descended on both sides from refugees, whom integration, brought about informally, without any official direction, served magnificently. Multiculturalism was not a doctrine in their day, a fact for which I am grateful, for otherwise I should now be in the clutches of social workers, housing departments and assorted political entrepreneurs.

PC AMONG THE DOCS

A CONSIDERABLE PROPORTION, if not an outright majority, of the medical profession is of conservative cast of mind: politically, that is, not technically. Perhaps a close and continuous acquaintance with human nature at its limits renders doctors, if not cynical exactly, at least circumspect about the prospects for human perfectibility.

It is surprising, then, that the major medical journals these days, edited entirely by doctors, are riddled with - I almost said rotted by - political correctness. It isn't easy to define political correctness with precision, but it is easy to recognise when it is present. It acts on me as the sound, when I was a child, of a teacher's nail scraping down a blackboard because his piece of chalk was too short: it sends shivers down my spine. It is the attempt to reform thought by making certain things unsayable; it is also the conspicuous, not to say intimidating, display of virtue (conceived of as the public espousal of the 'correct', which is to say 'progressive', views) by means of a purified vocabulary and abstract humane sentiment. To contradict such sentiment, or not to use such vocabulary, is to put yourself outside the pale of civilised men (or should I say persons?).

A recent edition of the *New England Journal of Medicine*, possibly the most august such journal in the world, exemplified the current grip of political correctness on the medical press. It was not by any means the most egregious example I could cite; it was interesting more for its subtlety than its blatancy. I should add, perhaps, that I do not object to the expression of certain views, which are themselves perfectly legitimate as opinions, as to the impossibility of publishing any other views.

Three items caught my eye. The first related to capital punishment, and the others to the epidemic of childhood obesity that afflicts America, and increasingly the rest of the world.

The article on capital punishment concerned an execution by fatal injection of a murderer in North Carolina. A special electroencephalograph was connected to him during his execution, and it suggested that he may have been more conscious during it than was previously supposed, and this in turn meant that death by fatal injection constituted the kind of cruel and unusual punishment forbidden by the Constitution. And since execution by lethal injection is about the most humane and painless that can be devised... Well, you get the drift.

Let me say at once that, on the question of the death penalty, I face both directions. Viscerally, I am in favour of it - in my professional life I met quite a number of murderers for whom it seemed to me that death was the only just and indeed humane punishment - but I do recognise a very powerful argument against the penalty, namely the tendency of all jurisdictions, which after all rely on merely human institutions, to make mistakes and execute the wrong person. You might argue that only those of whom we can be sure that they committed a brutal murder should be executed: but in our system of law, all convicted prisoners are supposed to be guilty beyond reasonable doubt, and in that sense all should be equally eligible for any penalty that the law prescribes for their particular offence. I am, moreover, a little squeamish about the increasingly clinical nature of executions, as if they were medical procedures. I remember reading an account of an execution by fatal injection, though I now cannot recall where the account was published, in which the injection was preceded by a swabbing of the skin of the person to be killed. This seemed to me both ridiculous and sinister, as if we were trying to pretend that an execution was actually a surgical operation. This (if the account of the execution was accurate) is a terrible slippage.

On the other hand, I cannot share any sense of outrage against the idea of capital punishment, such as is now widespread in Europe. From the assumption of European moral superiority *vis-à-vis* the United States with regard to capital punishment, you would have thought that capital punishment had been outlawed in all of Europe in about 458 BC. In fact, the country in which the outrage is strongest, or at least most vocal, France, was the last country in western Europe to abandon it, in 1981 - hardly an aeon ago.

The suffering of the murderer from North Carolina – a possibility, incidentally, rather than a certainty – can hardly have lasted so long as to be counted an atrocity such as the Constitution was intended to outlaw. A person to be executed by fatal injection is first given a barbiturate to render him unconscious, then a muscle relaxant to render him immobile, and finally a drug to stop his heart beating. If this is cruel and unusual, then almost any punishment is cruel and unusual. If you measured the physiological response of an accused as a judge sentenced him to a ten-year prison sentence, you might just as well conclude that this was cruel and unusual punishment. It is a short step to saying that all punishment is cruel and unusual - which, of course, has long been the predominant view among criminologists.

It seems to me unlikely that, had the EEG conducted on the murderer in North Carolina demonstrated that he was fully unconscious at the time of the injection of the muscle relaxant, the *NEJM* would have reported it with the subtext that we can now all accept capital punishment, it is all quite painless and humane, and therefore morally justified. In other words, we are dealing here more with politically correct propaganda rather than true argumentation. It is not as if the *NEJM* is (or indeed should be) in disinterested search of a painless method of execution; nor is it likely that it would use the same data as an argument against euthanasia. It is establishing its membership of the great family of the right-thinking.

In the same issue, there were two articles about America's − and now the world's − epidemic problem of childhood obesity. This has been brought about by physical inactivity and the consumption of junk food. (I once saw a striking illustration of the connection between junk food and obesity on the streets of Bangkok. I watched children emerge from an exclusive school there, and they grazed on huge quantities of junk food the moment they were free to do so. Not surprisingly, they were fat, startlingly so in a land where most people are elegantly slender.)

The articles in the *NEJM* discussed the responsibility of the government to forbid food companies from advertising, especially on television, directly to small children. Personally, I see nothing wrong with a proposal to censor such advertising. By definition, small children are not fully capable of making up their own minds about things, and it seems to me that advertisements directed at them to get them to do things which are likely to be permanently damaging to them, for the sake of making a profit, or rather an extra profit, are immoral.

What was very striking about the two articles in the *NEJM*, however, was the complete absence of reference in either of them to the responsibilities of parents towards their own children, or to the cultural context in which parents have largely abandoned such responsibilities. The articles mentioned that television advertisements had made it difficult for parents to control their offspring's diet, and that they somehow transferred the onus for making a choice about diet from the parents to the children. A majority of children now claimed that it was they, not their parents, who decided what they ate.

I hesitate to mention my own childhood in this context, in case I should be thought to be implying that I have turned out perfectly (I am, in fact, slightly overweight). But when I was a child I ate what I was given, or else I went hungry. As a result of this take-it-or-leave-it attitude, I increased my repertoire of what I would eat, learned to like many things that were good for me though they were not as immediately attractive as various unhealthy or nutritionally worthless foods, and learned moreover that my choice - or rather my whim - was not the beginning and end of the universe.

Of course, the question as to why so many parents have transferred authority from themselves to their children as young as three years old is a very interesting and important one, to which more than one answer can be given, and at more than one level of analysis. This transfer of authority is a mass phenomenon, otherwise the epidemic would not have taken place. Parents no longer seem in control of how much television their children watch, what their children buy with their money or even what they eat at home.

The problem might be, for example, that people have come to believe that the satisfaction of choice, no matter how ill-informed, whimsical or deleterious, however childish or childlike, is the whole meaning of existence, at all the ages of man, from the very moment of birth onwards. Clearly, this has a connection with the notion of consumer choice: it is the wrongful extension of a principle that, in the right context, is obviously an excellent one. The epidemic of childhood obesity is a precise illustration of Edmund Burke's famous dictum that men are qualified for liberty in exact proportion as they are (or have been in the past) prepared to place a limit on their own appetites.

We might ask what kind of society we have created in which so many parents do not control the diet of their own children, and what such a lack of control – surely not confined to diet – bodes for the future. Perhaps parents are just too busy nowadays to make the effort; or perhaps they subscribe to the sentimental (and lazy) idea that to give children what they want exactly when and how they want it is an expression of deep love.

But whatever the reason, the fact that two articles about the problem of childhood obesity in the *NEJM* could fail even to mention individual parental responsibility is indicative of what one can only call a totalitarian mindset. According to this mindset, it is for the government to solve every problem, either by prescribing behaviour, or forbidding it, or of course both. It is not that I think that the proposal that the government should ban the advertising of noxious products to small children is wrong; what bothers me is the failure to recognise that there is any other dimension to the problem, a dimension that is in fact much more serious.

No doubt the *NEJM* does not want to court unpopularity, or even notoriety, by suggesting that millions of American parents are, at least in this respect, failing their own children (I suspect that they are failing them in other respects too). It is always safer, from the point of view of gaining the esteem of the intelligentsia and of avoiding their censure, to blame those in authority or large corporations rather than 'ordinary' people, who are by definition blameless victims. But to absolve ordinary people of all blame for the obesity of their own children, by simply omitting to mention it altogether, is to deny them agency as full human beings. Far from being generous towards, or respectful of, ordinary people, it is extremely condescending towards them. Poor things, they are but putty in the hands of television companies and the food industry.

If the only publicly admissible or mentionable locus of responsibility for the diet of children is the government, we have accepted the premise of totalitarianism. The authors of the articles in the *NEJM* might answer in their own defence that their articles considered only those measures the government could take to affect the situation; nevertheless, the fact that they did not mention even in passing that parents had some active role to play in their children's diet suggests to me that the thought did not even occur to them. Here truly is the dog that did not bark in the night-time.

WHO CARES?

PUBLIC AFFAIRS, SAID DOCTOR Johnson, vex no man: by which, I suppose, he meant that, if we are honest, only those matters which touch us directly and personally have the power genuinely to move us. The rest is ersatz or assumed emotion that we fake or exaggerate in order to appear more concerned with public affairs than we really are; and true it is that an argument with my wife causes me more genuine upset than a distant war, however bloody, though I am perfectly aware that in the scale of human history the war weighs a million, or a trillion, times more heavily.

This means, or ought to mean, that I should by now have reached such a state of serenity that even the weekly arrival of the medical journals should not upset me. After all, my personal situation is about as satisfactory as it will ever be. I please myself, more or less, as to what I do; my work is also my pleasure. I am indeed fortunate.

And yet *The Lancet* in particular, once one of the world's greatest medical journals, never fails to irritate me. Its sanctimony makes Elmer Gantry seem like a self-doubter. It propounds abject nonsense with the self-conceit of the assuredly saved preaching to the assuredly damned. Dickens would have loved to satirise it.

For example, it published a paper at the end of July entitled, 'Is access to essential medicines as part of the fulfilment of the right to health enforceable through the courts?' The paper discussed whether, if individuals were denied access to important medicines, they could seek redress via the courts, particularly in Latin America, on the grounds that their rights were being denied.

The right to health was accepted in this paper as if it were a straightforward natural fact, like the roundness of the earth, for example, and no more disputable. Yet the notion of a right to health is plainly ridiculous, at least until man becomes immortal. A man who is dying of incurable cancer is unfortunate, but his rights are not being infringed.

Perhaps the authors of the paper meant by the 'right to health' the 'right to healthcare'. But this is scarcely any better. A right to a material benefit implies someone else's duty to provide it, irrespective of whether he wants to do so or indeed is actually able to do so. This is not to say, of course, that the world would not be a better place if everyone who needed it were able to obtain healthcare; but the world would not be a better place because everyone's rights had been observed or complied with, but because avoidable suffering had been avoided. There are more and better reasons, after all, to treat people medically than that they have a right to such treatment.

I could not help but notice that among the drugs deemed so essential that not to make them freely available to people who need them amounts to a breach of their rights was buprenorphine, a drug prescribed by doctors to opiate-addicts in the hope that they, the addicts, will thereafter stop taking opiates of their own, and take those of the doctor instead. In a way this was odd, because there was an item in the very same edition of *The Lancet* entitled, 'Designer drug Subutex [buprenorphine] takes its toll in Tbilisi [the capital of Georgia].' There, at least, there was no danger that the people's right to buprenorphine was being infringed.

The article starts with the following dramatic paragraph:

'Crushed on pavements, tossed by the road, or in the corners of apartment-block entrance halls, the used syringes tell a story of rising addiction. The needles seen across Tbilisi are discarded by the addicts of Subutex, a treatment for opiate abuse that has ironically become the country's most popular drug.'

The drug is manufactured in Britain and exported to France, where gullible doctors prescribe it to addicts who pretend to need it, and who then sell it on to dealers who smuggle it into Georgia at a profit of 600 per cent. Seven tablets in France cost £12, and £96 in Georgia. Among the smugglers of buprenorphine was the honorary consul of the Côte d'Ivoire in Georgia, who brought it into the country in his diplomatic bag. According to *The Lancet*, the problem is not a small one: 39 per cent of addicts treated in clinics in Georgia were addicted to buprenorphine, and the total number of drug addicts in Georgia was 250,000, which is to say one in twenty of the entire population. This represents an 80 per cent increase since 2003, and is largely due to the importation of buprenorphine.

Five pages later in *The Lancet*, the very same author wrote an admiring, even hagiographical article, about Dr Vladimir Mendelevich, a doctor who is trying to introduce the treatment of drug addicts in Russia, Georgia's neighbour and historical suzerain, with yes, you've guessed it, buprenorphine (among other drugs). Dr Mendelevich is described as a hero by the author without any hint of irony, or even of awareness of what he had written only five pages previously, or that to introduce yet another drug into a country notorious for its corruption and administrative chaos, contiguous with Georgia, is an idea that needs very careful consideration.

Just how essential is buprenorphine that, not to make it available to all who feel they need it constitutes an attack on their fundamental human rights? This question was in part answered by a paper in the *New England Journal of Medicine* that appeared in the same week as *The Lancet* that I have cited. The authors, who practised at Yale, wanted to establish whether extra counselling had any effect on the abstention of addicts who were prescribed a tablet containing both buprenorphine and naloxone.

This tablet is an extremely clever one. Naloxone when taken by mouth has no effect, but when taken by injection acts as an antagonist to opiates, and precipitates withdrawal symptoms. Thus its inclusion with buprenorphine discourages buprenorphine abuse (though I have little doubt that, before long, addicts and their acolytes will devise something to circumvent this precaution).

The researchers recruited 497 addicts for their study, but excluded 296 of them because (as addicts in real life tend to do) they took alcohol or other drugs as well as opiates, or behaved in a dangerous and antisocial way. A further 35 dropped out at preliminary stages, leaving only 166 of the original 497 for the experiment.

The 166 were divided, like Gaul, into three: those who received the drug on a once weekly basis, those who received it on a three-times weekly basis, and those who received it on a three-times weekly basis plus extra counselling. In the event, there was no difference in the outcomes between these three groups at 24 weeks.

What was most striking was that only 75 continued the experiment to the 24th week, which is to say that 422 of the original addicts did not get that far: and 24 weeks is not exactly an eternity. The average maximum duration of abstinence from illicit opiates among the 166 sterling citizens who were treated was between five and six weeks. More than half their urine specimens tested positive for the presence of illicit opiates.

Nor is this all. It is well known that the results of clinical trials are better than results obtained in a 'natural' environment, that is to say you cannot expect the same degree of success when you transfer a treatment that has been tried experimentally to normal, everyday practice. This is for several reasons, among them the enthusiasm and dedication of the staff involved in the trial, enthusiasm that often communicates itself to the patients who are therefore more optimistic and compliant with treatment than they would otherwise be.

It might well be that the very low compliance rate of the patients was caused by an awareness of the presence of naloxone in the tablets they received. It was precisely because the medication could not be abused, at least until someone devised a method of abusing it, that the compliance rate was so very low. But if so, it must cast doubt on the motives of the addicts for seeking and accepting treatment in the first place. And it should be borne in mind that the patients were selected among 497 addicts for their relatively 'good' behaviour: namely, their absence of additional substance abuse and lack of threatening, violent and criminal conduct. In other words, their prognosis was already better than average among the addicts.

Had the patients been prescribed buprenorphine alone, I think they might well have 'complied' with treatment better, but only because it would have had some economic or abuse value to them. The criteria for completion of the study were not exactly stringent: those who did not miss more than three counselling sessions or missed their medication for more than a week were deemed to have completed it.

In short, the whole business was an elaborate and sordid farce, from which the authors drew the conclusion that there is 'a need both to measure adherence in future research and to monitor and encourage adherence in practice in order to reduce the potential misuse of the medication and to improve the treatment outcomes.' The idea that the whole notion of treatment in a voluntary condition such as addiction might be inappropriate was quite beyond the authors.

But let us return briefly to the question of the supposed right to health. Can it be the right of anyone to obtain a treatment that is marginally effective, if it is effective at all? In fact, this is often the case in modern medical treatment. The chances of anti-hypertensive treatment doing you good rather than harm are small, though the harm it can do you is slight and the good it can do you is enormous. How certain does the good that treatment does you have to be before it becomes a right enshrined in, and actionable at, law?

I am astonished at how quickly the doctrine of rights has colonised minds, like bacteria on a Petri dish. Not long ago, I asked a young patient what she was going to do with her life (I am sufficiently interested in my patients to ask such things). She said she wanted to study law. Any particular branch, I asked, thinking she might want to do criminal law, which is the most interesting, if least lucrative, branch?

'I want to go into human rights,' she said, with that semi-beatified smile with which a girl of her age might once have claimed to have a vocation.

'Oh yes,' I said, 'and where do human rights come from?'

'What do you mean?' she asked.

'I mean, are they just there, like America, waiting to be discovered by someone going out and looking for them, or are they conferred by mere human agency, in which case they can be repealed at the drop of a law?'

She looked appalled, as if I were a deeply wicked man who had suggested that, for example, racial discrimination was just the thing.

'You can't ask that,' she said.

I didn't explore the question of why not, because a medical consultation is not a dialogue by Plato. But after that, I did begin to think that there was something to Richard Dawkins' conception of a meme, namely an idea that enters minds and spreads from mind to mind as a gene favourable to survival in a population.

The problem with memes, of course, is that they don't have to be good ideas, only ideas that are in someone's, or some group's, advantage. And the ever-expanding concept of human rights is of advantage to regulatory bureaucracies, of course, for how can positive rights be enforced without them? Not coincidentally, the paper in *The Lancet* with which I began this article emerged from that bureaucracy of bureaucracies, that meta-bureaucracy, the World Health Organisation in Geneva.

WHERE THE MEANS JUSTIFY THE END

ONE OF THE REASONS that I worked for many years as an ill-remunerated doctor in a prison, and used earlier in my life to visit countries torn by civil war, is that extreme situations help to clarify what is important in life. I never arrived in the prison but I wondered how I would react to incarceration, whether I would be a stoic and retreat into myself or be someone who kicked against the traces and made trouble for the authorities just to assert my own continuing humanity.

Of course, the prison in which I worked was nothing in point of inhumanity to the great political prisons and camps of the twentieth century. True, there was the odd sadist who worked there, because prison work is always attractive to sadists. I remember one warder who became angry when a prisoner had an epileptic fit in my presence.

'Don't you do that in front of the doctor!' he ordered the unconscious man, and I have little doubt that he would have kicked him hard and often – in short, given him what used to be called in prison warders' parlance 'the black aspirin,' which is to say the prison warder's boot – if I had turned my back for an instant.

Like most of the sadists working in prison, this man was extremely crafty, and took advantage of the labour laws that require concrete evidence of wrongdoing before dismissal. Though long suspected by everyone of cruelty towards the prisoners, suspicions alone were not enough for him to be dismissed. Eventually, he was caught infusing someone's eye with noxious chemicals, and went to prison himself. But it was the infrequency of such gross cruelty that struck me, not its frequency.

A recent anthology, entitled *From the Gulag to the Killing Fields*, edited by Paul Hollander, reminds us of how far man's inhumanity to man can go, and on what scale. It is a selection from the prison and other memoirs of victims of communist repression in the Soviet Union, Eastern Europe, China, Vietnam, Cambodia, Cuba and Ethiopia.

Professor Hollander, who provides a long introductory essay, is the author of the now-classic *Political Pilgrims*, a history of the way in which western intellectuals were duped, and wanted to be duped, by their visits to communist countries into believing that some kind of paradise was under construction and was already partially built: in sharp contrast, of course, to the living hells of their homelands.

Hollander knows whereof he speaks, since he spent some of his childhood in Hungary hiding from the Nazis and then escaped from the communists – but only after the window of opportunity to escape in the immediate aftermath of the revolution of 1956 had closed. These experiences no doubt serve to put the less pleasant aspects of daily life in the west into some kind of perspective.

When you read the accounts of the victims of the repression, you begin to feel that all other subject matter for writing is trivial or self-indulgent. Indeed, a single line can provide more illumination (provided you use your imagination a little) than reams of academic discourse.

For example, when Evgenia Ginzburg, author of the brilliant and terrible memoir, *Into the Whirlwind*, leaves her flat to go to the local headquarters of the NKVD, having been called there for a supposedly friendly chat about someone she knows, her husband says to her, 'Well, Genia, we'll expect you back for lunch,' and she replies, 'Goodbye, Paul dear. We've had a good life together.' She knows, as he does, that she is never going to see him again this side of the afterlife: which is to say never. Thus a fathomless world of pain and sorrow is expressed in those few simple words that shames our vociferous complaints about nothing very much.

We are not dealing here with an isolated case or two, such as the victims of the sadist who worked in the prison in which I also worked. The pain and sorrow as Evgenia Ginzburg expressed was a mass, everyday phenomenon. I remember what a professor told me when I visited the Baltic States just before the Soviet Union collapsed about his childhood in the late 40s: that he never went to bed other than fully-dressed, so that he would have clothes to travel in if the secret police came to the door in the early hours of the morning (they always came in the early hours of the morning). And another professor told me he remembered the trucks that would draw up at his school, whereupon names would be called out of those children who were to get in them and never be heard of again. A tenth of the population of the Baltic States was deported in those years.

Murders and deportations on the scale practised in the communist countries could not have taken place without the co-operation and even the enthusiasm of large numbers of people. Compared with the question of how radical evil on so large a scale became (and could once again become) possible, all other historical and sociological questions seem rather unimportant, especially as we cannot be certain that such radical evil will never again appear in the world. On the contrary.

In his introduction, Professor Hollander quotes Solzhenitsyn. According to Solzhenitsyn, the *sine qua non* of mass murder as a way of life, or as an industry, is ideology. Before the advent of ideology, people only did harm within a relatively restricted circle, for example in the ruthless furtherance of their own careers. Macbeth is a very bloody play, but only those who in some way stood between Macbeth and the throne had much to fear from him. Ordinary people, at least, could stand aside in the conflict.

There was no standing aside in the ideologised state: either you were for the government, the leader and the ideology, or you were against them. Indeed, once dialectics became the master science, being personally in favour of them was not enough; you had to be objectively in favour of them, that is to say to have no blemish on your record, such as a bourgeois birth, knowledge of anyone with such a birth, or intellectual interests.

Where the means justify the end, as they do for most ideologies, mass murder becomes more likely, perhaps even inevitable in ideologised states. The capacity for cruelty, and the enjoyment of cruelty, that lies latent in almost every human heart, then allies itself to a supposedly higher, even transcendent purpose. Original sin meets social conditioning. A vicious circle is set up: and eventually, viciousness itself is taken to be a sign both of loyalty and of higher purpose.

It is curious how even now, after all the calamities of the twentieth century, the lengths to which people are prepared to go to pursue an end is taken by others as a sign of the worthiness if not of the end itself, at least of the motives of the extremists. The fact that people are prepared to blow themselves up in an attempt to murder as many complete strangers as possible is taken as proof of the strength of their humanitarian feelings and outrage at a state of injustice.

The greatness of a crime is thus a guarantee of the greatness of its motive: for who would order the deportation of whole nations, for example, cause famines, work millions to death, shoot untold numbers, unless he had some worthy higher purpose? And the more ruthlessly he did all these things, the higher his purpose must be to justify them. To participate in the worst of crimes is then to be the best of men. It was under communism (as well as Nazism) that Norman Mailer's ethical injunction, to cultivate your inner psychopath, became government policy, as well as prudent.

Psychopaths there are, of course, in every time and every place. They are always dangerous, but in some circumstances they are more dangerous than in others. The very qualities that are loathsome at one time are praised as diligence, fervour, loyalty, honesty and so forth at others. Here is a description from Professor Hollander's book, written by a Cambodian physician who lived through the three years of Pol Pot's regime:

> ... a new interrogator, one I had not seen before, walked down the row of trees holding a long, sharp knife. I could not make out their words, but he spoke to the pregnant woman and she answered. What happened next makes me nauseous to think about. I can only describe it in the briefest of terms: He cut the clothes off her body, slit her stomach, and took the baby out. I turned away but there was no escaping the sound of her agony, the screams that slowly subsided into whimpers and after far too long lapsed into the merciful silence of death. The killer walked calmly past me holding the foetus by its neck. When he got to the prison, just within the range of my vision, he tied a string round the foetus and hung it from the eaves with the others, which were dried and black and shrunken.

The man who did thus was almost certainly imbued with a profound sense of purpose, given him by an ideology. By a terrible irony, the author, Dr Haing Nor, was shot dead in Los Angeles, where he had taken refuge, by a robber – a psychopath, presumably, of the ordinary sort, though possibly one influenced by the self-righteously angry intonation of modern pop music.

The worst brutality I ever saw was that committed by Sendero Luminoso (Shining Path) in Peru, in the days when it seemed possible that it might come to power. If it had, I think its massacres would have dwarfed those of the Khmer Rouge. As a doctor, I am accustomed to unpleasant sights, but nothing prepared me for what I saw in Ayacucho, where Sendero first developed under the sway of a professor of philosophy, Abimael Guzman. I took photographs of what I saw, but the newspapers deemed them too disturbing to be printed. Humankind at breakfast can bear very little reality. But I also found it difficult to persuade anyone by means of words of the reality of what I had seen: most people nodded and thought I had finally gone mad. On the plane back from Peru, I delighted a worker for Amnesty International when I described to him some of the bad behaviour of the Peruvian Army; but when I described what I had seen Sendero do, incomparably worse, I might as well have talked to him of sea monsters, and of giant squid that could drag nuclear submarines to the depths.

I wish I could have given him Professor Hollander's book. Perhaps then he would have caught a glimpse of what insensate cruelties can be inflicted in the name of utopias, and he would not have disbelieved me. In his introduction, Professor Hollander speculates as to why Nazi atrocities should, deservedly, be so well known and their lessons so well-absorbed, while those of communism, that are not exactly unknown, and on an even greater scale than Nazism's (no thanks to Nazism for that, of course, because Nazism was stopped in mid-atrocity), have comparatively so little emotional resonance: an unfortunate fact which it is the purpose of his book to change. Perhaps the difference exists because elements at least of communism still exert an attraction for so many intellectuals, and no one wants to acknowledge that his ideals justified and in part motivated mass murder on an unprecedented scale. Who would not rather deny the meaning of scores of millions of deaths, than abandon his illusions?

HEART OF DARKNESS

RECENTLY, I HAD OCCASION to re-read Conrad's *Heart of Darkness*. It is a short book, and I have now read it so many times that I seem to know whole paragraphs off by heart (and Conrad's paragraphs can be long).

By now, it is pretty well established that Conrad did not exaggerate the horrors of Belgian colonialism in his story, especially in its earliest phase when the Congo was but the personal fiefdom of the rapacious and utterly unscrupulous King Leopold (who, incidentally, so wished his capital, Brussels, to resemble Paris, that he knocked down the mediaeval Flemish heart of the city, that was as beautiful as Bruges, and had the grossly sub-Parisian city that we know today erected in its place).

Conrad describes the loose talk of the early colonialists as having been 'reckless without hardihood, greedy without audacity, and cruel without courage.' With contemptuous irony, he calls them 'pilgrims'. Whatever their mission, it was definitely not *civilisatrice*.

Heart of Darkness is often taken as being unequivocally anti-colonial or anti-imperialist, perhaps because such an interpretation would redeem its portrayal of Africans as cannibals at worst, and uncomprehending savages at best. Only in this way can Conrad, who is acknowledged by everyone to have been a great writer, be made to appear sufficiently in sympathy with our modern susceptibilities.

Actually, I am not sure that the story is quite as anti-imperialist as we should like to suppose. The narrator, Marlow, describes how he looked at a map of Africa just before being appointed to the command of a river boat on the Congo. In those days (just after the Congress of Berlin, that partitioned Africa between the European powers), areas of Africa were coloured according to the empires to which they belonged. Blue, for example, was French. Marlow says this: 'There was a vast amount of red – good to see at any time, because one knows that some real work is done in there.' Red, of course, was the cartographic colour of the British Empire.

Now of course Marlow was a fictional character, and it is an elementary mistake of literary criticism to identify too closely the opinions of a fictional character for those of an author. Yet the biographical parallels between Marlow and Conrad himself are too great to ignore completely. They went to the Congo at the same time. Some of the phrases in Conrad's diary of the time - the first of his known writings in English, his third language – appear in *Heart of Darkness*. And Conrad is known to have been a great admirer of the British. I think it unlikely that, at least on this subject, his views were too far removed from those of Marlow.

So it is specifically Belgian imperialism that Conrad condemns - though, of course, he is making a much wider point than that King Leopold and his acolytes were very bad men. The heart of darkness is the heart that beats within us all, awaiting its chance to express itself. Conrad was a materialist and an atheist but, in a sense, he believed in original sin. It was inscribed in our biological nature.

But what was 'the real work' of which Marlow spoke, when he saw large areas of red on the map of Africa? This is a question whose importance has not declined in the intervening years, indeed of late it has become more acute, despite the complete disappearance of the British Empire in the intervening century. Is it the job of any country in the world to do 'the real work,' indeed is any country capable of doing such work? Upon your answer to this question depends your attitude to foreign policy: is it the pursuit of your interests, or is it to do good ('the real work') in the world?

As a doctor and psychiatrist, I spent an awful lot of my professional life trying to change individuals in a direction that I thought appropriate and beneficial for them. I am not under any illusions about how far I succeeded. I think I succeeded very little. At the best, I implanted the seeds of change rather than caused change itself. It was often the case that my patients had adopted grossly self-destructive paths in life, that viewed dispassionately and with a minimum of common sense could lead to nothing but misery, despair and chaos. Indeed, my patients often acknowledged this themselves, at least intellectually.

'Yes, yes,' they would say, 'of course you are right.' And they would promise to change, and to take all the very obvious steps to amend and improve their lives.

When I was young and inexperienced, I believed them. I felt very pleased with myself. It then came as a shock to me that, despite all their protestations of desire to change, they persisted in their folly. My words had not produced their salutary effect after all. I might as well have said nothing at all. When I was young, I thought my pearls had been cast before swine; later, I realised the profound truth contained in La Rochefoucauld's maxim, that it is easier to give good advice than to take it. When I considered my own life, I saw that this was so; most of the wrong decisions I had made, especially the worst and most important of them, I had made knowingly, in full knowledge of the ill consequences to which they would lead. If I have been saved from disaster, it is by native cunning rather than by superior wisdom.

But if it is so difficult to change a comparative handful of individuals, most of whom have the strongest possible reasons to change, how do you change whole nations, let alone whole cultures?

Of course, it is easy – nothing is easier, in fact – for the powerful to have an effect upon the weak and the seemingly powerless. The trick is for the powerful to have precisely the effect upon the powerless that they want, and in my view this is never possible. The weak may bend before the powerful, and may change their ways for them, but rarely (actually, I think never) in precisely the way in which the powerful want.

The disparity in power between the colonising nations of Africa and the native Africans was much greater than that between the United States and the Iraqis. 'We have the Maxim gun and they do not,' sums this up. But it is unlikely that at any stage of the colonial enterprise in Africa, the colonisers had precisely (or even approximately) the effect that they thought they were having, and no other. In the late stage of British colonialism, for example, the British fondly imagined that they were bequeathing to various African countries institutions that would function in the same way without them as with them. In retrospect, this now seems an almost laughable belief. No better example of this could be had than Uganda, that land that Churchill called 'the pearl of Africa.' (Beware of pearls of continents, and above all Switzerlands of continents: for them, special horrors are usually reserved. The only exception to this rule known to me is Costa Rica, the Switzerland of Central America.)

This is not to say that the colonialists left nothing behind; the continent they invaded was changed for ever. For example, traditional forms of African political authority were destroyed once and for all, in favour of western-style nationalists, who spoke the language of freedom but dreamed the dream of power. Whether this constituted an advance or a deterioration depends not only on the facts, but on the values that you hold dear. It boils down, in a way, to the question of whether you think corrugated tin roofs are better than grass roofs. No definitive answer can perhaps be given to this thorny question.

What is certain is that the colonialists changed Africa for ever. The arrow of politics, like that of time, flies in one direction only. You can conserve, perhaps, but you cannot return. The impis of the Zulus will never again stomp the hills of Natal, nor will the Azande return to the prelapsarian state in which the anthropologist, E E Evans-Pritchard, found them, when they believed that all deaths were caused by witchcraft. The Sudanese government has made sure of that.

So where does that leave us? I have always thought it a mistake to suppose that our example is so utterly splendid that everyone will want to copy it on the first contact with us. For one thing, our example, while admirable in some respects, is not admirable in all others. And for a second, people are inclined to prefer their own path to the path we suggest for them, simply because it is theirs. As Dostoyevsky pointed out a long time ago, if there were a government that arranged everything for our own perfect good and nothing but our own perfect good, thinking nothing whatever of its own good, we should still rebel against it merely to express ourselves as human beings. In fact, of course, no such government has ever existed or will ever exist.

In Africa, where I spent a number of years, I saw that the best of intentions did not necessarily produce the best of results. (I worked for several years in Tanzania, where billions of Scandinavian, Dutch and World Bank money wrought nothing but economic and social disaster.) This is not, of course, an argument in favour of the worst of intentions. It does not follow from the fact that the best of intentions often produce bad results, that the worst of intentions produce good ones. It is, alas, a truth of human existence that the paths to disaster are many, the paths to success few. Tolstoy had it exactly right when, with regard to personal relations, he said that all happy families are happy in the same way etc. etc.

If what I am saying is true, then foreign policy should be the pursuit of interests and not of virtue, at least among others. Of course, one hopes that one's interests are not incompatible with benefits to others: trade is an example of this. The fact that I derive a benefit from selling you something does not obviate the benefit you receive by buying it. But when I sell you a pair of pyjamas, I do not suppose thereby that I am promoting your marital fidelity. With luck, I am making myself a profit, and you comfortable at night.

Should, then, we be seeking to instil our notions of democracy in the Middle East? The first thing to remember is that freedom and democracy are not necessarily the same thing at all. For instance, a people may easily vote into power a government that wishes to massacre part of the population.

Democratic elections in Palestine and Iran have not necessarily been to our advantage, as the late Emperor Hirohito might have put it. I am far from suggesting that our sonofabitch must be better than all other possible sonofabitches (or should it be sonsofabitch?), but it is worth remembering that the alternative to bad is not always better.

It is one of the common charges in the Middle East against the west that it has supported dictators and not promoted democracy. The latter, however, is desirable only where the people are infused with a spirit of tolerance and moderation. Freedom and democracy are not in the gift of anyone, and to suppose that they are is to hinder their only real, that is to say, indigenous, development. As the physician in Macbeth pointed out, sometimes the patient has to minister to himself. Our job is to make sure the patient doesn't spread any diseases to us.

OF MAILER AND MURDER

ON A RECENT VISIT to New Zealand, I happened across a book that I had long intended to read, *In the Belly of the Beast*, by Jack Henry Abbott. (Before the advent of the internet, which equalised world prices, New Zealand used to be the best place in the English-speaking world for second-hand books.)

The name probably faintly rings a bell. He was a career criminal, and had spent the vast majority of his life in penal institutions of one kind or another. At the time he first wrote to Norman Mailer, he was serving a sentence of up to nineteen years for having killed another inmate. Previously, he had broken out of jail and robbed a bank. For whatever reason, he was not a good man.

Mailer was much taken, however, by his literary ability, his prose style and his thoughts (among other things, he was a communist, and was of the opinion that the American penal system was far worse than that of the Soviet Union, even in the time of Stalin). Mailer supported Abbott's appeal for parole, and Abbott was duly released. His book was published, he became for a short while the lion of the New York literary scene, a kind of interesting specimen (a petty criminal would have been of no interest, of course), until, a couple of days prior to the publication of the favourable review of his book in the *New York Review of Books*, he killed again, only six weeks after his release. His victim was a young man, an aspiring writer, who was working temporarily as a waiter, with whom Abbott had an impulsive quarrel. He stabbed him with a knife that he 'happened' to have on him.

Abbott was on the run for a short while, but then returned to prison where, about twenty years later, he hanged himself. In his only other book, called *My Return*, he argued that he could not have intended to kill the young waiter, because he stabbed him only once, and a man like him would have stabbed him many times had he intended to kill him. This was not the argument of a good man.

In fact, there was a passage in his first book, *In the Belly of the Beast*, that might have alerted Mailer and others to his penchant for stabbing people. It describes how prisoners take revenge in prisons. It is worth quoting in full:

Anything Goes

Here is how it is: You are both alone in his cell. You've slipped out
a knife (eight- to ten-inch blade, double-edged). You're holding
it beside your leg so he can't see it. The enemy is smiling and
chattering away about something. You see his eyes: Green-blue,
liquid. He thinks you're his fool: he trusts you. You see the spot.
It's a target between the second and third button on his shirt. As
you calmly talk and smile, you move your left foot to the side to
step across his right-side body length. A light pivot toward him
with your right shoulder and the world turns upside down: you
have sunk the knife to its hilt into the middle of his chest. Slowly
he begins to struggle for his life. As he sinks, you will have to kill
him fast or get caught. He will say 'Why?' Or 'No!' Nothing else.
You can feel his life trembling through the knife in your hand. It
almost overcomes you, the gentleness of the feeling at the center
of a coarse act of murder. You've pumped the knife several
times without even being aware of it. You go to the floor with
him to finish him. It is like cutting hot butter, no resistance at all.
They always whisper one thing at the end: 'Please.' You get the
odd impression that he is not imploring you not to harm him,
but to do it right. If he says your name it softens your resolve.
You go into a mechanical stupor of sorts. Things register in slow
motion because all your senses are drawn to a new height. You
leave him in the blood, staring with dead eyes. You strip in your
cell and destroy your clothing, flushing it down the toilet. You
throw the knife away. You jump under the showers. Your clarity
returns.

No doubt the first thing that struck Mailer about this passage was its
quality as prose. It is very graphic. But the words, after all, are those
of a murderer, and suggest more than a merely vivid imagination. It
would have been as wise to take them literally as it proved to be foolish
not to have taken the words of *Mein Kampf* literally. But Mailer lived
in a world (that of radical politics protected by a bourgeois order)
in which words never really meant what they said or said what they
really meant, in which moral exhibitionism was the highest good and
the *sine qua non* of the regard of one's peers. So safe were they in their
literary enclave that reality didn't matter much; what counted was the
ability to use words in the approved fashion, and truth was nowhere.

Ten years later, Mailer indirectly recognised his mistake, saying that the Abbott episode was not one of which he was proud. But it seems that the disregard of reality that he displayed has now entered the New Zealand criminal justice system.

You probably think of New Zealand as an empty land of beautiful landscapes: and so it is. It is tolerably prosperous, it is egalitarian in ethos, it is uncrowded, even its fauna and flora are gentle. It has no native carnivores and no snakes. Its climate is temperate and in places among the most pleasant in the world. It should be peaceful.

And so it once was. In 1950, when it was one of the wealthiest countries in the world, it had almost no crime whatever, or at least an irreducible minimum of crime. Now it has one of the highest crime rates in the western world, including crimes of violence. It is very puzzling.

While I was in New Zealand, I learned of two cases that seemed emblematic of the Mailerian developments in the country's criminal justice system. The first concerned a man with 102 convictions, many for violence including rape. (I should point out that 102 convictions means many more offences, since the conviction rate is never 100 per cent of the offending rate, and is sometimes only 5 or 10 per cent of it.)

This man nevertheless became eligible for parole. As conditions of parole, the board told him he must not drink, smoke cannabis or frequent certain places. The man told the board that he would abide by none of these conditions, but he was released on parole anyway. Within a short time, he had killed three people and so maimed a fourth that she will never recover.

The second case was of a man with many previous convictions, some for violence, who abducted and murdered a young woman aged 24. He was imprisoned and applied for bail. Three times he was turned down, but a fourth judge granted him bail. He was sent to live at a certain address, where he befriended his neighbours, who did not know that he was accused of murder. Eight months later, while baby-sitting their children, he killed one of them.

Perhaps the most extraordinary twist of this terrible tale is that the parents of the murdered child then had another baby, which the social services then removed from them on the grounds that they had previously entrusted a child to the care of a murderer and were therefore irresponsible parents. The state blames its citizens for the mistakes – if that is what they are – that it makes.

What lies behind this terrible, wilful incompetence? I suppose some people might say that anecdotes mean nothing; that it is statistics we have to look at, and the majority of people sent out on parole, or on bail for murder, do not kill again. The questions we should be asking are what proportion of people who say in advance that they have no intention of abiding by parole conditions go on to commit serious crimes if granted parole anyway, and what proportion of accused murderers granted bail kill again while on bail. In the light of these questions, the decisions taken in the two cases I have cited might appear slightly less absurd.

This is dust in our eyes, however. The presumption must be against someone who has been convicted of 102 previous offences, many of them violent, or someone who has been convicted of many previous offences and is suspected on the strongest possible grounds of having killed. It is morally frivolous to suggest otherwise.

In other words, the moral frivolity of the New Zealand criminal justice system could not have been more plainly demonstrated than in these two cases. (On the day before my departure from the country, a young man, also with a long record, who attacked an old woman in her eighties, and fractured her facial bones in two places, having first given her what he called 'a king hit' – that is to say a single punch that felled her – was sentenced to a year's imprisonment, which, with remission, will mean he will be at liberty in less than six months.) The question arises, Where does this moral frivolity come from?

The judges in New Zealand are not entirely to blame, since they have to sentence according to guidelines laid down for them. They cannot impose any sentence that they happen to think is just. But they do not protest against guidelines that are patently absurd. Nor was there any reason why the fourth judge should have granted bail in the second case I described. Therefore the judges cannot absolve themselves entirely of responsibility.

Lying behind the frivolity of the New Zealand criminal justice system (which also infects the British system) is a willingness to ignore, or an unwillingness to take seriously, the most obvious prognostic signs, or even to take considerations of justice into account. Just as Mailer failed completely to recognise the significance of the passage in Abbott's book, which after all was composed of letters to himself, that I have quoted above, so the judges and others in New Zealand ignored the most obvious considerations in their dealings with the criminals before them. Their own reputation for generosity of spirit and lack of vengefulness was more important to them than protection of the public.

Lying in a layer of the mind yet deeper than this desire for approbation is the baleful influence of Rousseau's idea that Man is or would be good but for the influence of society upon him. If this is the case, then the murderers in the cases I have cited were as much victims as their victims, and the society which has thus victimised them has no moral right to treat them harshly. Rather, it must reform, indeed perfect, itself. Until it does so, it ought to expect cases of the kind I have described.

This, of course, was precisely Abbott's point in his letters to Mailer. He said that society had made him the way he was, and thus had no right to point the finger at him; throughout the book, he alluded in a moral fashion only to what had been done to him, never what he had done.

There is no doubt, of course, that most criminals come from a very bad background (though it does not follow, thank God, that everybody from a bad background is a criminal, else we should none of us be safe in our beds). Of course, where the bad background itself comes from is another question, and much disputed. I think in large part it comes from the intellectual and moral *zeitgeist* that intellectuals have created. But the undoubted fact cited above has confused us utterly, and caused us to confuse two questions: first, how do we prevent people from becoming criminals in the first place, and second, how do we prevent those who have become recidivist criminals from committing further crimes? The two questions have different answers, and there is not a single answer to them both. When, however, we mistake the first question for the second, and the second for the first, we end up making Mailer's, and the New Zealand criminal justice system's, mistakes, over and over again.

One thing is evident, however: those who make the mistakes do not pay the price for them. They feel the warmth of generosity without feeling the cool current of responsibility.

LET'S BE RATIONAL

NOT LONG AGO, I spoke at a colloquium attended mostly by American conservatives. They were, at least to me, a highly congenial audience, friendly, humorous, polite, cultivated and very well-read (not always, let us be quite frank, the first characteristic of conservatives in any country). I happened to mention on the platform during one of the sessions that I was not religious, unlike the other members of the panel. I cannot now remember the precise context in which I made my terrible confession.

I was surprised afterwards that several of the audience approached me and thanked me for it. What was there to thank me for? They said that they, too, were without religious faith, in short atheists, and it was a relief to them that someone, otherwise of like mind with the majority of the audience, had confessed it.

I found this strange, perhaps because I come from a country in which irreligion is now the norm and no one feels obliged to hide his disbelief, rather the reverse: it is faith that one feels obliged to equivocate about in polite company. In Europe, it requires more courage to be religious than irreligious, at least if one has achieved more than a certain level of education. One of the most important differences between Europe and America, we are often told (and I myself partly believe), is that in the former religion is dead as a live social force, whereas it is very much alive in the latter. I find myself in the rather peculiar position of thinking that this is much to the advantage of the United States, though I cannot myself assent to any kind of religious belief. It is, after all, the truth that is supposed to set you free, not a convenient myth.

An atheist who would disagree with me very strongly is Professor Richard Dawkins, the biologist and formidable polemicist. In his most recent book, which became a worldwide best-seller, though not in Islamic countries where it is needed most, he evinces a hatred of religion that I, who have no faith, and believe some at least of the things that he believes (for example, the rather unpleasant nature of the deity as portrayed in the Old Testament) am quite unable to feel. I don't hate religion, in fact I am rather in favour of it; I am like Gibbon, who said admiringly of Roman religious syncretism that the people believed that all religions were equally true, that the philosophers believed them all equally false, and that the magistrates believed them all equally useful, without any of them coming into conflict over the matter. Religion was useful, that is, from the point of view of improving human behaviour and keeping it lawful.

In his book, Dawkins maintains that atheist Americans are afraid openly to avow their disbelief; and because he seems temperamentally inclined to overstate his case, whatever the subject matter, I did not really believe him. On the other hand, I recalled my experience at the colloquium, and I telephoned an American friend of mine, a conservative intellectual in that modern Babylon, New York, and asked him what he thought. I was a little chagrined to discover that he thought there was an element of truth in what Dawkins had written; I was chagrined because I was reviewing his book, and wanted another stick to beat him over the head with.

Now of course a sample of one is not a very large sample, indeed it could hardly be smaller, even if supported by my experience at the colloquium. But my friend is a man with antennae that are sensitive to the American *zeitgeist*, as it were, even though he lives in Manhattan, and I believed him.

But still I have many points of disagreement with Dawkins. He is an unreconstructed believer in technical progress, as if such progress is not sometimes equivocal and does not bring in its wake new and unanticipated problems. He appears to believe that the more technical progress we make the happier we shall be. This seems to me to be unrealistic.

He cites the example of in vitro fertilisation (IVF), as a result of which many parents have experienced the inexpressible joy of parenthood who would otherwise not have experienced it. This is undoubtedly true, as far as it goes, but it is not the whole truth by any means, which is more complex.

IVF is successful in at best a quarter of those who undertake it. It is very expensive and time-consuming. It therefore has various effects, besides the joyous denouement of a new baby.

In the first place, it makes the condition of childlessness worse than it might otherwise be. What cannot be cured must be endured; by holding out the hope that childlessness can be cured, it prevents, or at least delays, the acceptance of what is destined to be a lifelong condition, and therefore prolongs suffering unnecessarily. It raises hopes that are more likely than not, by quite a wide margin, to be dashed. In the meantime, people will spend a large amount of money and focus their attention exclusively on a single object, to the detriment of their psychological balance. It is far from unknown for couples to break up when IVF finally succeeds or finally fails. The idea that life will be perfect on condition of x is rarely constructive.

IVF, moreover, has created moral dilemmas. Who should be entitled to it? Anyone who asks for it? Should there be any requirement that the mother-to-be (if the procedure works) has certain qualities that will make her a good, or good enough, mother? After all, people who wish to adopt children are made to jump through all sorts of hoops before permission is given to them, and justice requires that people should be treated equally in morally equivalent situations; should the recipients of IVF be made to jump through the same hoops as adoptive parents, therefore? We are faced with a dilemma: either we make no demands of the woman receiving IVF, in which case we are emptying behaviour of important moral consequences, or we make such demands, at the cost of inflaming ideological conflict about such matters as what it means for a woman to be a proper mother.

In Europe, we have seen the strange phenomenon of women in their 60s undergoing successful IVF. Of course, we do not yet know that women in their 70s make bad mothers: perhaps they will make excellent mothers, provided that they survive, because of their long experience of life.

But the overall cultural effect of such pregnancies is to propagate and reinforce the notion of life as an existential supermarket, in which you can live any way you choose by fetching a way of life down from the supermarket shelf, in the same way as you choose breakfast cereal. In this brave new world, there are no intrinsic limits that you must accept if you are to be free, balanced and happy.

The realisation that 'having it all' is not a realistic possibility, that every pleasure entails foreclosure on other pleasures, that hard choice is always necessary and that reality always bites back against those who refuse to make such choices, is an important stage in the achievement of maturity. Oddly enough, the acceptance of frustration is the precondition of happiness. One way to avoid permanent misery is not to demand more of life than it can yield.

Dawkins might answer in two ways. First, he might say that, with further experience, experimentation and technology, IVF will become more successful: indeed, it is the only way IVF can become more successful. At some point (perhaps, not certainly), the ratio of success to failure will change: instead of being 1:4, as it is now, it will be 4:1. Then there will be no possible doubt that the sum of human happiness will be increased by it, which must be doubtful now.

This is a good argument, but it relies more on faith than on reason, precisely what Dawkins, as a rationalist, would wish to avoid. When William Harvey made perhaps the greatest physiological discovery, the circulation of the blood, in the history of medicine, he had faith that eventually such knowledge would lead to benefits for humanity. In fact, it was centuries before it did so: his belief was faith-based, and for a very long time would have had no rational support in its evidence. It is of course possible, even likely, that the results of IVF will eventually improve, but we cannot know this for certain in advance of all experience. It is possible that they will not.

The second argument is that Man has made a Promethean bargain and it is impossible for him to go back on it, even if he wanted to. Just as time's arrow flies in one direction only, so there is no way where science and technology is concerned except forward. Moreover, it is a matter of empirical fact that our increasingly secular and technological culture has also brought, or at least co-existed with, genuine moral advance. There is no reason to suppose that such advance will not continue.

There are no decisive arguments about the moral effects of technology. It seems to me likely, for example, that nuclear weapons have so far saved more lives than they have taken: that without them, an armed conflict in Europe between east and west would have been much more likely, and that therefore millions of lives might have been lost if nuclear weapons had not existed. (This is quite apart from the argument over the justification for dropping atomic bombs on Hiroshima and Nagasaki.)

Proliferation of nuclear weapons, however, might in the end tip the balance against them, especially if they fell into the hands of terrorists or leaders with apocalyptic visions. The jury is out, and out for ever, at least until a nuclear holocaust actually takes place, when the verdict will be clear enough if anyone is left to hear it.

I do not disagree with Dawkins that, in some important respects there has been moral progress. The casual acceptance of racism in large parts of the world, for example, is now a thing of the past, and even people who still harbour racist ideas are afraid either to express them or to act upon them. I can't think of this as anything but moral progress.

And yet Dawkins disregards other important aspects of morality in which regression had undoubtedly occurred. To give only one example: the rate of indictable offences has increased 40 times in the country of his birth, Britain, in his lifetime, notwithstanding an enormous increase in wealth and the standard of living as measured by consumption of material goods. And this rise of crime alone has had a terrible effect on the quality of life of millions of people, who justifiably live in constant fear and who arrange their lives accordingly. Many of the old, for example, are under perpetual curfew, imposed by some of the young, in Britain.

In other words, matters are more complex than Professor Dawkins would have us believe. Progress is possible but not inevitable, and certainly not without its ironies either. (In our new-found happiness, 10 per cent of us feel constrained to take anti-depressants.) An old-fashioned rationalist, he does not acknowledge that a perfectly self-consistent way of life, based purely upon reason and nothing but reason, is not possible. And in his latest book he portrays the typical believer as an ignorant bigot who goes round shooting abortionists, or slaughtering people who deviate in the slightest from his doctrine. You might as well say that Lenin was the typical atheist, who wants to kill all priests - as Lenin had thousands killed in no time at all.

Dawkins's latest book is an example of the nothing-but school of historiography: European history is nothing but the history of warfare and genocide, American history is nothing but the history of exploitation and oppression of the blacks, and so forth. For him, the history of religion is nothing but the history of bigotry, savagery, ignorance, intolerance. Of course, all of these are to be found in the history of religion, and bigots still abound. The problem with the nothing-but school of history, apart from its incompleteness and untruth, is it fuels the very thing against which it rails, bigotry and hatred.

ON EVIL

I HAVE LONG BEEN preoccupied by the problem of evil. Not being a philosopher, I have no satisfactory explanation of evil to offer, nor even, indeed, a satisfactory definition of it. For me, evil is rather like poetry was for Doctor Johnson: easier to say what it isn't than what it is. All I know for certain is that there's a lot of it about - evil, I mean, not poetry.

Why? Is the heart of man irredeemably evil, or at any rate inclined to evil? What are the conditions in which evil may flourish?

My medical practice, admittedly of a peculiar kind, in a slum and in a prison, convinced me of the prevalence of evil. I was surprised. I had spent a number of years in countries wracked by civil wars and thereby deprived of even minimal social order, precisely the conditions in which one might expect evil to be widely committed, if only because in such situations the worst come to the fore. But nothing prepared me for the sheer malignity, the joy in doing wrong, of so many of my compatriots, when finally I returned home. Every day in my office I would hear of men who tortured women - torture is not too strong a word - or commit the basest acts of intimidation, oppression and violence, with every appearance of satisfaction and enjoyment. I would once have taken the opening sentence of Adam Smith's *Theory of Moral Sentiments* for a truism:

> How selfish soever man may be supposed, there is evidently some principles in his nature, which interest him in the fortune of others, and render their happiness necessary to him, though he derives nothing from it except the pleasure of seeing it.

But now I no longer think it is even a truth, let alone a truism. I would be more inclined to write:

> How good soever man may be supposed, there is evidently some principles in his nature, which interest him in the suffering of others... etc., etc.

69

I have seen so much, both at home and abroad, that I am not easily taken aback. When you have heard of baby-sitters who impale babies on railings in order to quieten them during a televised football match, or of men who suspend their girlfriends by their ankles from the fifteenth floor balcony, and this kind of thing daily for many years, you develop a kind of emotional carapace. One almost begins to take a pride in one's own unsociability, which one takes to be a kind of sophistication. It is a form of spiritual pride, I suppose. Still, I nevertheless read a book that shocked me. It was about the Rwandan genocide, called *A Time for Machetes*, by a French journalist called Jean Hatzfeld. He interviewed several men who had taken part in the genocide, probably the most murderous in human history, at least in terms of numbers of deaths per day while it lasted, and were now imprisoned. One of them was under sentence of death.

As it happens, I had been to Rwanda only a handful of years before the genocide. I was travelling across Africa by public transport, so that I could see African life from below, as it were. I passed through several extraordinary countries, for example Equatorial Guinea, where the first (democratically elected) president after independence from Spain had been overthrown and executed by his nephew. Francisco Macias Nguema was one of the great unsung political monsters of the twentieth century, the century *par excellence* of political monsters. He kept the national treasury under his bed, had all people who wore glasses executed on the grounds that they were dangerous intellectuals, introduced forced unpaid labour and killed or drove into exile a third of the population. His nephew who overthrew him, who until then had been his accomplice, was somewhat of an improvement, though still a dictator (and to this day is president): whenever he left the capital, the power supply was switched off as no longer being necessary. (An interesting history could be written of the murder or imprisonment during the twentieth century of people who wore glasses, merely because they wore glasses. Communists in particular were inclined to believe that people who wore glasses were their enemies, because – despite their own materialist conception of history, according to which the driving force of history is economic relations rather than ideas – short-sightedness is particularly prevalent among intellectuals, and intellectuals, at least outside the humanities of departments of western universities, have ideas that might cast doubt on the ultimate truth of communist ideology: a backhanded tribute to the fact that ideas ultimately rule the world.)

I am ashamed now of the superficiality of my understanding of the Rwanda of those days. I knew, of course, that Burundi (through which I had also just travelled) and Rwanda were mirror images of one another: that in Burundi it was the Tutsi minority that massacred the Hutu people, whereas in Rwanda it was the other way round, and that it was rather difficult to decide who had started this most vicious of vicious circles. But by comparison with many African countries, Rwanda seemed a well-run state, comparatively uncorrupt, its people industrious to a fault, and far from wretchedly poor, despite being one of the most densely populated countries in Africa, if not the world, with an astonishingly high natality. I knew, of course, that it was a dictatorship, the dictator being Major-General Juvenal Habyarimana, and that every Rwandan, *ex officio* as it were, was a member of the one party of the one-party state, the *Mouvement national révolutionnaire pour le développement* (MNRD), from birth. But at the time, I was not very optimistic that multi-party politics, of the kind that the dictator was forced to introduce in 1991, would necessarily represent an improvement. In a way, I was right: the most efficient slaughter in human history took place three years later.

In that slaughter, in the space of three months, neighbours killed without compunction those with whom they had been friendly all their lives, only because they were of the different, and reputedly opposing, ethnic designation. They used no high-tech means, only clubs and machetes. Women and children were not spared; husbands of mixed marriages killed wives, and vice versa. The participation of the general population in the slaughter was its most remarkable feature: usually in mass murder, it is the state that does the killing, or rather the state's agents, since the state is an abstraction without an existence independent of those who work for it. Hatzfeld, the African correspondent of the French left-wing newspaper, *Libération*, went to interview some of the perpetrators a few years after the genocide. They were friends who took part in the murder (if that is not too slight a word for it) of 50,000 of the 59,000 Tutsis who lived in their commune.

Oddly enough, being in prison gave them the ability to talk about what they had done, if not honestly, at least with some degree of freedom. I do not know to what degree Hatzfeld, who interviewed them individually and at length, edited the transcript of his interviews, and of course we have no way of knowing how representative his witnesses are: but their testimony is perhaps the most startling ever committed to paper.

There is no real remorse for what they did, only regret that it landed them in their current predicament. They feel more sorry for themselves than for their victims, or the survivors. They are not even altogether unhappy in prison, and look forward to resuming their lives where they left off (before the genocide) as if nothing too much had really happened - or should I say been done by them? They hoped for, and expected, forgiveness on the part of the survivors, amongst whom they would have to return to live, because resentment and bitterness are useless emotions and because they (the perpetrators) had all been gripped by a collective madness. This, of course, absolved them in large part from personal responsibility.

For three months, the men would get up, have a hearty breakfast, gather together, and then go on hunting expeditions of their former neighbours, who had fled to the nearby marshes. They would hack anyone they found to death; and then, when the whistle blew in the evening for them to stop their 'work' (they regarded it as such), they returned home, had a quick wash, had dinner and socialised in a jolly way over a few beers. Their wives would be − for the most part, though not universally − content, because Tutsi property was thoroughly looted, and distributed according to the individual efficiency and ruthlessness of the killers. One of the most haunting things in this book, if it is possible to pick anything out in particular, is that many of the victims did not so much as cry out when caught by the murderous *genocidaires*: they died in complete silence, as if speech and the human voice were now completely worthless, redundant, beside the point. I have often wondered why the people went into the gas chambers silently, without fighting back, but I suppose that when you witness absolute human evil committed by the people with whom you once lived, and who, at least metaphysically, are just like you, you see no point in the struggle for existence. Non-existence, perhaps, seems preferable to existence.

The murderers were pleased with their work, they thought of all the corrugated iron roofing, cattle and so forth that they were 'earning' by it. They had never been so prosperous as during this period of slaughter and looting. Unaccustomed to eating meat very often (the Tutsi were pastoralists, the Hutu cultivators), they gorged themselves upon it, like hyenas finding an abandoned kill in the bush. Very few were their pauses for thought.

Let us not console ourselves with the thought that these were unsophisticated Africans, without the mental capacity to know better: in short, mere savages. Again, I do not know how much Hatzfeld has edited their words, but his perpetrator interlocutors seem to me more articulate than most of the people with whom I have had to deal in Britain as patients over the last decade and a half. Indeed, their language occasionally becomes poetic: though poetic language in this circumstance is mere euphemism.

Besides, the few comments of the survivors, mostly women, that Hatzfeld inserts into the text, are of considerable moral and intellectual sophistication, and certainly not those of unreflecting primitives with few powers of cerebration. Here is Edith, a Tutsi schoolteacher, on the question of forgiveness:

'I know that all the Hutus who killed so calmly cannot be sincere when they beg pardon, even of the Lord. [Many now pray fervently: the Rwandans were fervently religious long before the genocide.] But me, I am ready to forgive. It is not a denial of the harm they did, not a betrayal of the Tutsis, not an easy way out. It is so that I will not suffer my whole life asking myself why they tried to cut me. [Cut is the euphemism used by victim and perpetrator alike for 'kill,' since most of the death was dealt with a machete.] I do not want to live in remorse and fear from being Tutsi. If I do not forgive them, it is I alone who suffers and frets and cannot sleep... I yearn for peace in my body. I really must find tranquillity. I have to sweep fear far away from me, even if I do not believe their soothing words.'

Francine, a Tutsi farm woman and shopkeeper, on the other hand, says this:

'Sometimes, when I sit alone in a chair on my veranda, I imagine this possibility: one far-off day, a local man comes slowly up to me and says, "Bonjour, Francine, I have come to speak to you. So, I am the one who cut your mama and your little sisters. I want to ask your forgiveness." Well, to that person I cannot reply anything good. A man may ask for forgiveness if he has one Primus [beer] too many and then beats his wife. But if he has worked at killing for a whole month, even on Sundays, whatever can he hope to be forgiven for? We must simply go back to living, since life has so decided... We shall return to drawing water together, to exchanging neighbourly words, to selling grain to one another. In twenty years, fifty years, there will perhaps be boys and girls who will learn about the genocide in books. For us, though, it is impossible to forgive.'

No, it is impossible to console ourselves with the thought that the Rwandans are so different from us that they and their experiences have nothing to say to us. Edith and Francine are, indeed, more dignified, more articulate, more intelligently reflective, than most of the victims of small-scale evil in an English slum whom I have met.

This book penetrates deeper into the heart of evil than any other I have ever read. The author makes no claims for his work: he is still mystified by it himself. But if you want to know what depths man can sink to – an important thing to know, when your argument is that things are so bad that they cannot get any worse, so prudence is unnecessary – read this book. At the very least, it will put your worries into perspective.

FREEDOM AND ITS DISCONTENTS

WHEN THE NAZIS MARCHED into Vienna, to the delirious welcome of the crowd, and not very long before the Gestapo escorted him off the premises as it were, Freud wrote two lapidary words in his diary: *Finis Austriae*. And since then it is true that Austria has not featured very prominently, let alone favourably, in the mental horizons of most educated people even in Europe, much less in North America. Despite its great beauty, its marvellous historical and artistic heritage, and its ascent to great and near-universal prosperity, a pall even yet hangs over the country, for the most obvious reasons.

When I think of modern Austria, here is what I think of: scenes from the film *The Third Man*, the writer Thomas Bernhard who so despised his native land that he directed in his will that none of his books ever be published there, and the diplomat Kurt Waldheim who covered up his own past, again for very obvious reasons. If pushed, I think also of a modernist artist whose brilliantly original idea was to cover everything in blood, and Elfriede Jellinek, the Nobel Prize winner whose view of her country is hardly more flattering than that of Bernhard. No doubt this is all very unfair, but we are seldom fair about anything.

Not long ago, however, Vienna was in the news, or at least in one of the British newspapers: for it reported from there the case of the youngest transsexual in the world. Once known as Tim, Kim started to receive treatment for a change of sex at the age of twelve. Tim (as he then was) apparently persuaded doctors that he was born in the wrong kind of body, and despite his youth, they accepted him at his word.

Later in the day of the publication of the story, the BBC telephoned me and asked me whether I would comment on the case for the World Service. They asked me what I would say, and the first thing that came to mind was the likelihood of a lawsuit against the doctors at some time in the future. The search for compensation sometimes seems to be modern Man's (or should I say personkind's?) deepest quest. After all, Man is born happy, but everywhere he's sad: so it must be that someone is to blame, and, as an advertising jingle for no-win, no-fee lawyers that I once overheard in a radio in a taxi put it, 'Remember, where there's blame, there's a claim.'

I was not very enthusiastic about appearing on the programme, however, for more than one reason. Although I believe that concision is next to godliness, and everyone should say what he has to say in as few words as possible, the distillation of answers to difficult philosophical questions into soundbites is not necessarily propitious to proper discussion and argumentation.

(The BBC, on the whole, doesn't go in for long discussions, believing that its audience has the attention span of – I nearly said a twelve-year-old, but of course, as we have seen, twelve-year-olds are now mature enough to take the most momentous decisions in life. On another occasion, a researcher asked me to appear on what it called 'a long discussion' on a subject that seemed to me an important one, but when I asked what she meant by 'long' she replied 'Six minutes,' and then said, when I remarked that six minutes did not seem so very long to me, that it was long for them. Long, after all, is a relative term. And when I asked how many other people were to appear on this long, indeed virtually interminable, discussion, she said three, not counting the presenter, which suggested to me that the winner of the discussion – for there must always be a winner – would be he who managed to shout the loudest and bully his voice into the microphone. If T S Eliot were alive today, I think he'd change that famous line to 'Human kind cannot bear very much discussion.')

Fortunately, I had a good excuse not to appear on the programme, though why I should have felt that I needed an excuse is itself a little odd. At any rate, I had a dinner engagement at the time of the broadcast, which released me of all sense of obligation. I felt an almost physical relief.

Immediately, in the manner of a professional intellectual, I began to analyse the reasons for this. The answer was neither flattering to me, nor reassuring about the state of our freedom.

If I had spoken my mind, without let or hindrance, I should have said what I suspect a very large majority of people think: that there is something grotesque, and even repugnant, about the whole idea of sex-changes, let alone of sex-changes for twelve-year-olds. A feeling of repugnance is not a complete moral argument, of course;

something deeper is required. Nevertheless, an intuition that an action or policy is profoundly wrong is the beginning, if not the end, of moral reflection.

However, the fact is (if I am truthful) that a certain fear or pusillanimity entered into my relief that I was not to broadcast on this subject. If I had done the broadcast, I would have had to sit opposite an advocate of trans-sexualism in the studio (so the producer had told me), and to be true to myself and my opinions I would have had to tell him/her, in front of an audience of many thousands if not millions, that I thought that what he/she had done was fundamentally egotistical and antisocial. Knowing the format for radio programmes, it was unlikely that I would have been able to give my reasons for thinking so; and I am in general reluctant to give gratuitous offence to a particular person, partly from moral cowardice and partly from a belief that the giving of such offence is a bad thing in itself.

But I was also aware that trans-sexuals now form a considerable lobby group, not because of their number, which is inconsiderable, but because of support from that part of the intelligentsia that sees the dissolution of boundaries if not as God's work exactly, then as the work of the morally elect. They have been fighting boundaries for years.

Well, what of that? We certainly don't live in a society in which one has to fear the midnight knock on the door because one has stepped out of line by expressing faulty opinions. Yet lobby groups and their allies nevertheless have a way of exacting a price for the expression of views very different from their own. They are able to portray that person that opposes them as unreasonable and bigoted, as some kind of pea-brained antediluvian. And the fact is that they are probably prepared to put more effort into doing this than the person who opposes them is prepared to put into defending his opinion, because he is not a monomaniac or a one-issue person, unlike at least some of his opponents. The truth is that I don't care very much about trans-sexualism, and so I didn't want to risk even a small amount of public opprobrium from right-thinking people on the subject. The heavens will not fall if one twelve-year-old Austrian boy gets a sex-change, after all; and there is, to adapt slightly a saying of Adam Smith's, a deal of ruin in a civilisation.

Thus we see how social change, of a kind opposed by the majority of the population, can come about: no one can be found to oppose it strongly, because the individual change doesn't matter that much, except to the beneficiaries, and the price of opposing it is made too high. Precedents are set, and once set, followed; there is no going back. Omelettes never can become eggs again; the genie never returns to the bottle.

It used to be that governments were the greatest threat to freedom of expression, but now it is social pressure of the kind I have described that threatens debate. I first realised this when I wrote an article about a condition known as Chronic Fatigue Syndrome, questioning - I must admit, in less than emollient terms - the firm view of those who suffer from it, namely that it is a viral rather than a psychosocial condition.

What I had not realised at the time I wrote was that the sufferers from chronic fatigue were, in fact, tirelessly active in defence of their view of their condition, and would entertain no other. No sooner was the article published than I began to receive protests by telephone and post, often cast in unpleasant and abusive language; my hospital received calls for my dismissal; even a government minister was contacted.

I discovered when I spoke to other journalists who had written or broadcast in similar vein about the same subject that the treatment I received at the hands of the chronically fatigued was comparatively mild, perhaps because of my obscurity and unimportance. Television journalists in particular were made to suffer, for long receiving calls in the middle of the night, a barrage of insults and so forth, often for month after month, so that their sleep was chronically disturbed. Not surprisingly, they resolved never to touch the subject again: for them, after all, it was only one subject among many, while for the protesters it was the subject of subjects. Even comparatively discreet researchers, who wrote in much more guarded terms, told me that if they deviated by one jot or tittle from the line propounded by the chronically fatigued, they were inundated with protests. One, an eminent professor, told me that he had felt almost under siege.

And thus the argument went by default: and only one view was allowed to enter the public consciousness. The point at issue is not whether the chronically fatigued are right in their views (they may yet be proved to be so), but whether they should attempt to curtail legitimate debate in this fashion.

Let us be honest: there are few of us who have never felt the temptation to silence those fools and scoundrels who have views different from our own. They must, after all, be either stupid or malevolent (or, of course, both). If the means to silence them were at hand, we would be sorely tempted to use them.

Which of us listens without impatience and even anger to the arguments of our opponents? If you believe in global warming as the result of man's activities, can you abide the obviously crooked arguments of the sceptics, who are in the pay of, or at least in mental thrall to, the polluting multinationals? Or if you believe that Al Gore only wants to increase the power of governments, preferably with him in charge of the largest of them, can you listen without a rise in pulse rate and blood pressure to the arguments of climatologists who insist that it is we – I mean, we humans – who are causing a rise in global temperature? What is truth? said jesting Pilate, and would not stay for an answer.

La Rochefoucauld said that love of justice in most men is only fear of suffering injustice. By analogy, love of free speech in most men is only fear of being shut up. If they were a bit stronger than they are, they would just have monologues, the most pleasurable of all speech forms. Who among us has not taken part in a conversation in which his principal concern was with what he was going to say next, hardly bothering in the meantime to listen to the others, except to await a pause into which he may interject his wonderful words?

The threat to free speech does not inhere, therefore, solely in governments, but in our hearts. And in the modern world, a peculiar threat comes from right-thinking monomaniacs who associate to form pressure groups. With the decline in the grand ideology of socialism, we have not seen the decline of ideology, but the rise of micro-ideologies. Ideology has been divided into fragments and privatised, as it were, but it remains just as ideological. And few pleasures are greater than those of the exercise of power, especially in the name of the greater good. To be both powerful and virtuous, how delightful!

Please don't reply to any part of this essay. I won't read it: I know I'm right.

DO THE IMPOSSIBLE: KNOW THYSELF

I ATTENDED A FASCINATING conference on neuropsychiatry recently. Neuroscience, it seems to me, is the current most hopeful candidate for the role of putative but delusory answer to all mankind's deepest questions: what is Man's place in Nature, and how should he live? What is the good life, at least in the western world?

The fact that there is no definitive answer to these questions does not mean that we cease to ask them. Some philosophers have argued that a question that is in principle unanswerable is not really a question at all, but the philosophical equivalent of verbigeration, the symptom in which some lunatics make word-like sounds that do not actually correspond to any language. But this strikes me as evasive, a kind of high class magical thinking, in which a person believes that a state of affairs can be brought about merely by wishing it to be brought about.

An equal and opposite temptation is to believe that the questions have already been answered, at least in principle (that is to say, everything but the detail has been worked out). Freudians and Marxists, for example, once believed that they knew not only what had gone wrong with human existence, but how to put it right. They believed this because they thought they had a complete and sufficient explanation and description of Man. This, of course, put them at a great advantage, at least in their own estimation, to the great mass of mankind that was neither Marxist nor Freudian. They had seen the light as clearly as any evangelical; and there are few states of mind more delightful than an awareness of superior understanding to that of the great mass of one's fellows.

It will not have escaped the notice of the observant that Marxism and Freudianism have become a little frayed around the edges of late, and that their adherents are reduced to recalcitrant membership of increasingly beleaguered sects. But the attraction of all-embracing worldviews that explain not only who we are but prescribe how we ought to live remains as strong as ever. Some of the neuroscientists to whom I listened at the conference implied that we were on the verge of such a breakthrough in our self-understanding, thanks to neuroimaging, neurochemistry and neurogenetics and so forth, that Man, proud Man, will no longer be a mystery to himself. The heart of all our mysteries will be plucked out wholesale, as it were; and to understand all will then be not so much to forgive all as to control all, especially our bad habits.

Let me not be taken as denying that the neurosciences have advanced stupendously in the last few years. Progress, indeed, has been so rapid that leaders in various fields now talk of the late 1990s as if of an era of prehistoric antiquity and ignorance, just as those in the late 1990s used to talk of the late 1980s.

During the conference, I heard one of the best lectures I have ever heard by a professor at the Salpêtrière in Paris. (This hospital, of course, has one of the most distinguished histories in neurology of any hospital in the world.) Not only did the professor speak brilliantly, with wit, learning and charm, but he showed astonishing before and after videos of patients treated surgically for a variety of conditions, from Parkinson's disease to Gilles de la Tourette's syndrome. It was difficult then not to succumb to a sort of euphoria, that consisted of the belief that at last we really did understand, at least in principle, what it was to be a human being. This was further reinforced by neuroimaging studies showing the areas of the brain that were active when a man in love perceives his beloved: the neurological basis of romantic love, as it were. Somewhat disappointingly for romantics, the parts of the brain that are activated during the encounter are primitive from the evolutionary point of view, and present in the pigeon and the lizard.

In fact, the professor from the Salpêtrière, being a cultivated man, was comparatively circumspect in his estimation of the wider significance of his work. The operations he described were performed on people with gross and relatively discrete pathology, who were abnormal in a very obvious way. In fact, for all the wizardry of the means used, the extension of our knowledge upon the basis of which the operations were performed was not of an order of magnitude greater than previous advances, nor was that knowledge different in kind from that which we had already long possessed.

Nevertheless, several speakers strongly implied that with the exponential growth of neuroscientific research, we were about to understand ourselves to a degree unmatched by any previously living humans. I confess that, whenever I heard this, I thought of the old proverb about Brazil: that it is, and always will be, the country of the future.

At the very end of the conference, a well-known professor of philosophy was brought in to confirm that man's self-understanding would soon advance by leaps and bounds, thanks to the neurosciences. The professor was a man of great erudition, and spoke fluently without notes, with enormous and beguiling wit. Many times before, he said, Man had believed that he understood himself; this time, it was going to be true.

The speaker was so convincing and so fluent that I could not but help recall the way that Michael Oakeshotte, the former Professor of Political Philosophy at the London School of Economics, and the greatest conservative thinker of his time, introduced Isaiah Berlin at the LSE where he had come to give a lecture. Isaiah Berlin, he said, was the Paganini of the lecture platform: the best compliment-cum-insult I know, approximated only by Disraeli's remark when champagne was served after a truly terrible public banquet. Thank God, said Disraeli, for something warm at last.

Two main questions arose in my mind during the neuropsychiatric conference. The first was whether any scientific self-understanding was possible. The second was whether, if possible, it was desirable. My answer to both questions was, and is, no.

In the first place I find it difficult even to conceive of what a scientific self-understanding would actually be like. My patients often used to ask me, 'Doctor, why am I like this?' or 'Why do I do the things I do?' I would sometimes then ask them what they would consider an adequate and satisfactory explanation, and not a single one (including the highly intelligent and educated) was able to tell me.

For example, alcoholics would ask me why they drank. I would give the various, not necessarily mutually exclusive, explanations, including that related to the price of alcohol. If the price of alcohol falls, the consumption in a population as a whole rises, and the normal distribution curve of consumption shifts to the right, with a disproportionate number of people then falling into the category of problem drinkers. In other words, more than half of alcoholics drink too much because the price of alcohol is too low.

It will not perhaps surprise readers to learn that this explanation, while statistically sound, failed altogether to satisfy my patients; for, as they quite rightly asked, why then did some people drink and some not, whatever the price of alcohol? Even at high prices, some people become alcoholics; and even at low, most people never do.

Well, of course there is a genetic component. People with family histories of alcoholism are more inclined than others to drink to excess, and this is a genuine genetic effect, as twin studies have shown (identical twins are more likely to show similar patterns of drinking than are non-identical twins). But even identical twins show dissimilar drinking patterns more often than they show similar ones.

The fact is that, however many factors you examine, you cannot fully explain behaviour, not even relatively simple behaviour. And if you cannot explain relatively simple behaviour, how are we to explain the immense, indeed infinite, variety of human behaviour? How are we fully to account for the infinite variety and originality of human utterance, for example? (It is vanishingly unlikely that the last sentence, or for that matter this one, has ever been written before.) How does one develop a universal law that explains an infinite number of unique events that are infused with meaning and intentionality? It was on this question that the programme of behaviourism, that (as everyone now completely forgets, though it was not so very long ago) promised a complete and sufficient explanation of human behaviour, foundered.

A neuroscientist might reply that he is not trying to develop a theory that explains everything in detail, but only in general: that is to say, to explain the important and significant generalities of human thought, feeling and conduct. But on a purely scientific or naturalistic view, nothing is more important than anything else, in the sense in which the words are being used here. In a universe deprived of intentionality as a whole, a volcano is no more important than the death of a beetle, or the explosion of a star. Nothing is important or significant but conscious thinking makes it so: the type of thinking, moreover, that employs moral categories that are inherently non-natural.

What people consider important varies according to their interests. In imaginative literature, for example, some authors take the broad sweep of history as their subject, while others take the minor fluctuations of a single person's emotional state. (Only the very greatest, such as Shakespeare, successfully take both at the same time.) There is no way of deciding which approach is correct or better, though I have my preferences.

Those who say that we are on the verge of a huge increase in self-understanding are claiming that enlightenment will suddenly be reached under the scientific bo tree. The enlightenment will have to be sudden rather than gradual because, if it were gradual, we should already be able to point to an increase in human contentment and self-control brought about by our already increased knowledge. But even the most advanced societies are just as full of angst, or poor impulse control, of existential bewilderment, of adherence to clearly irrational doctrines, as ever they were. There is no sign that, Prozac and neurosurgery notwithstanding, any of this is about to change fundamentally.

In other words, I think that life will continue to bewilder us for as long as we are self-conscious, thinking, feeling beings.

Let me briefly turn to the question of whether complete self-understanding, if attainable, would be desirable.

It would entail an ability not only to explain but to monitor and predict all human thoughts whatsoever. It would be possible, in theory, indeed necessary, that we should have an implement capable of access to everyone's thoughts. For example, I would have a scanner that, directed at you, gave me access to your thoughts that you would not be able to hide from me. Of course, you too would have such a scanner to give you access to my thoughts.

You might say, of course, that while such a device would be possible, it would not be universally available; but it is a moot point whether such a device would be more horrible in its consequences if it were available only to some people than if it were available to all. What is certain is that, if our self-understanding reached the point that such a device were possible, life would be hell.

In my opinion, the great philosopher David Hume understood why human self-understanding was forever beyond our reach. It is not a coincidence that he always expressed himself with irony, for the deepest irony possible is that of the existence of a creature, Man, who forever seeks something that is beyond his understanding.

Hume was simultaneously a figure of the enlightenment and the anti-enlightenment. He saw that reason and consideration of the evidence are all that a rational man can rely upon, yet they are eternally insufficient for Man as he is situated. In short, there cannot be such a thing as the wholly rational man. Reason, he said, is the slave of the passions; and in addition, no statement of value follows logically from any statement of fact. But we cannot live without evaluations.

Ergo, self-understanding is not around the corner and never will be. We shall never be able seamlessly to join knowledge and action. To which I add, not in any religious sense: thank God.

OLIVER GOLDSMITH
AND THE THIRD WORLD

DOCTOR JOHNSON WAS VERY good at encomia. (Or should it be encomiums? I think both are correct, but I prefer the former on the grounds of euphony, though I await with eagerness the correction of pedants.)

Speaking of the great portraitist, Sir Joshua Reynolds, Johnson said, 'Sir Joshua, sir, is the most invulnerable man I know; the man with whom, if you should quarrel, you would find the most difficulty how to abuse.' I cannot think of many people of whom such a thing could plausibly be claimed, and because Johnson implied that abuse had to contain at least an element of truth (or else why should it ever be difficult to abuse anyone?) his tribute is a sincere and moving one.

Doctor Johnson's epitaph for Oliver Goldsmith was handsome too: 'Oliver Goldsmith: Poet, Naturalist, Historian, who left scarce any style of writing untouched, and touched nothing that he did not adorn.'

Johnson also knew how to damn with faint praise, of course. He said of Goldsmith's poem, 'The Traveller', that it was the finest poem that had appeared since the time of Pope: but Johnson's low opinion of the intervening poets was well known. He thought even Thomas Gray, of the Elegy in a Country Churchyard, dull, and called him 'a mechanical poet'.

Goldsmith's most famous poem, and I suspect the only one ever read nowadays, is 'The Deserted Village,' written in pleasant, and occasionally moving, rhyming couplets. Perhaps it is not a coincidence that Goldsmith, who usually wrote with great speed, expended more time and effort over this poem than over anything else he ever wrote. I re-read it recently, for reasons both complex and dull, and my response to it was deeply ambiguous, for reasons more to do with the ideas expressed in the poem than with the felicity or otherwise of the manner in which they were expressed.

'The Deserted Village' could have been written by contemporary anti-globalisers were they inclined to write poetry, which thankfully they are not. For the poem (published in 1769) is a lament on the

86

modern world, and on the destruction of an older, kinder, better world by that vile activity, trade.

First, Goldsmith praises the village as it once was and as he once knew it:

> Sweet Auburn! loveliest village of the plain,
> Where health and plenty cheer'd the labouring swain,
> Where smiling spring its earliest visit paid,
> And parting summer's lingering blooms delay'd...

The village was once a virtual paradise, though (or because) life there was simple:

> A time there was, ere England's grief's began,
> When every rood of land maintain'd its man;
> For him light labour spread her wholesome store,
> Just gave what life required, but gave no more;
> His best companions, innocence and health;
> And his best riches, ignorance of wealth.

Alas, a worm enters the bud:

> But times are alter'd; trade's unfeeling train
> Usurp the land, and dispossess the swain;
> Along the lawn, where scatter'd hamlets rose,
> Unwieldy wealth and cumbrous pomp repose...

The land having been sequestered by 'unwieldy wealth', the rural population goes to the city, both driven and attracted thither, the latter by its luxury and glitter:

> If to the city sped – What waits him there?
> To see profusion that he must not share;
> To see ten thousand baneful arts combin'd
> To pamper luxury, and thin mankind;
> To see each joy the sons of pleasure know,
> Extorted from his fellow creature's woe.

Goldsmith expresses his disapproval of this process in the most famous lines of the whole poem:

> Ill fares the land, to hastening ills a prey,
> Where wealth accumulates, and men decay;
> Princes and lords may flourish, or may fade;
> A breath can make them, as a breath has made:
> But a bold peasantry, their country's pride,
> When once destroy'd, can never be supply'd.

And Goldsmith then addresses himself to the great ones of the earth and asks them important questions:

> Ye friends to truth, ye statesmen, who survey
> The rich man's joys increase, the poor's decay,
> 'Tis yours to judge how wide the limits stand
> Between a splendid and a happy land.

It is, of course, very easy to pick holes in Goldsmith's arguments, or presumptions. The idea of a prelapsarian past, during which a little light labour procured for mankind a simple but healthy subsistence is a recurrent delusion. When Goldsmith describes agricultural labour before the machine age, it is clear that he has never done much or any of it himself. It was hard, repetitive, dull, boring and dangerous. And it is highly unlikely that many agricultural labourers were ignorant of the advantages of wealth: they simply had no idea of how to go about acquiring it.

As for 'trade's unfeeling train', it was to be only a few years before Adam Smith definitively pointed out what in fact had been pointed out before, that the tradesman, in acting selfishly, had to please his customers. To do so, they had to enter imaginatively into their worlds: so tradesmen could not afford to be unfeeling in the same way as a feudal baron could afford to be unfeeling.

And Goldsmith is clearly a believer in zero-sum economics: that one man's loss is another's gain, that in order for one man to be fat many others must be thin. This supposition underlies a lot of Third-Worldist thinking, according to which part of the world is rich because the other part is poor. This noxious idea springs eternal, because the economy – of a country or indeed of the whole world – is conceived statically, as a cake, rather than dynamically, as a growing organism.

It is not very difficult to prove that the wealth of the world has increased dramatically, that impoverishment has declined, and that it is simply not true that the wealth of one requires the poverty of another.

Yet I did not respond to the poem as if it were simply a catalogue of vulgar errors, long since corrected. This is because, looking at developments in my own lifetime, I think there has been regression as well as advance; and perhaps it is because of my advancing years, but I often think the former has been greater than the latter, despite the enormous increase in prosperity I have witnessed. The idea that wealth can accumulate and men decay is not inherently a foolish one.

Many, if not most, advances are not pure and unadulterated; there is rarely gain without loss. I can illustrate this with a very trivial example from my own experience.

In my childhood, fruits were still seasonal; there were summer fruits and winter fruits. With the tremendous advances in methods of cultivation, transport, distribution, marketing and so forth, there is only one season of the year: and that is now.

As a child I used to look forward with longing to the short raspberry season (raspberries were, and are, my favourite fruit). This longing was equalled only by the joy, the rapture, when the first raspberries of the season appeared. How I wanted the season to go on for ever, and yet I knew it would last only three or four weeks. Never has fruit given me such pleasure.

Nowadays, I can buy raspberries all year round. They arrive from every corner of the globe: it is astonishing that raspberries from Chile appear in my local supermarket 48 to 72 hours after they have been picked (and they are far from bad, too). This is a miracle of organisation that only the market could have achieved.

And yet: much as I still like raspberries, I will never recapture the joy I experienced in my childhood which consisted as much of the eager anticipation as the fulfilment of my desire. I do not approach the fruit counter of my supermarket with any great excitement.

Nor do I expect my supermarket one day to put up a notice to the effect that it is no longer importing raspberries because it wants its customers to experience the joys of longing and anticipation. I suspect that I would be quite cross if it did. So Goldsmith is right: some things, some pleasures, some joys, once destroy'd, can never be supply'd.

Nor does it seem to me self-evident that the flight to the city is always an unmixed blessing, or that people do not lose something important when they move. One of the things that I have remarked on my travels, for example, is the almost instant loss of visual taste when peasants move from the country to the city. I have seen it in Asia, in Africa, in South America.

I do not want to indulge in any Noble Savagery, yet I have noticed that peasants often have a remarkable eye for form and colour. They give beauty even to utilitarian objects. Most African huts, for example, have an elegance about them, a delicacy of form and – where colorations are used – they also display a colour sense that is moving in its refinement. But as soon as the peasants move to the city, they accumulate kitsch, not because kitsch is all that is available to them, but because they come at once to like it. Delicacy and refinement are replaced by crudity and garishness. Perhaps they associate all that is kitsch with modernity: I have no real theory why the transformation of taste should take place, but it does.

Of course, you might say that if their tastes change, what is it to you? If they are happy with plastic roses and cheap enamel bowls instead of beautifully woven mats and elegant pottery, who are you to complain? It is their right to make choices about their own lives. If they think living in a squalid slum in a city of umpteen million offers them a better life than eking out an existence in the remote countryside, what right have you to complain?

Fundamentally I agree; I don't think you can keep people by force in an anthropological museum for the aesthetic delectation of refined people such as I. And yet it would also be false to say that I look forward eagerly to a world in which all the instinctive, or at least unselfconscious, artistry of peasant life has been extinguished in favour of mass-produced artefacts of doubtful aesthetic worth.

Again, when Goldsmith asks whether a splendid or a happy land is more desirable, he is only uttering a commonplace: that, within quite wide limits, money does not buy happiness.

Finally, Goldsmith – who trained as a doctor – tells us that the peasant life was healthy by comparison with that of the city. From our present standpoint of unprecedented good health, this sounds absurd. Yet when Goldsmith wrote, a half of all children in London died before the age of five. For some hundreds of years, London could not have maintained, much less increased, its population by reproduction alone: it needed immigrants from the countryside. Otherwise, its population would have shrunk.

Furthermore, cities remained obviously noisome places for a hundred years to come. In the poorer parts of Liverpool, for example, the median age at death was 18. Even when my father was born, in the slums of London, the infant mortality rate, that is to say the numbers of children dying in their first year of life, was 125 per 1000. And London was then among the healthiest capital cities in Europe.

So Goldsmith's attitude was not self-evidently ridiculous, though in the event it proved to be mistaken. Of course it was modernisation, with its concomitant urbanisation, that produced not just the enrichment of mankind, but its vastly improved life expectancy. Goldsmith was not to know that; what he saw was the break-up of a way of life that was apparently in equilibrium with its surroundings exchanged for conditions that were truly horrific. Furthermore, it would have been of no consolation to him to know that future generations would benefit from this exchange; for we live predominantly, if not entirely, in the present.

I think the anti-globalists are making the same mistakes as are made in 'The Deserted Village', but they are not entirely to be despised for it. For the truth remains that there is always loss as well as gain in any advance. That is why melancholia recurs in successive generations at a certain point in their life cycle.

WHY INTELLECTUALS LIKE GENOCIDE

SEEMINGLY ARCANE HISTORICAL DISPUTES can often cast a powerful light on the state of our collective soul. It is for that reason that I like to read books on obscure subjects: they are often more illuminating than books that at first sight are more immediately relevant to our current situation. For, as Emily Dickinson put it, success in indirection lies.

In 2002, the Australian freelance historian and journalist, Keith Windschuttle, published a book that created a controversy that has still not died down. Entitled *The Fabrication of Aboriginal History*, it sets out to destroy the idea that there had been a genocide of Tasmanian aborigines carried out by the early European settlers of the island.

For about the previous quarter of a century, it was more or less an historical orthodoxy that there had been such a genocide. Robert Hughes accepted the idea in his best-selling history of early Australia, *The Fatal Shore*. I accepted it myself, because when I first visited Australia in 1982 I read several books on the subject by professors of history at reputable universities, and rather naively supposed that their work must have been founded on painstaking and honest research, and that they had not misrepresented their original sources.

Windschuttle argued in his book that they had fabricated much of their evidence, and that, contrary to what they claimed, there had been no deliberate policy on the part of the colonial authorities or the local population either to extirpate or kill very large numbers of aborigines. He showed that the historians' reading of the obscure source materials was either misleading or mendacious.

He sifted the material very carefully and found that there was evidence for the killing of 120 Tasmanian aborigines, either by settlers or by the military and police. Although this does not sound many, in relation to the population of Tasmanian aborigines it was a lot. It is the equivalent in the United States of upwards of 7,000,000, for there were only about 4,000 aborigines (or so it is thought) at any one time in Tasmania.

However, a similar number of settlers were killed by aborigines, and perhaps it is not so very surprising that there was conflict between people of such widely different conceptions of life as the aborigines and the early British settlers. But conflict is not genocide, which entails a plan deliberately to rid the world of a certain population. There was no genocide in Tasmania. The Tasmanian aborigines did indeed die out in the nineteenth century, but largely of disease and as a result of the loss of fertility caused by the venereal disease introduced by the settlers.

After the book was published, there were furious challenges to Windschuttle. Slurs were cast upon him: he was, for example, the Australian equivalent of the Holocaust deniers. A book of essays in refutation of his point of view was published; a refutation of the refutation was also published. He appeared all round the country in debates with some of his detractors. As far as I understand it, the massed ranks of the professional historians were unable seriously to dent his argument. A few small errors (which he acknowledged) were found in his book, but not such as to undermine his thesis; in any case, they were very minor by comparison with the wholesale errors of his opponents. He had been much more scrupulous than they.

What struck me at the time about the controversy was the evident fact that a large and influential part of the Australian academy and intelligentsia actually wanted there to have been a genocide. They reacted to Windschuttle's book like a child who has had a toy snatched from its hand by its elder sibling. You would have thought that a man who discovered that his country had not been founded, as had previously been thought and taught, on genocide would be treated as a national hero. On the contrary, he was held up to execration.

Why should this be? Here I confess that I am entering the world of the *ad hominem*. I will not be able to prove my assertions beyond reasonable doubt, and other interpretations are possible. However, when it comes to questions of human motivation, it is difficult altogether to avoid the *ad hominem*.

It is, of course, possible, that the professors and the intelligentsia were so convinced that there had been a genocide, and believed that the evidence that it had taken place was so overwhelming, that any person who denied it must have been an extremely bad man. On the other hand, if the evidence was so overwhelming, they should have been able easily to produce sufficient of it in public to convince someone like me (and many others). This they have not done, and so one must conclude that, at the very least, the historical question is an open one. And if the question is still an open one, the fury directed at Windschuttle was quite disproportionate.

I think the explanation lies elsewhere. Australia is known, not without reason, as the Lucky Country. It has virtually every resource known to man. It is a liberal democracy and has been for most of its existence. No one in Australia has ever feared the midnight knock on the door. To live well there requires a good deal less effort than in most places, perhaps anywhere else. The climate in much of the country is generally very pleasant. Overall, it is probably the best place, certainly among the best places, on earth to live. The fact that it is lucky is not, of course, a consequence of its natural endowments alone, but of what human beings have made of those endowments. Australia is a triumphant success.

This is not to say that everyone in Australia is deliciously happy, or that Australia is a prelapsarian Garden of Eden. People who live there, like people everywhere, have their problems. They go bankrupt, divorce, neglect their children, have accidents, die prematurely, kill themselves, overeat, drink too much, get bored, suffer illnesses, and so forth, just like people everywhere else.

The fact is, however, that political reforms in Australia, whatever they might be, are very unlikely to add much to the sum of human welfare there. Australia confronts human beings with their existential responsibility to make happiness for themselves, and this is sometimes a hard responsibility to face up to. For if you are unhappy in a country like Australia, you have to consider the possibility that the problem lies with you rather than with the conditions that surround you.

This is a disagreeable thing, particularly for an intelligentsia, which is deprived by it of a providential role for itself. What does an intelligentsia do when a country is already as satisfactory in its political arrangements and social institutions as any country has ever been? Intelligentsias do not like the kind of small problems that day-to-day existence inevitably throws up, such as termites in the woodwork or conflict at work over desk space: they like to get their intellectual teeth into weightier, meatier problems.

What could be a weightier problem than a prosperous, fortunate country that was founded upon genocide? Clearly, if it was so founded, an intelligentsia is urgently needed to help it emerge from the dark moral labyrinth in which it exists, hitherto blindly. For only an intelligentsia is sufficiently used to thinking in abstractions to be qualified to act as guide to the nation.

Of course, an intelligentsia needs allies, for it is rarely strong enough by itself to dominate and control a society, and oddly enough the genocide school of Tasmanian history has created allies in people who now call themselves Tasmanian aborigines. But – I hear you object – I thought you said that Tasmanian aborigines died out in the nineteenth century (the last one being called Truganini)? Yes, I reply, but that is full-blooded aborigines. Because there were sexual relations between the first settlers and aborigine women, there exist people in Tasmania with aborigine blood running in the veins. Admittedly, that blood is almost as dilute as a homeopath's medicine, but it is enough for some purposes.

Where there has been genocide, it is only right that there should be apology and, more importantly, reparation. In the case of the aborigines, this can only be restoration of the land to them as a collectivity. Indeed, it has been suggested that half the territory of the island of Tasmania be reserved to aborigines.

These aborigines live indistinguishably from their non-aboriginal neighbours. They speak no language other than English; they do not forage in the bush for food; they have the same jobs and are under no social disability, perhaps because they are also physically indistinguishable from non-aborigines. In fact they are descended to a much greater extent from the perpetrators and beneficiaries of the alleged genocide than from the victims of it. It would therefore be difficult to think of a more obvious attempted fraud perpetrated on a political entity than the claim by Tasmanian 'aborigines' to ancestral lands.

Actually, Tasmanian historiography of the genocide school has parallels elsewhere. I remember when I lived for a time in Guatemala reading the most currently-celebrated account of colonial Guatemala, called *La patria del criollo*. In all of its eight hundred pages the role of epidemic disease in reducing the number of Indians after the arrival of the Spanish was not mentioned even once, not even in passing, though it is almost certain (that is to say as certain as it can be) that the overwhelming cause of the decrease was epidemic disease.

Why was it not mentioned? Because the author wanted to present the current, supposedly lamentable state of Guatemala to be a direct consequence of the colonial era, which was itself a time of genocide. This being the case, there was only one thing to be done: to found the state anew, to start all over again, to build a new state from a better blueprint. It is not very difficult to see what role the intelligentsia would have in constructing the new society: a very powerful, indeed directing one.

The same is true in Australia, of course. If the current state was founded on genocide then, however superficially satisfactory it might appear at first sight, it is necessary to re-found it on a sounder, more ethical basis. And the architects and subsequent owner-managers will, of course, be the intelligentsia; for only they are qualified.

Now Australia is a country that in general, until recently at any rate, has not cherished its intellectuals. It has not accorded them the respect to which they think they are naturally entitled. Indeed, until a couple of decades ago it was common practice for Australian intellectuals to flee their country and live elsewhere, so strong was the anti-intellectual atmosphere of their country. Australia was not a lucky country as far as intellectuals were concerned.

That has changed quite a lot recently, but still intellectuals in Australia are not taken as seriously by the public as they take themselves. Besides, there are now more of them, and competition for attention is therefore greater. And there is nothing much more attention-grabbing than the claim that your current happiness and good fortune is founded on a pile of bones. With a bit of luck, this claim will even turn people neurotic and increase the need for therapists.

It is hardly surprising, then, that when someone came along and challenged the version of history on which their new-found importance in society was to be based, they threw their dolly out of the pram, as the prison wardens in the prison in which I worked used to put it to describe the actions of a prisoner who had lost his temper. The dispute was not just a matter of the interpretation of the contents of old newspapers in Hobart libraries: it went to the very heart of the intelligentsia's self-conception as society's conscience and natural leaders.

A conflict over the veracity of footnotes was thus a conflict also over the proper place of intellectuals in modern society. And Windschuttle was vastly more often right about the footnotes than he was wrong. This was quite unforgivable of him.

THE QUESTION OF ISLAM

IT IS THE BEST of faiths, it is the worst of faiths. It is the faith of tolerance, it is the faith of hate. Opinions of Islam in the world could hardly be more diverse or more opposed.

However many times one hears it said that Islam is not a unitary phenomenon – that the Sufis are as different from the Salafists as chalk is from cheese – almost everyone, after pronouncing this caveat, proceeds to speak or to write as if Islam were a unitary phenomenon. This is the great achievement of the Islamists: they have turned the nastiest imaginable form of their religion into the only one that counts for non-Moslems – and for an increasing number of Moslems too. It is as if the Spanish Inquisition had been made the sole legitimate representative (to use the cant term of the 1960s and 70s) of Christianity.

The claims that Islam has in its history been religiously tolerant are difficult to disentangle in an honest fashion. Without an axe to grind, you would hardly even consider the question. Islam is a religion but Moslems are people, and their conduct may not always have been what religious enthusiasts would have wanted it to be, or believed was religiously required. Then again, what is religiously required has been a matter of dispute: and extremism has not always prevailed over pragmatism.

Perhaps I should start with a personal experience. Not long ago in Istanbul, I bought something in a shop owned by a Jewish family. The language in which I spoke to the proprietor was Spanish: he was of the last generation that spoke Ladino, the mediaeval Spanish that the Jews expelled from the Iberian peninsula brought with them to Istanbul and spoke for half a millennium there. The language was dying out, but not because of any persecution: the young, obsessed with the fripperies of modernity, were no longer interested in maintaining the tradition (so much the worse for them, of course).

I discussed history a little with the proprietor. He felt nothing but affection for and gratitude to Turkey: for the Jews there had suffered nothing like what they had suffered in Croatia or Salonika, that is to say extermination. As for the near-extermination of the Armenians by the Turks, it occurred precisely as the Ottoman empire was remodelling itself along European nationalist lines. It was secularisation, not religious fanaticism, that led to this most appalling episode.

Now let me turn to a book published last year in France, entitled *Les trois exils*, The Three Exiles, by Benjamin Stora. This book illustrates and answers the question with the greatest clarity.

Professor Stora was an Algerian Jew who moved to France at independence in 1962. In his beautiful book, he recounts both his family history and that of the Jews in Algeria, whose two thousand year presence in the country (or perhaps I should say part of the world) ended definitively in the year that the author himself left.

For about two-thirds of their history in Algeria, the Jews lived under a Moslem dispensation. They were, of course, dhimmis, but at various times some among them achieved great prominence in the government, such as it was. When Europeans in the sixteenth century mounted invasions of Algeria and Morocco, the Jews helped to repel them, both because they thought they were destined to fail and because they thought they were better off as dhimmis than under European rule. Indeed, the Jews of the Maghreb commemorated these events annually in what was called the Purim Kettanim.

They were nevertheless subject to violence, persecutions and discrimination; in 1805, 48 Jews were murdered in Algeria in a pogrom, and in the following year 300. European and American travellers of the first third of the nineteenth century remarked on the wretchedness of the Jewish populations of the Maghreb, and the exactions to which they were constantly subject.

Then came the French occupation of Algeria, and the start of the long process of westernisation of the Algerian Jews. (There are photographs in Stora's book, showing the change from Turkish to western costume, complete, irreversible and universal by 1938, though in 1914 half of his family had still posed in Turkish costume.)

Napoleon III considered granting French citizenship to all Algerian Jews, but was overthrown before he could do so; one of the first acts of the new Third Republic, however, was the Cremieux Decree, which turned all Algerian Jews into French citizens.

Here was a reversal of fortune indeed: the Jews went from being dhimmis, that is to say second-rate citizens, to being first-rate citizens, while at the same time the Moslems went from being, if not first-rate citizens in the western sense, at least top dog to underdog.

But the colonial French were not altogether delighted by the Cremieux Decree. In the years that followed it, French anti-Semitism reached one of its apogees, and the Algerian French (the majority of whom were actually of Spanish and Italian origin, and were therefore somewhat insecure in their own citizenship) were in this respect more Catholic than the Pope. In the 1900s, there was a pogrom carried out against the Jews, not by the Algerian Moslems, but by the colons. Their complaints against the Jews were the usual ones.

The prevalence and virulence of French colonial anti-Semitism notwithstanding, there was also room for outbursts of Algerian resentment against the Jews, and in 1934 there was a pogrom in the city of Constantine carried out by a large Moslem mob. That it was an organised and not a spontaneous affair is suggested by the fact that there were simultaneous attacks on villages in the hinterland, not normally in intimate contact with the city. Some Moslems behaved with great ethical courage, however, in protecting their Jewish neighbours. (The author of a book about the pogrom, Robert Attal, owed his life to one such, who told the rampaging mob that the young Robert, his mother and sister, whom he had hidden in his house, were already dead; the mob, who had already killed Robert's father, were satisfied and went away.) As for the colonial police, they failed to restore order until it was too late.

With the defeat of France, a *Pétainiste* regime was instituted in Algeria, which reversed the Cremiuex Decree: that is to say, the Jews became not merely second-rate, but nth-rate citizens. That regime lasted until the liberation, when they became first-rate citizens again, in contradistinction to the Moslem Algerians. This was truly a dizzying historical trajectory.

Nor was it quite over. The nationalist movement gained strength, and the violence increased enormously; a million people were eventually killed. Officially, the FLN, the *Front National de Libération*, was a secular movement; it appealed to Algerian Jews to join the struggle against the French, and promised them equal treatment after independence. However, the Algerian Jews did not believe it, for they had the examples of other Jews in other Arab countries before them; the famous Jewish-Algerian singer, Raymond, was assassinated in 1961, and Moslem attacks on Jews increased; the Jews naturally thought that the Moslem tradition would prevail over the secular nationalist ideology, and in 1962 they left *en masse* for France. If they had not, it is not difficult to imagine their fate in the civil war waged between the military government and the FIS, the *Front Islamique de Salut*.

But what is the moral of this history, if there is one? It is certainly not one of the immemorial goodness and tolerance of the western tradition and the immemorial wickedness and intolerance of the Islamic one. I suppose a Martian, on reading this story, might come to the conclusion that human beings were a bad lot, and that he had better leave Earth as soon as possible.

But there is another moral to the story, and I do not think it is one that is encouraging about Islam as a force in the modern world. For many centuries, the record of Islam was probably no worse, and might even have been better, than the western one, at least in point of religious tolerance (the Jews of the Maghreb in the sixteenth century certainly thought so). Unfortunately, this is a pretty dismal standard to measure anything by. There was, in fact, plenty of room for the Islamic record to be as good as or better than the western one, and still be very bad. Between dhimmitude and death, who would not choose dhimmitude? But that is not to say it was an enviable or morally defensible fate.

By 1962, however, things were very clear: for Algerian Jews, France, its chequered record notwithstanding, offered hope for the future and equality under the law, while Algeria offered the prospect of future pogroms, the promises of its leadership notwithstanding. And there was a reason for this: while France had a theory of legal equality, Islam did not. And the Jews of Algeria thought that the hold of Islam over the *pays réel* would more than outweigh the hold of secular nationalist ideology of the *pays légal*. The former, and not the latter, would determine their fate in Algeria. They did not believe the promises of the FLN, not because the individuals who made them were insincere, but because the forces against their being kept were simply too strong.

This suggests that there is a conflict between Islam and modernity, at least if one of the important components of modernity is equality under the law. Such equality means that Moslems would have to accept that, even in polities where they were in the immense majority, Islam would have no special claim to consideration, and that (for

101

example) apostasy would have to become a normal and acceptable part of life. Whether, under these circumstances, Islam would remain truly Islamic is a question for scholars, not for scribblers such as I.

Personally, I doubt whether the auguries are good. When the now-President Sarkozy asked the second-hand car salesman of Islamic fundamentalism, Tariq Ramadan, whether he believed in the stoning of adulterers (that is to say, no doubt, of the majority of French politicians or their wives), he replied that he was in favour of a moratorium.

A moratorium, indeed! The dilemma is this: if the answer is no, that we are no longer in favour of the lapidation of adulterers, any more than we are in favour of burying them up to their necks in sand and letting the sun and the ants do the rest, then the injunctions of our religion are not eternal truths, and the whole of its sacred basis must be questioned; if the answer is yes, that we are in favour of the lapidation of adulterers, as an example of the merciful correction of wrongdoers to be expected of the righteous, then we reveal ourselves as primitives unfit for the modern world. Islam is not the only religion about which such questions might be raised; but it is the only one that has not made a concerted attempt to deal with them (and its decentralisation, or lack of structure, makes it difficult for it to do so).

The question of adultery is a much less important one than that of apostasy, of course, because if open apostasy were allowed, who knows where it would end? In all likelihood in the secular society, complete with music and dancing, that so appals Moslem fundamentalists (and which in truth does have unpleasant aspects but which, taken all in all, is the best we can, or at any rate do, hope for).

In other words, the moral of Professor Stora's book is that Islam, whatever its past glories, achievements, strengths and even tolerance by comparison with extremely low standards prevailing at different times elsewhere, has no means as yet of dealing with the modern world in a constructive fashion, and perhaps (though here it is impossible to be dogmatic) never can have such a means without falling apart entirely. I leave it to the experts to decide.

HOW TO HATE THE NON-EXISTENT

BY NATURE AND INCLINATION I am an aesthete: I can hardly think of Venice or Siena, for example, without an access of emotion. And yet I have spent a great deal of my life among the utmost ugliness, both physical and moral. Moreover, I must confess that the problem of evil has preoccupied me.

One of the reasons for this, perhaps, has been literary ambition. It is far easier to make evil interesting than good. Depictions of good people are inclined very soon to decline into mawkishness, and make their objects as dull as they are unbelievable. Too much good repels us; we long for the feet of clay to be revealed. As Oscar Wilde said, only a man with a heart of stone could read of the death of Little Nell without laughing.

A fascination with evil is pretty widespread. When, at social gatherings, I tell people what I once did for a living, namely that I was a doctor in a large prison, it isn't usually very long before someone asks me, slightly shamefacedly, who the worst, most evil man I ever met was. They also want to know what he did in as much detail as possible, of course. No story is so horrifying that it ever bores people; and even the most demure cannot for long entirely resist the thrill of the barbarous.

More recently, perhaps on account of my advancing age, the problem of good has begun to preoccupy me. How is extraordinary goodness possible? Where does it come from? Is it innate? And if it is innate, is it real goodness? For there cannot be real goodness where the possibility and temptation to its reverse is not present.

Suffice it to say that I have met in my life a few people who are the very opposite of those men whom I met in the course of my work who gave off a powerful aura, that seemed to me almost physical, of evil. I don't believe in satanic possession, because I don't believe in Satan, but these men gave me an insight into how someone not completely stupid might come to believe in such a thing.

One of the formative experiences in my life was working for a British surgeon in Africa who for me was all that a doctor should be. In those days, and in that place, there were very few aids to diagnosis; observation, logic, experience and instinct were all. The surgeon was such a brilliant diagnostician that his opinion was like a final court of appeal for all other doctors in the hospital (to say nothing of the patients). I never knew him to be wrong. He was a meticulous technician and seemed capable of operating with equal skill and facility on all parts of the human body. The knowledge and intellect necessary for this is insufficiently appreciated by those who have never seen it up close. In these days of ever greater specialisation, such surgeons are rare.

But his technical accomplishment was, if anything, less impressive than his moral character. He was a man of perfect temper: I never knew him to be other than calm, even when in the middle of an operative crisis, or be less than polite to anyone; called up from his bed in the middle of the night, he was as equable and self-contained as by day, and this despite the fact that he must have had at least two nights' disturbed sleep a week for many years. His patients – mostly poor Africans – trusted him utterly, and were right to do so.

I do not know what religious belief he had, if any; he was too much of the old school to obtrude on such matters where they might have caused offence. Although highly respected in his hospital, he gained no wider renown through his work; the satisfaction for him was in doing good. I never knew a better man.

And yet I found his example intimidating to me: not, of course, because of anything he said or did, but because I knew, indubitably and at once, that I should never be as good a man as he. My problem was ego: I wanted to make a mild stir in the world, and doing good for others was not enough for me, not that I was bad enough to wish them any harm (and, in the event, I did my fair share of getting up in the middle of the night on their behalf). But the good of others could never be my sole motive, or entirely satisfying to me. I could never be wholly benevolent, as he was. And now I feel guilty that I, not as good a man as he, am somewhat better known than he. The judgment of the world is not infallible.

Oddly enough, I have something in common in the above respect with a man whom I do not in general find congenial, that is to say Michel Foucault. Foucault's father was a surgeon of local renown, who gave the young Michel an example of practical compassion for others (namely, getting up in the middle of the night to save their lives) which he, Michel, knew that he would never be able to live up to because he did not care enough about their lives to do so. There was one recourse left to him, if as an egotist he was to equal or surpass his father, namely to adopt the Nietzschean position that such compassion as his father showed is really disguised weakness, contempt or drive for power, but not real compassion. Thus, everything is the opposite of what it seems, and progress, so called, is really regress, or at best sideways movement.

It was in Africa also that I met my other examples of extraordinary goodness. For a time I gave my services one afternoon a week to a Catholic mission station about fifty miles from where I myself was working. The hospital was run by an elderly Swiss nun, neither a doctor nor a nurse, who managed a large hospital on her own with a staff of nurses. The hospital was spotless, astonishingly so, and the number of patients seen there prodigious. The hospital was much preferred to any government-run facility, with their accretions of squashed mosquitoes and smeared blood on every wall.

The nun had an almost physical air of invulnerable serenity about her, and she had an aura that struck me, of course in the opposite sense, in the way that the aura of evil later struck me. She was not a plaster saint, however, and had a good sense of humour; nor was she any kind of fanatic, for she gave me the contraceptive injection to give to the women with heart disease already exhausted by repeated childbirth, which I administered under a portrait of the Pope. I never tackled her on the subject of the apparent contradiction, because it has often seemed to me that no purpose is served by ideological confrontation in the service of complete intellectual consistency, where concrete good might be endangered by it.

I met other nuns in remote parts of Africa who seemed completely happy in humbly serving the local people: a community of Spanish nuns whose cheerful and selfless dedication to the ill, the handicapped and the young caused them, rightly, to be loved and revered. In Nigeria, I met an Irish nun, in her mid-seventies, who was responsible for the feeding of hundreds of prisoners who would almost certainly have starved had she not brought food to them every day. In the prison, a lunatic had been chained for years to a post; many of the prisoners had been detained without trial for a decade, the files of their cases having been lost, and they would never leave the prison, even when a judge ordered their release, unless they paid to the gaolers a bribe which they could not afford. They believed they would spend the rest of their lives in detention, seventy to a floor space no larger than that of my sitting room.

The nun moderated the behaviour of the prison guards by the sheer force of her goodness. It was not a demonstrative or self-satisfied virtue; one simply would have felt ashamed to behave badly or selfishly in her presence. She is almost certainly dead now, forgotten by the world (not that she craved remembrance or memorialisation). I sometimes find it difficult, when immersed in the day-to-day flux of my existence, to credit that I have witnessed such selflessness.

I recognise that there must be ways of being good that do not involve such total self-abnegation. After all, even in the poorest and worst-off countries, there are only a certain number of disabled, despised and dispossessed who need to be looked after; we cannot, therefore, all be good in the way of the Irish nun. Indeed, the world needs other types of people at least as much as it needs people like her; and I am sure that there are cynics who will assert that immersing oneself in the kind of work she did is simply a way of overcoming one's personal psychological problems, and is therefore ultimately selfish. But this is a metaphysical, not empirical, statement about all human behaviour, because any behaviour whatever could be explained in precisely the same way. It is simply a way of saying that altruism is logically impossible, and that all human actions must be selfish.

I once made the mistake of writing an article in a left-wing publication saying that, in my experience, the best people were usually religious and on the whole religious people behaved better in their day-to-day lives than non-religious ones: and I wrote this, as I made clear, as a man without any religious belief.

As a frequent contributor to the public prints, I am accustomed to a certain amount of hate mail, and can even recognise the envelopes that contain it with a fair, though not total, degree of accuracy. Of course, e-mail has made it far easier for those consumed with bile to communicate it, and on the whole it exceeds in vileness what most bilious people are prepared to commit to paper. I don't think I have ever hated anyone as much as some of my correspondents have hated me.

Suffice it to say that I have never received such hate mail as when I suggested that religious people were better than non-religious in their conduct. It seemed that many of the people who responded to me were not content merely not to believe, but had to hate. Although I had not denied that religious motivation could motivate very bad behaviour, something which indeed can hardly be denied, I was treated to a summary of the historical crimes of religion such as many adolescents could provide who had recently discovered to their fury that they had been made to attend boring religious services when the arguments for the existence of God had never been irrefutable.

Not long ago, while I was in France, the centenary of the final separation of church and state was celebrated. It was presented as the triumph of reason over reaction, of humanity over inhumanity, and I am not entirely out of sympathy for that viewpoint: I certainly don't want to live myself in a state in which a single religion has a predominant or even strong say in the running of it. And yet the story was far more nuanced than that triumphantly presented.

For example, a fascinating book was published on the occasion of the centenary reproducing the iconography of the anticlerical propaganda that preceded the separation by thirty years; and on looking in to it I saw at once that it was exactly the same in tone as anti-Semitic propaganda. There was the wickedly sybaritic hook-nosed cardinal in diabolical scarlet, the thin hairy spider, representing the economic interests of the church, whose sinister legs straddled the whole globe, and the priest who welcomed innocent little children into the fold of his black cloak. One has to remember that almost the first consequence of secularism in France, as in Russia, was unprecedented slaughter.

Perhaps one of the reasons that contemporary secularists do not simply reject religion but hate it is that they know that, while they can easily rise to the levels of hatred that religion has sometimes promoted, they will always find it difficult to rise to the levels of love that it has also encouraged.

OIL ON TROUBLED WATERS

QUITE OFTEN ONE READS that such-and-such a country – the Congo, for example – is impoverished in spite of its abundant natural resources. The tone is usually pained and a little surprised; the writer seems to think that natural resources ought to benefit populations without human intervention, by jumping out of the ground and developing and distributing themselves equitably, for example.

Without political wisdom, however, abundant natural resources are more often a curse than a blessing. Many of the most prosperous and best-governed areas of the world, by contrast, are not at all well-favoured by nature. Man is not at his best when he receives or hopes for something for nothing.

I first realised this on an island called Nauru, which was in the Central Pacific. It was about ten miles in circumference, and had a population of only 4000 indigenous inhabitants, but was for a time the richest country in the world *per capita*.

For almost all their history, the Nauruans had lived off fish and coconuts, in a state of what anthropologists called a generous subsistence. But their island was covered in phosphate rock that was valued as a fertiliser. Appropriated by Germany at the end of the nineteenth century, the island passed under Australian, British and New Zealand rule during the First World War, and the phosphate was mined by the British Phosphate Commission, an amalgamation of British, Australian and New Zealand interests.

Then, in 1968, the Nauruans received their independence and gained control over their own resources. Overnight, more or less, they became very rich, but the results were not altogether happy. Foreigners worked the mines, while Nauruans received the proceeds. Everything became a free gift, though some had more free gifts than others, since land ownership and therefore phosphate royalties were unequally distributed. But everyone received a house, water, electricity and telephone free of charge.

This was not a recipe for industriousness. The Nauruans became physically inactive and ate enormously, on average 5000 calories per day (one person was found who managed 14,000). They liked sweet drinks, and drank Fanta by the carton of 24 tins, and also Chateau d'Yquem. Within a short time, about half of them were diabetic.

Unfortunately, the phosphate ran out, leaving their island a moonscape. Only too predictably, they were swindled by conmen out of their financial reserves, and their traditional way of life had in the meantime been destroyed. The tragedy would never have happened but for the phosphate.

Nigeria was another country that I visited that was cursed by the existence of natural resources, in this case oil; or rather by political inability to take proper advantage of them. What seemed like good fortune was soon turned into ill-fortune.

Like most countries in Africa, Nigeria was a geo-political expression. While it has undoubtedly developed some identity of its own, it contains within itself a very large number of distinct ethnic and language groups. The oil, which soon became overwhelmingly its most important export, other than people, was concentrated in one small part of the country.

Nigerian politics became the struggle for the control of the oil revenues. The foreign exchange receipts from oil meant that Nigeria could import everything cheaper than it could produce it itself, including food. A Nigerian minister famously once said that Nigeria's problem would not be how to obtain money, but how to spend it. Nigerian agriculture, previously promising, went into decline and a hideous urbanisation ensued.

While the Nigerian oil revenues were huge, they were not adequate to ensure a high standard of living for everyone even if they had been distributed equally rather than appropriated by political and military elites who struggled for the control of them. This struggle was the principle business of Nigerian public life.

I used to visit Nigeria regularly, and knew the writer, Ken Saro-Wiwa, who was subsequently hanged by the dictator, General Abacha. Saro-Wiwa, who wrote a wonderful novel of the Nigerian civil war called *Sozaboy*, came from the Niger Delta, where the oil also came from, and he started a political movement to try to obtain oil revenues for his particular tribe, the Ogoni. Although much of the oil came from Ogoniland, the Ogoni had received almost no financial benefit from it whatsoever. Instead, their native creeks, forests and fishing grounds had been largely destroyed by oil leaks.

I discussed his movement with him when I went to see him in Port Harcourt, the largest city in the area, and took the pessimistic view that it was bound before long to provoke violence; but Saro-Wiwa, a non-violent man with a wonderful sense of humour, told me that the situation was already so bad that it could get no worse. Alas, I was proved right; and Saro-Wiwa not only lost his life, but violence became endemic in the area. (Of course, it is possible that it would have done so even without his initiative.) At any rate, oil proved a blessing to no one in Nigeria who did not get his hands on a large part of the loot.

This brings us to Messrs Putin and Chavez, whose positions surely depend on the existence in their countries of huge oil and gas reserves. Would either of them have been possible without oil and gas? And are they not both of them leading their respective countries to disaster?

It is true that Chavez lost the referendum that would have granted him the presidency for life, if he felt like it, by a small margin, and congratulated his opponents on their victory. But his most significant words after his defeat were, 'For now, we could not do it.' In other words, if at first you don't succeed, try, try, again. It is in the nature of plebiscitary regimes that plebiscites are held until the population gets the answer right according to the leader or to the right-thinking elite, whereafter there is no further plebiscite, at least on that subject.

Chavez is a Latin American *caudillo* whose populist measures are possible only because of oil revenues. In other respects he reminds me of the nineteenth-century Bolivian president, General Melgarejo, who once said 'I'm going to rule in Bolivia as long as I like and I'll have anyone who doesn't like it hanged from the nearest tree.' Chavez also reminds me of the nineteenth-century Guatemalan dictator, Rufino Barrios, who was once seen to take the Guatemalan constitution out of his pocket, fold it in four, place it on a chair and sit on it.

Chavez is the most flamboyant and extravagant of Venezuela's corrupt squanderers of oil revenues, promising huge numbers of people the illusion of a share of the unearned wealth that will melt away like snow in the spring sunshine. Chavez is the product of a combination of oil money and political unwisdom, the latest twist in a vicious spiral of past corruption and present resentment, that produces more corruption and then more resentment. Venezuela has had oil bonanzas before and squandered the money on schemes not wholly different from Chavez's, leaving the country no better off when the oil price collapsed than it would have been had the oil price never risen in the first place. The tragedy (if lost opportunity is a tragedy) is repeating itself, though this time with the possibility of a true dictatorship emerging.

Putin is altogether a more serious and sinister figure. When all is said and done, there is about Chavez the air of the preposterous and posturing buffoon, as there was about Mussolini. Moreover, Venezuela will never be able to threaten the peace of the world in any serious way.

Russia is different. It is true that Russia is as dependent upon oil and gas for its exports as any tinpot country, but that does not mean that it is itself tinpot. The Upper Volta didn't make and never would have made rockets, but the Soviet Union did. Russia is resurgent thanks to its oil and gas, and this is good news neither for Russia nor for the rest of the world.

Oil and gas revenues have allowed Mr Putin to appear to the Russian people as if he were the answer to Russia's chronic economic woes, and they have been more than willing to trade a little freedom, of whose benefits they were never fully convinced anyway, for a little order. But without oil and gas, Mr Putin's record would have looked very different, and there would have been no compensation for his authoritarianism. The most that one can say of him is that he did not entirely ruin the hand that chance dealt him. At any rate, oil and gas have played their part in preserving the Russian authoritarian tradition which, while it might suit the Russian temperament, has not brought them much happiness.

So huge have been the Russian oil and gas revenues - Russia now has the third largest foreign currency reserves in the world - that it has been able to pursue a guns and butter policy. Not only is Western Europe now utterly dependent upon Russia for its gas supplies, Germany alone to the tune of 80 per cent (and Russia has already tried the weapon of reducing the gas supply to its weaker neighbours), but it has the only considerable military force left in Europe. The combination of deep pockets, monopolies of energy supply and military force, resentment at defeat in the Cold War and its pre-existing political traditions is not a reassuring one.

It is not even as if the Russian people can expect much good to come of this. Military power has always seemed more important to Russian regimes than the welfare of the people, a long-term effect, perhaps, of the Mongol invasion. And if, for some reason, Russian exports of oil and gas decline, the scene will be set for real turmoil.

By contrast, Norway has used its oil revenues with considerable wisdom. This is not to say that the Norwegians are a supremely happy nation, that they laugh for joy as they walk around in Oslo; they have never struck observers as being very jolly, perhaps for reasons of geography and climate. But they have not squandered their oil money, preferring to invest it against the day when it will run out.

The Norwegians have not permitted any of the money to be invested in Norway itself, for fear of distorting the local economy, and neither are they using the income that the money brings: in other words, the Norwegians have had to live as if there were no oil money. Given their rather puritanical view of life, it may be doubted whether they will ever feel entirely at moral ease living on the dividends that their foresight and restraint will have entitled them to. I somehow rather doubt it, in which case they will just go on accumulating more and more assets, like old-fashioned misers in their counting houses, while spending a certain amount of their wealth on bad causes such as aid to Africa.

But their miserliness will at least give them choices that Chavez's populist squanderomania will never give to the Venezuelans. The point, however, is that the Norwegian caution and good sense preceded the arrival of the oil money, and were not created by the oil. They grew out of the pre-existing culture.

This, it seems to me, is an important lesson: that there is no single formula for success or failure in the world, and that good sense and wisdom come from within, not from without. In current circumstances, Venezuela could no more behave like Norway than Norway could behave like Venezuela, though both have huge oil and gas revenues. If Chavez were overthrown, I do not think that the oil money would be vastly better spent, though the regime might be decidedly less dictatorial, any more than I would expect Norway to become a sink of light-hearted and frivolous corruption if the opposition were elected to power.

I hesitate to quote Marx, but when he said that while men made their history they did not make it in any way they liked, I think he was right. And this is something that framers of foreign policy should always bear in mind.

THE PLEASURES OF ASSASSINATION

WHEN PRESIDENT BUSH DESCRIBED the assassination of Benazir Bhutto as cowardly, he chose precisely the wrong word. (He was not the only person to do so, but he was the most important one to do so.) In fact, it was a very courageous act: for it requires great courage to assassinate someone in the middle of a large and volatile crowd favourable to that person, and above all then to blow yourself up just to make sure that you have succeeded. Not many people have that degree of courage: I certainly don't.

The two Islamic militants whose telephone call was putatively intercepted by the Pakistani security services, and who are claimed by them to have been the organisers of the assassination, were quite right when they called the two men who did it 'brave boys.' They were brave all right; I do not see how it can very well be denied. Even if the transcript of the telephone call turns out to be a complete work of fiction, the authors of it got something right that President Bush got wrong.

So why, in this respect, is the leader of the Free World wrong and the Islamic militants (assuming for the sake of argument that the intercept was genuine) right? I think it is because of a confusion about the nature of certain virtues, bravery among them. Bravery is generally counted a virtue, something that we admire; while the assassination of Benazir Bhutto was despicable, something that we deplore. Therefore, we have to deny the assassins bravery, and call them cowardly, or else we concede that they are, at least in one respect, virtuous. For what is it to be virtuous except to exercise one or more of the virtues?

But in fact, courage or bravery is not a virtue irrespective of the circumstances in which it is exercised. Courage in pursuit of a despicable goal is no virtue, quite the reverse in fact; and most virtues, indeed, are virtuous only when exercised correctly, that is to say when in pursuit of laudable goals. There are few that are right in all circumstances whatsoever.

This confusion does not concern only political rhetoric: it invades other spheres of life as well, for example art criticism. One often hears the word originality used as a term of praise in respect of a work of art, without any assessment of whether the originality has produced anything worthwhile in itself. In fact, it is easy to be original; there is nothing easier than to think of something that someone else has never done; you could probably draw up a list of a hundred such things in half an hour. But there are often extremely good reasons why no one has ever done them, chief among which are that it would be of no aesthetic or intellectual value to do them. Originality is thus no virtue in itself when applied to a work of art (or to anything else): and it is not surprising that a striving for originality in art in itself, unconnected to any other purpose, leads to work of little value, or even to work of negative value. No one would think an original scientific theory of any value, unless it had some evidence in its favour (though, of course, it might, in spite of itself, provoke some thought).

Most virtues are conditional upon the circumstances in which they are exercised. Only a strict Kantian would argue that it is morally obligatory to point a murderer in the direction of his victim, for example, on the grounds that one should always tell the truth. (Once, while out walking my dog, a car full of young men drew up to me, and I thought they would want directions to a road nearby. Instead, the driver said to me, 'Excuse me, mate, can you tell me which way the prostitutes are?' At that time, there were streetwalkers not very far away, and all of them drug addicts: was it right or wrong to tell the young men where to find them? I compromised, and gave them only the vaguest of directions.)

Virtues exercised irrespective of the circumstances become frightening. Extreme or habitual bravery often, but not always, turns into recklessness: the assassination of Benazir Bhutto was a case in point, in which extreme bravery was not recklessness. The latter is indifference to danger; but the suicide bomber was not indifferent to danger, indeed for him the only danger was that he should not succeed in dying for the cause. He was not reckless: he was determined.

Almost all of the virtues that you can think of are conditional on moral judgment for their correct exercise. Truthfulness, generally a virtue, can easily become the sadistic enjoyment of uttering painful truths for no reason other than that they give pain and distress. Generosity or kindness when too overflowing humiliates the recipient and can degenerate into the exercise of power over others. Prudence can become pusillanimity and a cover for cowardice and inactivity. Politeness when invariable and invariant becomes insincerity. And so on and so forth.

All this is perfectly obvious, at least on a moment's reflection. But we often forget it in the heat of the moment and therefore, when not wishing to ascribe a quality to an enemy that is a virtue in some circumstances, we ascribe to him the vice that is the opposite of that virtue, though in fact there is no evidence that he suffers from that vice at all, quite the reverse in fact.

The opposite of bravery is of course cowardice. And here we see an asymmetry: while bravery is not always a virtue, cowardice is always a vice. A lack of positive bravery is not always cowardice, however: we do not call the decision of someone to run away and fight another day cowardice, we call it prudence. Of course, in practice human motives are often mixed, or slide into one another. A man may claim to act from prudence when really he is concerned only to save his own skin, not to fight another day but for its own sake. But the fact that this is often the case does not mean that there is really no such virtue as prudence, which is the opposite of foolhardiness.

We do not find it enough, then, to deny our enemy the quality that in some circumstances is a virtue, for fear that we should be thought to be sympathising with him; we seek to endow him with the opposite vice, cowardice in the case of the assassins of Bhutto, though the evidence for this is completely lacking, indeed points in the other direction.

It is, of course, much easier to imagine someone who perfectly incarnates vice than virtue, which is why in literature villains are so often more memorable than heroes, and so much more believable. It is far easier to find fault in Benazir Bhutto, for example, than it is to find anything good to say about her murderers. (It didn't take long after her death for people to point out that she was haughty, with a strong sense of hereditary entitlement, possibly corrupt or at least very tolerant of corruption, and only equivocally a democrat.) As we have seen, the bravery of the assassins does not count as a virtue, and any minor virtues that they might have had - that they were good to their mothers, for example, or that they were considerate brothers - are nugatory by comparison with the evil they have wrought.

It would just be possible, I suppose, to characterise those who planned the assassination as cowards, in the sense that they were sending a young man or young men to a near-certain death that they themselves did not risk. But it would be easy to see how they would justify it to themselves: that the young man was expendable to the cause in a way that they were not expendable because of their experience and ability, and that in any case the young man or men in question would ultimately benefit from their acts. Besides, it seems to me unlikely that the planners were in any real sense cowards or cowardly: I have travelled a little in that area of the world and cowards are very few there. They are no more cowards than are generals who do not routinely expose themselves to the line of fire.

Does it really matter if assassination of Benazir Bhutto is incorrectly described by the president and other notables? The important thing is the event itself, after all. Words are but counters, as Hobbes says; but they are the money of fools.

Here I am with Confucius: I think words matter. If what is said is not what is meant, then in the end cynicism corrodes everything.

To call the assassination cowardly indicates a lack of clarity of thought, not only about the event itself but about the virtue of courage and perhaps even about virtue in general. And we want our leaders to be clear-sighted, not to misapprehend what confronts them and us. We are certainly not confronted by a band of cowards.

There are many ways in which the assassination could with justice have been characterised, without resort to the one word about it that was simply not true. It was, of course, an act of great brutality. What kind of people think that it is right to kill twenty people more or less at random during a peaceful rally (unless mere attendance at the rally were sufficient justification for killing them, in which case many thousands of people could rightfully be killed, perhaps many millions)? People who are brave are not necessarily good or clear thinkers.

Clarity of mind is perhaps not the most widely distributed of human attributes, though La Rochefoucauld tells us that we are all well-satisfied with our own powers of reason. What, for example, did the rioters who smashed shop fronts and burned cars after the assassination think they were achieving by their activities? What purpose did they think they were serving?

Having attended a riot or two (as an observer, I hasten to add), I should say that they were not so much serving a political cause as enjoying themselves. Moral indignation is, of course, a pleasure in itself, one of the few that costs nothing, and likewise one of the few that never lets you down; but it is as nothing compared with the pleasures of destruction in the name of a good cause. What greater pleasure is there in the world than to smash a large pane of glass for the good of one's country? It was the nineteenth-century Russian aristocratic anarchist Bakunin who said that the destructive urge was also a creative urge; he would have been more accurate if he had said that it was a pleasurable one.

For myself, I can say that when I give vent to anger, which I try to do as rarely as possible precisely because of this, a still small voice that is located (physically, it seems to me) at or in the back of my head, says to me, 'You are enjoying this.' And I know that the still small voice is telling the truth.

I do not, of course, wish to say that anger is never justified, even on some occasions extreme anger. But on many occasions, perhaps most, when we are angry, we are really rather enjoying ourselves, giving vent disproportionately because the expression of anger is enjoyable in itself. To burn cars in the street and smash shops is simply not a reasonable response to the assassination of Benazir Bhutto: it is a pretext to allow the vandal that lurks inside every civilised man to emerge and act out. The tinkle of glass, the crackle of flames: are there any sounds more soothing to the human ear, at least for a time?

The unexamined enjoyment of moral outrage is what killed Benazir Bhutto. Moral outrage is the only pleasure allowed to religious fanatics, but they can indulge it in full and unfortunately it is inexhaustible.

I think I begin to see, as through a glass darkly, why the ancient Greek injunction, to know thyself, was so cardinally important.

A COST BENEFIT ANALYSIS
OF COST BENEFIT ANALYSIS

IT GOES WITHOUT SAYING, I hope, that I am utterly opposed to murder. If it were possible to eliminate this, the oldest and most terrible of crimes, from the face of the earth, I should most certainly rejoice at it. So why is it that, when asked to prepare a medico-legal report in a case of murder, whether for the defence or the prosecution, I am extremely pleased and look forward immensely to receiving and reading all the documentation? Why is this, when I know full well that a world without murder would be much better than the one in which we live?

Most murders are merely sordid, of the kind that Sherlock Holmes would have despised as presenting no difficulties, at least from the point of view of the detection of the perpetrator. They take place in grim circumstances. They are, in his terminology, no-pipe problems. But most of them nevertheless contain disputable points, often of a medical nature, and if a point can be disputed, lawyers will dispute it.

I like the discipline that the court procedure imposes. There is nothing like the prospect of being cross-examined by a clever lawyer for the other side to make one very careful about what one says, never going beyond what is strictly defensible on the evidence available. It is rarely in life that we are so constrained, and what is unusual often has the charms of novelty. The fact is that pedantry has its pleasures and psychological rewards.

Testifying often turns into a battle of wits, which is another reason why I find it so enjoyable. I have learned over the years that loquacity in the witness box is disastrous, and that taciturnity is by far the best policy. When asked for advice by people who are about to go into the box for the first time, I tell them to be as near to monosyllabic as they can manage. The longer you speak, the more likely it is that you will say something foolish; and one foolish remark in the box has more effect on a jury than a hundred wise ones.

You must agree immediately if you have overlooked something that is pointed out to you by the opposing lawyer, for nine times out of ten such agreement takes the wind out of his sails and makes you look reasonable in the eyes of the jury - as well, of course, as being in accordance with the truth.

But the real pleasure of involving myself in these cases is the contact that they bring with extremes of human experience and emotion, and the knowledge they provide of the human heart. Furthermore, there is no dinner party whose conversation cannot be revived with anecdotes of murderers one has known, and I don't think I've ever met anyone uninterested in the subject of murder (or they have disguised their lack of interest very well).

If there were no murder, which of course would be a good thing, my life would be somewhat less rich than it is. This is not to say that I could not find an alternative source of interest; obviously I could. The world is so full of interest that a thousand lifetimes could not possibly exhaust it. But thoughts about murder, and re-reading Shakespeare's Henry IV, has set me thinking about man's rather peculiar constitution, according to which a problem-free world would be extremely problematic. Heaven on earth would, in fact, be hell on earth.

Falstaff, you will remember, is a man who is lazy, a coward, a boaster, a fornicator, a would-be thief, a sponger on others, a glutton and a drunk. There is not much virtue in him, and he casts doubt on the very possibility of virtue; 'What is honour?' he asks, and replies, 'A word. What is in that word honour? What is that honour? Air.'

And yet, far from hating or despising him, we feel the deepest affection for him. When he says, 'Banish plump Jack, and banish all the world,' we not only know exactly what he means, but agree with him. It is the perfect rejoinder to the puritan or moral enthusiast who wants a world that is perfect, without the slightest moral blemish, for whom peccadilloes are indistinguishable from mortal sin or radical evil.

There is a difficulty here. We want the world to be large and broad enough for there to be a Falstaff in it, but we don't want a huge number of Falstaffs. We certainly don't want everybody to be Falstaff, and we would never take Falstaff as a model for our children, and tell them to imitate him. We see Falstaff when as a man of fifty (old by Elizabethan standards), not as a young man, when he might well have been seriously disconcerting and unpleasant.

Many times in my career I have noticed that people who are reprehensible judged by rational criteria nevertheless contribute something positive to the world. I remember a small and very happy little hospital in which I once worked in which there was a drunken porter. He was lazy and unreliable, and many times other people had to do his work for him. Yet far from being hated or despised, he was universally loved; somehow he contributed to the *esprit de corps* of the whole hospital, whose staff was happy to carry him (sometimes literally). From the point of view of rational management, he should not have been employed; and yet the attempt to remove all 'characters,' from the workforce, that is to say all those inefficient people whose contribution is being what they are rather than doing what they do, usually ends in a miserable and demoralised staff.

Not long ago I was shown a short video made about a notorious Dutch family called the Tokkies. The Tokkies were what I suppose in America would be called white trash. They lived in public housing and had made the lives of their neighbours hell. They were noisy and dirty. They were involved in many battles, involving the use of baseball bats (no baseball is played in Holland), samurai swords, Molotov cocktails and guns, a selection of weaponry suggesting that poverty was the least of their problems.

Eventually, they were evicted from their home. It was just before Christmas. They got into their large van with a trailer, and drove down to Spain for a holiday. An entertainment company had the idea of filming them, dressed in Santa headgear, singing a Christmas song as they drove down to Spain. Husband and wife were utterly blowsy, beer and cigarettes made flesh.

The trouble was that the video was irresistibly comic. Try as I might not to laugh, I couldn't stop myself. One ended up thinking that a world in which there were no Tokkies would be a poorer one, however glad one was not to live next door to them.

It was the great French sociologist, Durkheim, who suggested that societies had need of their criminals, for their existence has a binding effect upon societies. It is far easier to unite against an enemy, after all, than in favour of something. Criminals are the enemies of society against whom the rest of us can unite, though we may be disunited about everything else. There is a great deal of consolation to be had from universal condemnation. So the criminal also contributes something to society, as Falstaff and my drunken hospital porter did.

Of course, this does not tell us precisely how many criminals we need for the purpose of social unification; perhaps only a few will do and we have many. Even if we had precisely the minimum number necessary to produce the society-binding effect, we would still feel aggrieved if we were personally the victims of a crime: for while it is possible that crime in general has a social function, no crime in particular has such a function.

We want a virtuous society, but not a society that is so virtuous that Ella Wheeler Wilcox is the only poet that means anything to it. As everyone knows, or at least should know, the attempt to enforce absolute virtue results in great evil.

When I read the medical journals these days, I feel I am reading the medical equivalent of Ella Wheeler Wilcox. They speak only the best of good sense (one doesn't argue with a poem by Ella Wheeler Wilcox). They tell us how we, or rather they, that is to say the general public, ought to live. Not too fat, a certain amount of exercise, no smoking, drinking in moderation of the right kind of wine taken purely as a medicine to ward of heart attacks and strokes, in short, every activity and comestible to be treated as a medicine to be taken in the correct dose.

It is not easy to argue against this rationalistic tyranny, just as it is not easy to answer a puritan without sounding as if you are positively in favour of sin, the more of it the better. No doubt properly conducted studies have shown precisely how much alcohol one should take to achieve the greatest possible longevity; or if they have not been conducted yet, they will be conducted in the very near future. Science will establish precisely how much butter one is allowed per week. Epidemiology will hunt down all the dangers lurking in our habits. From this, prohibitions and imperative duties will inevitably follow. It is only natural, after all, that doctors should advocate whatever saves and prolongs life.

I read recently a wonderful refutation of this outlook on life by the great Belgian Sinologist, Simon Leys. It was he who, throughout the Cultural Revolution in China, mocked and excoriated, in prose so witty that it made you laugh out loud despite its horrifying subject, the western sympathisers, who were legion, of that dreadful revolt against civilisation. It was he who during those locust years defended the immemorial refinement of Chinese civilisation from the brutality of the assault upon it in the name of ideological purity, and who defended intelligence and decency from stupidity and cruelty. He was almost alone and it required courage to say things that subsequently became obvious.

He is also a marvellous and laconic literary essayist, both in English and French, and in a book entitled *Le bonheur des petits poissons*, he writes of the pleasures of tobacco. In this little essay, only five pages long but pregnant with the most important questions about the purpose of human existence, he mentions a moving letter by Mozart in which Mozart says that he thinks of death every day, and that these thoughts are his inspiration. This habit of Mozart explains both the infinite joy and the infinite sorrow of his music.

When Leys, therefore, sees those terrible warnings that now appear on cigarette packets all over the world, he says that he is tempted, for strictly metaphysical reasons, to take up smoking again. He does not claim, of course, that an early death will make us all Mozarts; that is scarcely possible. But it probably is the case that an excessive interest in the rational means by which we can avoid premature death will prevent a Mozart from ever arising again, perhaps in any field of human endeavour (I know people who know more about music than I who say that in any case, serious music in the west died with Schonberg, that a tradition was killed once and for all, beyond any hope of resurrection, by him and his followers).

Leys is saying that the 36 years of Mozart's life are not to be regarded as half as valuable as that of someone else who achieved little and who lived to be 72: that is to say that the value of life is not to be estimated by its length or by any other mechanical measure beloved of rationalists.

So, as a doctor, I deplore it when you smoke or otherwise disobey the dictates of good sense; but as a man, I rejoice and am glad that you are incalculable.

AN ILL FOR EVERY PILL

I ONCE HAD A CONVERSATION with an eminent professor, of great and even intimidating erudition (though, of course, erudition is not quite the same thing as talent), about the degree of man's self-understanding. I maintained that it had not increased in any fundamental way, notwithstanding our startling technological progress, and that, in this respect, the neurosciences were greatly oversold, as in the past physiognomy, phrenology, social Darwinism and other doctrines had been oversold.

This was not to deny, of course, the very real achievements of science, but for the great majority of the time, and for the great majority of people, they were peripheral to the central issues and problems of human existence. As for Darwinian explanations of human conduct, they seemed to me of very limited use and power of illumination. Darwinians could always, often with great and admirable ingenuity, fit anything that actually happened into their explanatory schema, *ex post facto*; but as to giving us a guide as to how to conduct ourselves in the future, they were practically useless. At the most, theoretical Darwinism might tell us the limits of the possible in human conduct, but in fact most of these limits were already pretty well known to people of common sense (who may, of course, be not all that common).

The professor was not surprised by any of this; in effect, he had spent much of his life in a Laputan effort to extract sunbeams out of cucumbers. But he was surprised when I said that in any case I looked forward to man's complete self-understanding, in the sense of complete neuroscientific knowledge of mentation, with dread and trepidation rather than with eager anticipation: not that I thought that that day was coming any time soon (or ever, in fact).

He asked me the reasons for my dread. I said it sprang from the abuse of power that would almost certainly result; and I asked him to imagine an instrument so sensitive that it could 'read' human thoughts, and anticipate them. Would he want such an instrument applied to him? Would he want others, or even a single other person, to know exactly what he was thinking all of the time? It would surely be hellish, and incompatible with normal human relations. This explains

124

why life cannot and ought never to be lived in complete sincerity and honesty, as an open book; disguise, insincerity and hypocrisy are what make life bearable for self-conscious beings like humans. The art of living is in large part that of knowing when and when not to speak one's mind. Voltaire said that the way to be a bore is to say everything; he might have added that it is also the sure way to be a monster.

We are quite often told, however, that man's self-understanding is, at long last, just around the corner. We are especially inclined to believe this because it is certainly the case that our science and technology has produced many marvels for us, and we think that self-understanding is a mere matter of the exponential increase in the powers of technology, like that which has taken place in the power of computers. Progress in self-knowledge is inevitable.

In 1993, for example, a psychiatrist called Peter Kramer published a best-selling book entitled *Listening to Prozac*. In this book, he suggested that our scientific understanding of brain chemistry has advanced so far – as witnessed by the development of the serotonin reuptake inhibitor, fluoxetine (Prozac) – that we would soon be able to make up our personalities and characters (there is an often-neglected difference between the two) much as make-up artists make up the faces of actors in films and on the stage. Dr Kramer quoted cases in the book of people who had taken Prozac and had become better than well. Formerly shy and retiring types became outgoing and boisterous (personally I prefer shy and retiring types, but that is a different question). Yes, soon we could be all we wanted to be, and merely by swallowing a pill!

This was always nonsense, of course, though exactly the kind of nonsense that people wanted to hear because it is only too human to want all our problems and anxieties to disappear with what in effect is a wave of a wand. After all, in the not very distant past people held on to the idea that if only the buried psychological treasure that lay within them could be found, that is to say the repressed trauma that had caused their undesired characteristics and behaviour to develop, with the help of course of a technically-proficient therapist, then the latter would disappear spontaneously, without further effort or ado on their part, and the beautiful real person that laid buried inside them would emerge as a butterfly from a pupa and fly off into the sunshine of eternal happiness.

All this was just as superstitious as magical incantations ever were. The idea that Prozac (and drugs still to come) would solve all of life's little problems was no more realistic than the following, which I found in John Aubrey's *Miscellanies upon the Following Subjects: Omens, Dreams, Apparitions, Voices, Impulses, Knockings, Blows Invisible, Prophesies etc.*, published first in 1696 (my edition is the second, of 1721):

> To cure the Biting of a Mad Dog, Write these Words in Paper, Viz.: Rebus Rubus Epitescum, and give it to the Party, or Beast bit, to eat in Bread. A Gentleman of good Quality, and a sober grave Person, did affirm, that this Receipt never fails.

From the very first, Prozac was presented by its praise-singers as a fundamental advance, when it was perfectly obvious that it was nothing of the sort. It was no more effective than antidepressants which had been known since the early 1960s, though its side-effects were different and, for many people (though not all), more tolerable. The neurochemical theory that accounted for its very limited superiority over placebo in serious cases of depression was crude and reductive, to say the least.

Unfortunately, Prozac came on to the market just at the time when another product of a rather crude and reductive theory, or attitude, the *Diagnostic and Statistic Manual of the American Psychiatric Association*, became the object of almost universal superstitious awe and veneration. Here I rely on a brilliant book published last year by two professors of sociology, Allan V Horwitz and Jerome C Wakefield, entitled *The Loss of Sadness: How Psychiatry Transformed Normal Sorrow into Depressive Disorder*. They point out what should have been obvious to any person with the most minimal knowledge of human nature, that the definition of depression in that manual is complete disassociated human mood from the actual lived circumstances in which it was experienced. It was sufficient to be diagnosed with depression to have a certain number of symptoms for a certain length of time: two whole weeks!

This not only was a retrogression in our understanding of human life by comparison with that held in the past by almost everyone, including psychiatrists, but had the effect of turning practically the whole of the human race into psychiatric casualties. The World

Health Organisation has recently stated that depression is the condition which imposes the second greatest burden of illness and disability on mankind, to believe which requires more suspension of critical faculties than to believe that Peter Pan is a real person, or that Father Christmas is currently in Lapland preparing for his next forays down our chimneys.

Now if people are depressed, it follows that what they need is Prozac, or a drug very similar to it. And of course, since one might define mankind as the only creature that is susceptible to the placebo effect, in many cases the drug will have worked (it is inevitable that someone will write to say, 'Well, it worked for me, and that's enough,' just as it probably was enough for the Gentleman of good Quality, a sober grave Person). On the other hand, although the positive effects of these drugs are largely imaginary, many of their side-effects are only too real. Indeed, it is the reality of these side-effects that persuades people that the therapeutic effects must be real too: for it is a deeply-ingrained belief in most humans that effective medicine must be nasty to take.

The beneficial effects of drugs such as Prozac were grossly overestimated because the results of trials in which they proved not to be effective went unpublished, partly because negative results are uninteresting, undramatic and unexciting, and no doubt partly because of deliberate suppression. At any rate there is no evidence, and never has been any evidence, that Prozac favourably affects ordinary unhappiness. And if mass prescription comes, can class action be far behind?

Does it really matter, though, in any wider sense, that huge numbers of people have been given drugs that don't work to cure a condition that does not exist? (Let us leave aside the question of expense.) As we have seen, there are sometimes matters more important than intellectual honesty and consistency; and if in fact large numbers of them have benefited from a placebo response, why should we worry? As the late Deng Xiaoping said, what does it matter if a cat is black or white, so long as it catches mice?

To quote another luminary, Albert Einstein, not everything that is measurable is important, and not everything that is important is measurable. I think there is a harm to seeing life as a technical problem to be solved by neurochemical manipulation, namely that it is unrealistic, crude, uncivilised and ultimately cruel. It induces a kind of wilful blindness in people, who see their own disastrous decisions as being the result of disordered chemistry rather than as that of inadequate thought and character, and places the responsibility on others - particularly, of course the medical profession - to repair the damage and prevent it from recurring.

Although there has recently been an upsurge in anti-religious writing, the scientist view of human behaviour, that it is all a matter of too much or too little serotonin, represents a decline in understanding by comparison with that of the best divines (and I say this as an unreligious person). I wish I had a hundred pounds for every time I had overheard people saying to each other that their brains were chemically unbalanced, which explains why their lives were less than fulfilled.

The combination of the *DSM* and the availability of many different antidepressants has turned many doctors into checklist clerks: a sufficient score indicates treatment with Prozac. Judgment, let alone attempts at sympathetic understanding - which is not necessarily the same as complete agreement with the patient's view of things - and compassion, are rendered completely redundant. And since a lesser number of symptoms than that required by the checklist might indicate depression of lesser severity, and it is best to nip depression in the bud before it develops into a more serious form, almost all degrees of expressed dissatisfaction, and indeed some that are not expressed, end up being treated with the pills. The unhappiness of their patients now acts on doctors as the ringing of the bell once acted on Pavlov's dogs.

The American doctor and writer Oliver Wendell Holmes (whose son was the famous judge, and who was himself not only one of the first people to give anaesthesia but also one of the first to appreciate the infective nature, spread by doctors, of childbirth fever) once said that if the whole of the pharmacopoeia were thrown into the sea it would be the better for man but the worse for the fishes. I don't think this is true any more, but if all the Prozac in the world were thrown into the sea, I doubt that man would be more miserable and the fishes happier.

Not that I expect mankind to have learnt anything from the wretched Prozac story. In a few years' time, if not before, someone will come forward with claims that he has found the technical solution to man's dissatisfaction with his existence, will be believed for a time, and possibly make a fortune. Illusion and disillusion spring eternal in the human breast.

ROMAN REMAINS

IT IS OFTEN SAID that we know nothing of Shakespeare's personal views. This is largely because he had such a genius for expressing almost every possible human type from within, as it were, as if he had experienced everybody's thoughts and emotions for himself and as his own; and, just as we supposedly cannot know the true personality of an endlessly versatile actor because he is always playing a part, so (it is supposed) we cannot know what a man thought who was able to see every question from every possible angle, and who never once appeared in his own guise or spoke in his own voice. Moreover, his plays show moral problems; they do not preach their solutions. Shakespeare never thumps a tub, or buttonholes you like a drunk at a cocktail party.

I think, however, that the unknowability of Shakespeare's views can be exaggerated. We can safely deduce, for example, that he was not puritanical in his views, but neither was he an amoralist. In politics, likewise, he was neither a utopian nor a complete cynic.

Moreover, since the dramatic effect of his plays depends on the plausibility of his depictions, when he shows the crowd (always more or less of a mob) as foolish, fickle and frenzied, we must suppose that he thought this to be at the very least a plausible depiction. Shakespeare was no friend of tyranny, but neither did the multitude ever appear heroic in his works.

In his last tragedy, *Coriolanus*, Shakespeare examines political life in as unsparing and unsentimental a way as Machiavelli. Coriolanus is a patrician warrior who serves Rome with unequalled military prowess and bravery, but he is devilishly proud and utterly disdainful of the lower orders. He even blames them for smelling: which brings to mind a German saying, 'It smells of poor people here,' and George Orwell's observation that to accuse people of smelling is the most hurtful insult that you can direct at them.

Unfortunately, after his great victory at Corioli (hence his honorific title), Coriolanus stands for the office of Consul, one of the most important political offices in Rome. To be elected he needs the approbation of the plebeians: and, rather as in a general election in a western democracy, to obtain it he has to abase himself before them for a short time.

He has difficulty in doing even this because he is so haughty; for although the plebeians know full well he has fought many battles and been wounded many times, they want him to expose his scars to them in person. This, of course, is much beneath his dignity, but Coriolanus manages to come to some kind of accommodation with the plebeians, until their own representatives, the tribunes, inflame them against him by telling outright lies about him. They do this because they see it as a way to increase their own power, to which Coriolanus is an obstacle. They succeed in having Coriolanus exiled from Rome.

He does not take his banishment lying down, however; in revenge, he joins the forces of Rome's enemies and soon has Rome at his mercy. The plebeians who, at the behest of their tribunes, had called for his banishment now blame those same tribunes for Rome's plight and seek to kill them.

Coriolanus has been welcomed into the enemy camp, but the leader of the Volscians (the enemy), Tullus Aufidius, is jealous of Coriolanus's popularity with the Volscian people. Formerly Number 1, he is now very much Number 2. Coriolanus spares Rome when he is in a position to capture and destroy it, merely because of the appeal made to him by his mother; Tullus Aufidius, jealous of his power, accuses him of treason and has him done to death. The Volscian crowd that formerly adulated him switches in an instant into a murderous mob. Having had him killed, Tullus Aufidius then extols him in the last speech in the play.

I think it fair to say that no one comes out of this well. Coriolanus has virtues of course – he is extremely brave – but he is mulishly inflexible and his disdain of the common people, merely because they are the common people and not, like him, noble, is not very appealing, or even very intelligent. Moreover, he seems to have no inner life, only an external role to play, that of the hardened warrior, braver, stronger, more unyielding than anyone else; he is, like so many modern politicians, unappealingly one-dimensional. He has, as they say, no hinterland; one cannot imagine him being interested in philosophy or art, or having a strange and passionate hobby, such as collecting things; if there were no wars for him to fight in, he would cease to exist for himself; and one would no more wish to spend an evening in his company than in that of, say, Mrs Clinton.

Shakespeare, who knew how to depict the internal life of people better than anyone who ever lived, has not simply made a mistake with Coriolanus, in showing him to be an empty vessel filled up by activity. He is showing us a type that appears to me to be becoming more common: someone for whom public adulation, though always on his own terms, is a kind of scaffolding that keeps the whole edifice of the personality upright, that prevents the ego from crumbling into nothingness.

Tullus Aufidius is that very commonly encountered figure, the mediocrity whose ambition and ruthlessness is greater than his capacity: the type that now seems to rule the world, or a very large part of it (and perhaps always has done so).

The common people are far from adulated by Shakespeare. No *vox populi, vox Dei* for him, far from it. The first scene opens with the mob, the stage direction being 'Enter a company of mutinous Citizens, with staves, clubs and other weapons.' The First Citizen addresses the crowd:

> You know that Caius Marcius [Coriolanus] is chief enemy to the people.

The crowd replies enthusiastically that they know it.

> Let us kill him [continues the First Citizen], and we'll have corn at our own price.

This idea seems a very good one to the mob, who agree with him:

> No more talking on't! Let it be done!

Then the First Citizen enunciates what might be called the first principle of socialist economics, upon which (implicitly, of course) Shakespeare pours scorn:

> What authority surfeits on would relieve us. If they would yield us but the superfluity while it were wholesome, we might guess they relieved us humanely; but they think we are too dear.

132

In other words, the fundamental problem of economics is one of distribution; and if it were sorted out, all would be well. The redistributionists have ye always with you.

As for the tribunes, they are archetypical demagogues, unscrupulous and cynical. They understand that their constituents, the plebeians, are as the wheat through which the wind blows, bending in whatever direction the latest gust comes from. They also understand that hatred is by far the strongest political passion. The fact that Coriolanus deserves well of his country because he has won a famous victory will not satisfy the people for long:

> Doubt not [says Sicinius, one of the tribunes The commoners, foe whom we stand, but they Upon their ancient malice will forget With the least cause these his new honours...

The other tribune, Brutus, then suggests that they tell the people lies about Coriolanus:

> We must suggest the people in what hatred He still hath held them; that to's power he would Have made them mules, silenc'd their pleaders, and Dispropertied their freedoms, holding them, In human action and capacity, Of no more soul nor fitness for the world Than camels in their war, who have their provand Only for bearing burthens, and sore blows For sinking under them.

These lies are plausible; Coriolanus does indeed hold the people in contempt; but it is not true that he wishes to establish his own dictatorship, as the tribunes later pretend. And the tribunes, while goading the people on, pretend that they are moderates, intent upon holding the people back.

Has political life really changed very much since Shakespeare's day, at least as portrayed in Coriolanus? If anything, it seems to have regressed towards it, having perhaps (but only perhaps) moved away from it for an interlude of a century or two.

Demagogues and war heroes we have with us still, while discernible principles seem very few and far between. The crowds are still demanding that the candidates display their war wounds: when Mrs

Clinton 'mis-spoke' (in claiming untruthfully that she had once landed in Bosnia under sniper fire) she was trying to demonstrate that she, too, knew what it was to be under fire. The desire and willingness to present others in the worst possible light, as a sufficient argument in itself, is still with us. At the same time, a man of utter consistency, such as Coriolanus, would still be chewed up and spat out by the whole political system, just as he was nearly two thousand five hundred years ago.

The fact is that Coriolanus is not an attractive man, even though he's honest as the day is long and his integrity is unshakeable. When he captures Corioli, he denies himself any share of the spoils, but grants it in its entirety to his soldiers (later in the play, the tribunes allege that the spoil was never given in fact to the soldiers, thus implying that Coriolanus is not only a hypocrite but materially grasping, neither of which is true). Even his good qualities send shivers down our spine; he is cold and humourless.

In other words, it seems that integrity, like all other moral qualities, is best in moderation. Of course, we abhor complete unscrupulousness such as the tribunes display; it is contemptible; we want our politicians to be more honest than they. But we wouldn't want our politicians to be as inflexible in their integrity as Coriolanus either.

So if we had to write a job description for politicians, with all the qualities that we require of them, what would we put? Must be honest but not too honest? Must have principles but be prepared to abandon them as the occasion requires? Must be truthful but know when to lie and dissimulate? Must love the people but not be guided by them? Must be strong but without obstinacy? And how do we find such people?

Who will be prepared to stand up and say, 'Yes, I am an honest man, but not too honest?' On the contrary, we force every candidate to present himself as if he were the paragon of all virtues, each virtue being inflexibly adhered to; and, when he presents himself as such, his enemies then proceed to examine his past record and demonstrate that he failed to reveal those discreditable episodes in which all human lives are so rich.

This amounts to a megalomaniac's charter: and only human pachyderms, those with the thickest skins, need apply. I don't know about others, but one of the reasons I would never put myself forward for high office is that I would not want my life picked over by people who disagreed with my views, although, as human lives go, mine has been only averagely bad. I would need to want power very badly indeed to risk having my worst actions exposed to public view, though my worst actions have not been so very terrible.

Is there any lesson to be drawn from Coriolanus, that is to say a lesson that can be compressed into a line or two? I always feel nervous about trying to compress a work of literature into a two line moral: for if the point of such a work can be satisfactorily boiled down into such a moral, what is the point of the expanded version?

Well, Coriolanus teaches us that politics is an irredeemably dirty business, made dirtier by sea-green incorruptibility on the one hand and utter lack of scruple on the other. These extremes are often in dialectical relationship to one another: therefore, elect no one without a sense of humour, or at least of irony.

But which of the candidates has a sense of humour?

AUSTRIA AND EVIL

THE CASE OF JOSEF FRITZL evoked many lively, one might even say enthusiastic and joyful, animadversions on the Austrian national character. It was no coincidence, said the finger-pointers, that it should be in Austria, land of *Die Fledermaus*, Mozart-kugeln and Gemütlichkeit in general, in which so extraordinary a case should have occurred.

Fritzl, a 73-year-old retired electronic engineer, imprisoned his own daughter, Elisabeth, in a specially-constructed cellar of his house for 24 years, raped her repeatedly and had seven children by her, all born in there without medical assistance. One of them died very young. Three of them, aged 5, 18 and 19, had never in their lives left the cellar, their only contact with the outside world being through television – perhaps the only service that television has rendered humanity.

The other three children had been delivered to the doorstep of Herr Fritzl's house, as foundlings of old were once delivered to orphanages, by Herr Fritzl himself, accompanied by a note written in Elisabeth's hand (she supposedly having left the parental household a long time before) to the effect that, having had two children already, she could not cope with any more, and asking her parents to look after them and bring them up.

Had the oldest of the children kept in the cellar not suffered from a mysterious illness requiring hospital care – she was delivered to the hospital unconscious, with a note attached to her body asking that she be looked after – and had she not been visited in the hospital by Herr Fritzl and his daughter posing as his wife, the situation could have continued indefinitely, at least until Herr Fritzl's death.

The Austrian police were soon convinced that Frau Fritzl – the real Frau Fritzl, that is – knew nothing of what had been going on, and neither did any of the neighbours or townsfolk of the small and prosperous town of Amstetten where all this took place (Austria is nothing if not prosperous).

It was inevitable, I suppose, that the ignorance both of Frau Fritzl and of the townspeople of the evil taking place under their very eyes, as it were, or in the midst of their placid, well-ordered and comfortable existence, should have been taken as a real-life metaphor for Austria's attitude to its own past: for, in fact, no one really believes in his heart that either Frau Fritzl or the people of Amstetten could have been genuinely and totally ignorant of what had been going on there for so long. No, they both knew and did not know, or rather chose not to know: and choosing not to know something implies a degree of knowledge of it. Their ignorance, if such it can be called, of Herr Fritzl and his cellar was culpable.

This ambiguity, or (to put it less kindly) dishonesty, if it really exists, replicates in symbolic fashion the attitude of Austria to its historical record in the 1930s and 40s. Officially, Austria was a victim of Nazi aggression; in reality, it was an enthusiastic participant in Nazi crimes. But whatever crimes Austrians as individuals committed during the war, they committed them as Germans, not as Austrians. They were responding only to *force majeure*; the Austrian state was not implicated.

Suspicion of Austria runs deep, and with good reason. Everyone thinks (though it cannot be proved or disproved) that Kurt Waldheim, the former Secretary-General of the United Nations, was elected president of the country not in spite of his Nazi past, but because of it. The Austrians claim that they insisted on voting for him because they resented the hypocritical reaction of the outside world to his candidature – surely, they said, powers with the combined intelligence resources of the United States, the Soviet Union, Britain and France must have known of his Nazi past when they accepted him as Secretary-General, so why should the Austrians themselves not accept him as president? Once again the Austrians were able to conceive of themselves as the injured party in the whole business.

Even the Austrian prohibition of Holocaust denial, under which the British Nazi-supporting historian David Irving was (in my view wrongfully) imprisoned until he recanted, or at least pretended to recant, is ambiguous. On the one hand, of course, it is a recognition of the moral monstrosity of what the Nazis did, and of the Austrians' special responsibility for it; but on the other, it implies a deep mistrust of the Austrian people, who (it must have been feared by those who framed the law) might recant their anti-Nazism if they could.

Of course, there have been Austrians who were deeply disgusted by their countrymen. The greatest Austrian writer of the post-war period, Thomas Bernhard, inserted a famous clause in his will that repays reflection. He ordered that, for the duration of his legal copyright after his death, nothing he had ever written, including his plays, should ever be published or performed:

> within the borders of the Austrian state, however that state describes itself. I categorically emphasize that I want to have nothing to do with the Austrian state and I safeguard myself concerning my person and my work not only against every interference but also against every approach by this Austrian state to my person and my work for all time to come.

'For all time to come': that is a pretty strong injunction, implying as it does that the Austrian soul, or whatever you want to call it, is so tainted by its original sin, or sins, that it is irrecoverably and irremediably evil. And Austria's recent Nobel Prize winner for Literature, Elfriede Jellinek, does not seem to have a much higher opinion of Austria than did Bernhard.

Whatever the justice or injustice of these speculations, I think it wrong complacently to suppose that such horrors as the Fritzl case can occur only in countries other than the one in which one happens to live. I have seen enough of human evil, in many different countries, to know that evil is not neatly confined to borders. For example, I was once consulted by the police in Britain in a case that was, in its own way, as terrible as the one in Austria.

A couple had set up a sexual torture chamber in their own small house in a small and otherwise unremarkable town in Britain, where they proceeded to rape their own naked children, suspended upside down from the ceiling, while filming it on video. It was the man who filmed and the woman, herself naked, beat and raped the children; they sold the videos of these appalling proceedings, which continued for years unbeknown to the neighbours or to any authorities, at great profit to themselves. In order to protect his partner in the business, the man claimed that he had drugged the woman with opiates, to make her do his bidding; I was asked to give an opinion as to whether this made pharmacological sense. Of course it did not.

I do not think it is possible to say whether all this was worse than the Fritzl case: but even if it were, I should be reluctant to do so, because men often excuse their evil by claiming that at least it is not so bad as some other evil they could mention. This is not a way of thinking that should be encouraged. And yet one cannot help thinking about such cases.

A journalist acquaintance of mine asked me recently why this should be so, why evil fascinates in a way that good rarely does. To this question I do not have a definitive answer. Is the interest morbid? Maybe, but it is inescapable for creatures constituted as we are. You might as well pass a law to prohibit gossip as inveigh against our interest in the outer reaches of human conduct.

Although I think that most people are capable of evil under certain circumstances, I do not believe that many, as a proportion of the population, have any inclination to behave in the way that Fritzl or the two parents behaved. Vicarious wish fulfilment is not, therefore, the explanation of our fascination with radical evil.

I think that such cases bring into sharp focus our continual but continually failing attempts to understand ourselves and our place in nature. It is odd that we should have been equipped by that nature with a desire that (in my opinion) can never be satisfactorily fulfilled.

Of course, there has been a lot of propaganda recently to the effect that, thanks to a combination of Darwinian theory and neuroscience, we are about to understand ourselves in a radically better way than we have ever understood ourselves before. This seems to me to be nonsense: the latest post-religious attempt, after the failure of Marxism and Freudianism, to find an explanation of everything human. As for religion, it doesn't satisfy me either.

In other words, the only honest way to live is with a sense of mystery. It is not merely that no particular explanation satisfies me, I cannot conceive of what an entirely satisfactory explanation of ourselves would be like. (I also fear such an explanation, were it possible, because it would give enormous power to him who possessed it. But would he understand his own motives and behaviour in making use of it? By definition he would have to do so; he would have to have also a completely coherent, consistent and true ethical theory, such as no one has yet found.)

A case such as that of Fritzl confronts us with a question in the following form: 'At what point are we able to say to ourselves, ah, now we understand, that is to say truly understand, why he behaved like that?' How much of his genetic endowment, his early life history, his neuroanatomy and chemistry, his social position, his cultural inheritance, will we need to know before we can say that no mystery remains for us?

I think the answer is obvious. We will never reach that point. Our understanding of ourselves will remain largely at the periphery of our lives. We will be able to perform all kinds of technological miracles – we will make the blind see, the deaf hear and so forth – but we shall never understand our own subjectivity, or be able to connect it conceptually to the physical ground of our being. When Hamlet tells Rosencrantz and Guildenstern that they will not so easily 'pluck out the heart of his mystery', he was, in effect, speaking for all mankind. We are all of us mysterious not only to others but to ourselves, and will remain so.

Because of this, our ability to control events will always be very limited. Those who claim that human self-understanding has marvellously increased of late, and the search for it is all over bar the shouting, have been remarkably unable to predict the future or tell us how to live. Their explanations of human conduct are all *ex post facto* and provide no guidance as to what we should do next, in the way that (for example) medical science sometimes tells us what to do next when we have such-and-such an illness.

No doubt there will be a lot of official activity in Austria in the wake of the Fritzl case: first recriminations and then proposals to ensure that nothing like it ever happens again (everything that happens in the modern world being an opportunity to increase bureaucratic interference in lives). If only enough good procedures are put in place, nothing untoward will ever occur to disturb our illusion of control.

From what I know of the infinite variety of human self-destructiveness, which is itself an expression of the Dostoyevskian urge to depart from the dictatorship of good sense, I should say that the disturbers of the peace will always be able to outwit the keepers of the peace. Political wisdom consists of knowing what is predictable and what is unpredictable, what is controllable and what is uncontrollable, and all the gradations in between. If you waste your time in thinking that everything is predictable and controllable, you will miss what is there to be seen.

OF DEATH AND TRANSFIGURATION

ONE OF THE ADVANTAGES of rehearsing your thoughts (or, more accurately, some of your thoughts) in public is that you often enter into friendly correspondence with interesting people. Of course, you also expose yourself to cranks and pedants, the latter ready to pounce upon the slightest error either of fact or grammar in what you have set down. They who have never published a word seem to read solely for the pleasure of finding something over which to pull authors up. (They would defend themselves, of course, by quoting Doctor Johnson on the right of people who never made a table nevertheless to criticise a table.)

Actually, I am aware of the temptations of pedantry myself: as an occasional book reviewer, nothing gives me greater pleasure than to spot a mistake, the smaller and more arcane the better. Whether I refer to it or not in my review depends upon my overall attitude to the book. If I agree with or approve of the book in general I overlook it, but if I think the book is wrong-headed in a serious or reprehensible way I am sorely tempted to emphasise it beyond its intrinsic importance as a way of calling attention to the author's deficiencies. Only a vestigial attachment to fairness, and the fear that readers might consider me pedantic, restrains me.

The pedants of the world do serve a useful function, however: they instil a respect for facts among those who might otherwise be inclined to play fast and loose with them. (Does the latter sentence contain any facts, I wonder? Even thinking about pedants causes one to reflect upon what one writes.) Cranks, though, are another matter entirely: there is nothing to be said for them.

I started writing in the days – which I can now scarcely recollect, though in fact they make up the great majority of my earthly existence – before the internet, when cranks could not e-mail to you. Instead, they sent you letters, the madness of whose contents was often deducible by their envelopes alone. A fair proportion of the world's cranks, for example (at least of the kind that wrote to me), are extremely parsimonious, and recycle envelopes, blanking out the name and address of the original addressee with a black felt-tip pen, and the re-addressing them in unusual-coloured inks, violet being a particular favourite. As if this were not enough, they try to save envelopes – or is it the planet? – by cutting them in two and sealing them with Sellotape.

I am not sure whether access to the internet has increased the number of cranks or whether it has merely increased the ease with which they can express themselves. Writing a letter requires a degree of determination and even forward planning that sending an e-mail does not. Since most human characteristics grow more marked when they are expressed than when, for whatever reason, they are denied expression (contrary to the hydraulic model of self-expression that was fashionable for a time), it is possible to surmise that the internet has increased the prevalence of cranks in society.

But what of correspondents of the other kind? Two or three years ago, I started to receive letters from a doctor in California in his late eighties who was still in part-time practice (his specialism was not a physically-demanding one). He was clearly an erudite and witty man, something of a classicist in fact, for he often quoted – wholly appropriately, I might add – the Latin poets. He wrote of this and that, often of modern follies that he dissected with detached amusement rather than bitterness, for of course he had experienced a lot of folly in his time and he knew that life continued, usually with enjoyment, in spite of it. I looked forward to his letters.

Two weeks ago, I received another letter from him, alas the last I shall ever receive. It was, in a sense, a letter from beyond the grave. He wrote it to be sent to all his friends by his widow in the event of his death. This occurred suddenly and (I hope) without suffering.

It was an admirable letter, again full of the poet Horace (everything worth saying about life in general has already been said, it is just – the salvation of writers - that we forget). He spoke of his own exit from the world calmly, with no rage at the dying of the light. He had had a long and interesting life, and he had no wish that it should be prolonged for ever, beyond the age at which he could make a contribution. Oblivion held no fears for him.

I was reminded of the death of David Hume, who also met his end with complete equanimity, one might almost say with an amused equanimity. Of course, Doctor Johnson thought it was all affectation, that no one died like that, but Doctor Johnson, admirable as he himself was, might have been wrong on this occasion. Humanity is broad enough to include a few non-pathological souls who look on death without terror.

The doctor from California said in his letter that he was leaving his body to science, or at any rate for medical students to dissect (which is not quite the same thing, of course). And then he said something with which I could not agree, however much I liked and respected him. He said that his body was worthy of no more consideration or veneration than a rotten pork chop.

I would dearly have loved to take him up on this subject. It seems to me that it is necessary to venerate human remains in some way, and this (I admit) is odd because I am not religious, and do not believe in the immortal soul however much I would like to do so.

As the doctor knew very well, medical students do not always treat the bodies of those they dissect with veneration or respect: on the contrary, they give them nicknames and even play with body parts. This seemed to please him, as it was for him a sign of rationality. Man is a physicochemical being and nothing else, and when the physics and chemistry break down, there is nothing, or rather nobody, left to venerate or respect.

Although I do not think man will ever be able fully to explain himself fully in physicochemical terms, and I think the mystery of consciousness will continue to elude us, scientistic philosophers who are forever jumping the gun notwithstanding, it does not follow that I think that man is something more than a physicochemical being, such that his soul leaves his body on death as a butterfly emerges from a chrysalis. In other words, I do not believe in an afterlife, unlike (for example) some of those adolescents who attempt suicide, imagining that they will attend their own funerals in some ethereal way and observe all those grieving for them who took insufficient notice of them during their lives.

Yet, at the same time, I cannot agree with the rotten-pork-chop view of human bodies. Thinking back to my own time as a medical student at the dissecting table, I think our irreverence was in fact an inverted form of reverence. The fact that medical students by tradition were plunged on arrival straight into the dissecting room, as a kind of rite de passage, establishes this.

Doctors have to be involved in the lives of their patients, of course, and must be compassionate; but at the same time they must be objective and detached. (That is why there have been so many good doctor-writers.) They cannot break down with every tragedy they encounter, otherwise their careers would last not more than a week or two. How is the necessary detachment to be brought about?

In dissecting a human body, medical students have to overcome a strong initial revulsion against what they are told, and what they know, they have to do. The social pressure to exhibit sangfroid is great; the irreverence of medical students is (except for those few among them who are psychopaths) an attempt to persuade themselves that, in breaking a taboo, they are doing no evil. Their lack of respect is inverted respect.

Likewise, the mutilation of bodies after a battle appals us. It strikes us as more savage than the killing in battle that is, alas, sometimes justified or necessary. We would not expect the mutilators to behave well in other circumstances; if you knew a man who had behaved like this, you would instinctively keep your distance from him, though you would not keep your distance from a man who had simply shot someone dead in battle.

Of course, there have been primitive peoples (if one is still permitted to use the term primitive to describe anyone) who have made a thing of mutilating their enemies killed in battle. But this is also an inverted way of demonstrating that a human body is not just a rotten pork chop, that its significance is much greater. You do not go to the trouble of mutilating something that you consider of no account.

If I think that man is no more than a physicochemical being, or at any rate that there is no firm reason to think that he is, why do I nonetheless think that his inanimate remains ought to be treated with reverence? The answer exposes the reason why rationality is not enough in human life.

We have to live as if some things were sacred, for if we do not we become savages, or rather beings without limits. We cannot (or at least ought not) to condone necrophilia, for example, merely because no one is harmed by it, because the body on which it is practised is inanimate and has neither interests nor wishes, and is therefore not the kind of being that can give or withhold consent.

The precise boundaries of the sacred are always disputable, but we cannot do without an awareness of the sacred, even when we know that sacredness is not a natural quality, that it is not just 'there' in the way that natural qualities such as weight and density are, that it does not inhere as a natural quality of anything, that it is imposed upon the world by us in a way that other qualities are not. And that is part of the reason why a purely scientific attitude to life is both undesirable and impossible.

Unfortunately, people have often tried to adopt an impossible attitude to life. The mere fact that the attitude is impossible doesn't mean that the attempt is without effect, quite the reverse. Attempts to desanctify human life in the name of rationality have, in my view predictably, resulted in the most terrible of crimes.

If I am right, we also have an explanation of why art that consciously attempts to be transgressive or to break taboos is unlikely to be any good, either morally or aesthetically: because the impulse to break taboos, irrespective of what they are, and merely because they are taboos, is a very bad one, indeed it would hardly be going too far to call it evil. This is not to say that under no circumstances should taboos be broken: but they should be broken for reasons other than that they are taboos.

Doctor Johnson knew this: he said – in his life of Swift - that a man who obeyed conventions was more moral than a man who broke them, unless he was better. In other words, conventions may be wrong, but we cannot therefore do without them; and they should be broken only with good reason.

I mean no disrespect at all when I say that the letter from beyond the grave of my much-revered correspondent contained something in it that I consider deeply and profoundly wrong. He was the kind of man who would have welcomed a discussion on the subject, and I think was open to argument even at his advanced age. That is high praise of a man indeed.

THE TRIUMPH OF EVIL

I'VE BEEN ARRESTED ONLY three times in my life: which, as a prison guard once proudly said to me, in explaining that he had been assaulted by prisoners only three times in his forty year-long career, I don't think is bad, do you?

The first time I was arrested was as a South African spy in a small town in Gabon, West Africa. I knew at once, of course, that the policeman arresting me did not really believe that I was such a spy; but it could not have been all that often that a man so eminently shakeable-down arrived in this back of beyond.

Fortunately for me, he had a deep respect for the medical profession, and once he learned that I was a doctor he walked round the chair on which I was sitting in his police hovel, and said admiringly, as a very great compliment, 'Vous avez beaucoup de papier dans la tête' (You have a lot of paper in your head).

Luckily, also, he needed a prescription for his venereal disease, so in return for this, he set me free. I did think of giving him something that made him feel ill: surely, putting corrupt West African policemen out of commission for a while did not count as doing harm, in the Hippocratic sense. But then charity took over: he probably wasn't paid for months on end, and latching on to people as he had with me was his only source of income.

The second time I was arrested was at the border of Honduras and El Salvador, on the Honduran side. I was driving a pick-up I had bought in Guatemala, and was on my way to Sandinista Nicaragua. I had a lot of books with me that I had bought in San Salvador, at a bookshop called La Catedral del Libro (the Cathedral of Books), and the Honduran border guards immediately concluded that I must be a very dangerous person.

Although El Salvador was commonly supposed at the time to be a vicious dictatorship, La Catedral del Libro had such an eclectic mix of books that it could scarcely have been more various had El Salvador been the purest of liberal democracies. Works by Marxist guerrilla sympathisers were cheek-by-jowl with *Mi Lucha* (*Mein Kampf*) by Adolfo Hitler, and (I remember this very well, for I had not heard of such a thing before), Cafemancia, the art of telling the future by coffee grounds.

Anyway, I was given over to an armed guard who was instructed to come with me as far as the Nicaraguan border: I was under car arrest, so to speak. Evidently, I presented so terrifying an aspect to him that he fell asleep immediately, with his gun poking intermittently into my ribs. He never knew the irony that the Honduran authorities had managed to arrest practically the only foreign intellectual in the whole of the Central American peninsula who was anti-guerrilla. When I stopped for lunch, it would have been churlish not to have paid for my guard's lunch too, although natural justice suggested, to me at any rate, that it should have been the other way round.

The third was the only time I have ever been arrested in anything like anger. It was on my second visit to Albania, my first after the downfall of communism. The government of the anti-communist cardiologist, Sali Berisha, was in power, though he was soon to be toppled. A demonstration against the government by communists took place on the morning of my departure, and the police waded into the crowd – not a very big one – with truncheons. Of course, not long before they might have beaten anti-communists, had they dared demonstrate. The crowd broke and ran towards one of Tirana's few hotels.

I rushed out myself to take photos of what was happening and soon found myself in the iron grip of a policeman. He was like a weightlifter and I have never felt such strength. He bundled me into the back of a police pick-up with a cage, oblivious to my protests, those of a spoilt brat, that I had a plane to catch (which was true), and therefore could not afford the time to be arrested. Even had he understood English, I do not think he would have relented just because Austrian Airlines waited for no man.

Another three onlookers were bundled into the pick-up besides me, one of whom turned out to be an Albanian intellectual with good English. The cage was locked, and we were driven, sirens blaring, through the not very busy streets to the police lock-up.

We were bundled out of the truck, and I was given a bash on the back with a truncheon just to encourage me not to dawdle. We were all locked into a small whitewashed cell. From there we could hear the police beating someone in another cell, his animal cries of pain rending the air. It was a horrible sound, but it did not surprise me. I assumed that this was the kind of thing that went on in Balkan police stations, and perhaps not just Balkan ones.

The Albanians in our cell began to shout and wail. Obviously, they thought they were going to be next for the treatment. For my benefit, the intellectual shouted 'This is Albanian democracy! This is Albanian democracy!' They rattled the bars on the steel door of the cell, and I decided to intervene.

'Look,' I said to the Albanian intellectual. 'This is no time to be Albanian. You have to become British. Stay quiet and keep calm, and don't draw attention to yourselves. Otherwise we'll all be beaten.'

To my amazement, and relief, it worked. No doubt they were so astonished by this ridiculous foreigner that it took their breath away. They went silent.

Fortunately for me, some of my friends, with whom I had dined with an important government official the night before, saw me being arrested and called on the government official to intervene. This he quickly did.

After no more than half an hour's imprisonment, during which we heard in silence a variety of human cries, the door of the cell opened and an officer, this time all consideration and even obsequiousness, beckoned to me to come out. It had evidently been made clear to him that he and his men had made a mistake in arresting me, potentially a serious one since I might write a damning article on the human rights situation in Albania for British and American publications.

The officer put his hand on his heart, bowed slightly and had a look of utter ingratiation on his face. The boot was now clearly on the other foot, and I was in a position – or so he obviously thought – to ruin his career. I left the prison cell and was driven back to my hotel like a visiting dignitary. I caught my plane. Francis Drake said he had time to finish his game of bowls and defeat the Spaniards; I had had time to be arrested in Albania and catch the Austrian Airlines flight.

At the moment of my release I had faced an acute dilemma. What of my fellow-prisoners? Now that the whirligig of time had brought in his revenges, should I use my position to refuse to accept release until they too had been released. After all, they were guilty only of having done what I had done, namely watched the demonstration. I knew nothing of them, but I certainly did not want them to get the treatment clearly being meted out in the police station.

Once I was released, I did make sure before I left Albania that representations were made to the high official about my three co-detainees, and in fact they were subsequently released, I believe without event. But still I could not quite get it out of my mind that, even if accepting release had been obviously the most sensible thing to do, and that I was of more use to my fellow detainees outside the cell than in, I had accepted it for the wrong reasons: out of a mixture of selfish relief and cowardice. True enough, I had only a split second in which to decide, but on this one occasion when my situation required and enabled me to make a stand, I had failed.

Since then, I have found it a little more difficult to say exactly how I would behave if I had to live in an evil tyranny. My behaviour in the cell in Tirana had been sensible, perhaps, but hardly heroic. I am not the stuff from which, for example, a Solzhenitsyn is made. I am too attached to my ordinary existence for that, and too afraid of the worst that can be done to me.

Of course, the question of how to behave under an evil tyranny is one that much of the population of Europe in the twentieth century had to decide. In France, to take only one example, millions of people had to decide whether just to get on with their lives as best they could, join the resistance or take advantage of the new dispensation to get on in life. Even today, the interpretation of the ubiquitous black-marketeers under the Occupation is much disputed: were they ruthless predators concerned only for their own good, were they quietly undermining the occupiers (who were trying to extract as much economic surplus from France as possible, which diversion of goods on to the black market reduced, thereby improving the lot of ordinary Frenchmen), or were they in fact assisting the occupiers by making the whole system viable, which it would not have been without the black market? Or were they all of these things at once?

It is one of the evils of evil tyrannies that they seek to implicate everyone in their system, by means of spying, the granting of privileges, etc. But it is not only tyrannies that do this: modern bureaucracies, even in liberal democratic states, do this also. For example, in the British state hospital system (and no modern state does entirely without public hospitals), doctors undergo a compulsory annual appraisal by a colleague, decreed and designed by the administration, without any evidence that it improves performance in any way whatever. Its purpose is not to improve performance; its purpose is to destroy independence.

The very fact of participating in a process that is universally recognised to be useless is harmful, for everyone who does so is 'only obeying orders' for the sake of his own peace and quiet and for the sake of his career; in other words, by taking part, he has already lost some of his integrity.

One of the *pro forma* questions is very cleverly-worded, so cleverly that I actually admire its cleverness (which I think is instinctive rather than conscious, because apparatchiks, however much they believe in forms and procedures, operate and work by instinct when it comes to extending their own powers). The question is this: 'Are there any concerns about your probity?'

The first time I was asked, I said that I would reply only on condition that the person who asked would answer two questions. The first was what kind of person would answer such a question. The second was what kind of person would ask it. My appraiser got the point at once and laughed nervously. He told me that it was all nonsense, that nobody took any notice of it anyway. But then I asked him what kind of person took part unprotestingly in processes that were worse than merely a waste of time.

It isn't often that we face acute moral dilemmas such as the one I faced in the Albanian cell. More often our moral integrity is eroded bit by bit until there is none left. Edmund Burke said that freedom is seldom lost all at once, but freedom is not the only thing that is seldom lost all at once.

This helps to explain why the professional management of public institutions is so dangerous and corrupting. What is needed is amateur (though not of course amateurish) management.

NEITHER A LENDER NOR A BORROWER BE

I ARRIVED IN NEW YORK the day after Lehman Brothers, the investment bank which had been in business for 158 years, collapsed. By the time I left a few days later, Merrill Lynch had undergone a distress sale and the American government, given the choice between apocalyptic financial panic and the bottomless pit, had chosen the bottomless pit and bailed out (and taken over) the giant insurance company, AIG.

I arrived back in Britain, the land of my residence for six months of the year, to learn that one of the country's largest banks, Halifax Bank of Scotland, had been taken over by Lloyds Bank to prevent an undignified and potentially catastrophic run on HBOS, which would otherwise almost certainly have happened. It seemed as if my arrival in countries was a bad augury for the financial markets, and I decided to stay put for a while, just in case there really was a causative relationship.

Canvassing the opinion of friends and acquaintances as to the meaning of all this financial turmoil, I began to feel like a share in one of those vulnerable companies that would seesaw wildly in value on the stock exchange, according to the latest rumour, the day before it either collapsed completely or was rescued by one expedient or another. Some would say that the crisis was at most an epiphenomenon, and that the real economy, the one that baked bread and made nuts and bolts, would continue unaffected. Others would say that this was the beginning of the end, that we should all spend the rest of our lives struggling to make ends meet, eking out a bare subsistence, and that we should never feel secure and prosperous again. I swung between complacency and terror, until I finally took refuge in the thought, implanted in my mind by a scribbler of my acquaintance some time during the last episode of financial panic, that during recessions and depressions the demand for journalism and other forms of writing goes up rather than down, reading being a comparatively cheap form of entertainment. Wishful thinking easily attains the status of truth, and so I concluded, on the basis of what was no more than an

151

obiter dictum, that at any rate I should be all right. This conclusion, of course, did not take into account the epidemic of education-induced illiteracy since the last panic.

By no means a financial wizard – my love affair with money has thus far remained unrequited – I could not help thinking that the episode, whether it proves fleeting or of limited duration and minor consequence, was not without an important cultural dimension. Everything that happens tells us something about the way we live now, even when what happens is not entirely without precedent (every banker, broker and hedge fund manager ought to read, mark and inwardly digest Charles Mackay's *Memoirs of Extraordinary Popular Delusions and the Madness of Crowds*, first published in 1841 and scarcely out of print ever since, itself a powerful evidence of the inability of most of mankind to learn from the experience of others).

Of course, one's assessment of the cultural significance of events depends upon one's understanding, whether true or false, of their causation. Therefore, in what follows, I am depending upon my no doubt somewhat schematic understanding of the turmoil on the Anglo-American markets. It is therefore only right that I should state what my understanding is, before launching out on my main observations. If my understanding is fundamentally wrong, then my other observations are null and void.

Large quantities of money result in easy credit, and easy credit inflates the value of assets such as houses. This in turn means that houses, whose prices appear to be rising effortlessly like a good soufflé, become collateral to loans to people who would otherwise not merit loans.

The banks and mortgage companies, whose business, after all, is lending money, did not enquire too closely into the biographical record of their borrowers. Indeed, those who sold mortgages often had little connection to those who lent the money: rising prices would take care of any risk inherent in ignorance or fraud.

Financial instruments were concocted that successfully hid the very hazardous nature of this way of recycling money. I remember receiving a few years ago a brief tutorial from someone by no means stupid on the way in which mathematically gifted people on Wall Street had found a formula that successfully eliminated all risk from extending large loans to numbers of people who had never previously displayed any tendency to prudence or probity. I didn't believe it;

but, not being mathematically gifted, I found myself rather in the position of Diderot when Euler, according to legend, presented him with a mathematical formula allegedly proving the existence of God. Diderot had nothing to reply because he didn't know mathematics; I also kept my counsel about the lending of money to people with no capacity, let alone inclination, to pay it back.

However, the instruments created were so convoluted and distant from any concrete reality that those who believed in them were ignorant of their foundations. They believed in them as peasants used to believe in miracle-working Virgins.

Pyramid schemes of this nature work splendidly for a time, and those who get out before the *dénouement*, or manage to extract enough from them before they collapse, make a fortune. That, of course, is why they recur through history: many lose in the end, but a few gain, and gain astronomically, in the meantime. Mankind is a herd to be fleeced, and luckily the wool always grows back.

Let us now consider some of the cultural implications of what has happened. A few words seem to sum it up: improvidence and lack of probity. But whose, exactly, and in what proportion and with what implications?

The butcher and the baker, upon whose benevolence Adam Smith famously told us that we do not rely for the quality of our meat and bread, are kept in line by the evident and close connection between how they conduct themselves and the profit that they make. In other words, their self-interest guarantees their providence and probity; assuming they have no natural or unnatural monopoly, they would go out of business very quickly if they passed off measly pork and adulterated bread as the finest that money could supply.

But the connection between such virtues as providence and probity on the one hand, and reward on the other, is – it must be confessed – somewhat attenuated in the modern world of capitalism. There are so many steps between raw material and final product, or between the initiator of a productive process and the final consumer of whatever it is that is produced, that there is plenty of opportunity for the vices corresponding to providence and probity to operate and flourish, at least long enough for those who display them to line their nest with feathers of gold. This makes providence and probity all the more desirable, of course.

I don't think there is much doubt that the banks, in Britain at any rate, have been improvident and lacking in probity. If I may descend for a moment from abstraction to anecdote, I will recount my experiences with my own bank over the years that illustrate a change not just in its attitude to credit, but in our culture.

Shortly after I opened an account there, forty years ago, I received a letter from the manager drawing my attention with some asperity to the fact that my account was almost £3 overdrawn, and that he trusted that I would soon rectify the situation by the end of the week. Forty years later, when I was again overdrawn, I received a telephone call from the manager – the bank's motto being, 'Don't call us, we'll call you' – asking to see me. Indeed, the manager said he would come to my house.

Gosh, I thought, now I'm in trouble. When he arrived, I told him that I was about to pay the amount by which I was overdrawn into my account. He looked extremely crestfallen.

'You mean you don't want to borrow more?' he said. 'I've come here to offer you more.'

A wasted journey, obviously.

A short time later, I went to my bank to borrow money to buy a house while I sold another. Within five minutes I was offered a sum the like of which I had never previously handled, and in excess of anything I needed. While it was smaller than my total nominal assets, as I enumerated them, the bank made absolutely no effort to verify that I was indeed the owner of these assets.

With a large loan outstanding, I continued to receive, about every month or so, offers of a further loan of £30,000, no questions asked and mine for the borrowing by mere telephone call, just in case there were any little extras or extravagances I happened to feel like treating myself to (but apply now, before next month's offer of precisely the same thing!). The principal example given of the little extras or extravagances to which I might want to treat myself was the holiday of a lifetime.

Two considerations led me to turn down all of these kind offers. The first is that my taste in holidays of a lifetime runs more to observing civil wars than to lolling in the lap of luxury, and, while sometimes expensive to go to, civil wars offer little in the way of sybaritic possibilities (though there was a surprising availability of pink champagne during the Liberian civil war, even if it was difficult to chill).

The second consideration was the faintly puritanical belief, no doubt the psychological consequence of having been born only a few years after the end of the Second World War, that if one could not afford to pay cash on the nail for the holiday of a lifetime, one could not afford the holiday of a lifetime. One did not go deeply into debt for the sake of evanescent pleasures, such as that of a couple of weeks' sitting under palm trees by a lighted pool in the tropical sunset, waited upon by obsequious, and no doubt secretly resentful, flunkies.

Even allowing for the change in my personal circumstances over the forty years, the irresponsibility of the bank (and other financial institutions) seemed to me – if one absented a knowledge of history, that is – astonishing. There is no doubt, however, that many people, in fact many millions of people, listened to the siren song of easy credit, of fritter now, pay later.

The interesting question for me, then, is not that of the foolishness or dishonesty of the financial institutions, but that of the population. At what point did the population come to believe that it was possible (to cite the advertising slogan of a new credit card launched in Britain in the 1970s) to 'take the waiting out of wanting'?

Let us try to imagine what it is to be a sub-prime borrower, or indeed a borrower of any kind who over-extends himself and goes into debt for trifles light as air, for the procuring of what will predictably bring him no more than a few moments' satisfaction, soon to be followed by a further fevered search for a few more moments' satisfaction.

When I sought my large loan from the bank, I – who have by no means maximised my economic opportunities throughout my life, or behaved with squirrel-like wisdom and foresight, believing in my twenties, for example, that I would never survive to my present great age – considered such matters as to whether, in the event of not selling my other house, I should still be able to service my debt; whether I could find other means of paying the loan back; what happened if interest rates rose and my income fell; etc., etc. These did not seem to me to be terribly difficult thoughts, indeed they seemed rather obvious ones, almost coterminous with the decision to seek the loan, and certainly with the signing of the agreement. Yet it now appears that millions of people, in my own country and elsewhere, have not thought such thoughts, and this is really rather depressing. I suppose they thought they were getting something for nothing; the more sophisticated among them probably realised that, since they had no assets to speak of, they had nothing to lose. But I am not sure that mass lack of probity is much better than mass lack of providence (the question would make an interesting one for a student research paper).

Be that as it may, all these people are voters, who have the future direction of their country in their hands, at least in so far as a choice between candidates for office makes any difference to the direction their country takes. The future, it seems, depends upon the dishonest and the improvident. This is not altogether reassuring, at least in the abstract, until one considers the behaviour of the class from whom the candidates usually emerge. It takes a thief to elect a thief; and, in the imperfect sublunary world, perhaps that is the best to which we can aspire. At any rate, I prefer it to the unrestricted reign of honest men.

OF BIBLIOPHILIA AND BIBLIOCLASM

IN 1936, GEORGE ORWELL published a little essay entitled *Bookshop Memories*. In it, he recalled his time as an assistant in a second-hand bookshop, a time that was happy only when viewed through the soft-focus lens of nostalgia. Irony might be defined as disgust recalled in tranquillity, and Orwell's essay is nothing if not full of irony. He was glad to have had the experience, no doubt, but more glad that it was over.

Not much has changed in the three-quarters of a century that have elapsed since Orwell's experience as a bookseller. Second-hand bookshops the world over still tend to be inadequately heated places, Orwell says because the owners fear condensation in the windows, but also because profits are small and heating bills would be large. There is a peculiar chill, quite unlike any other, to be experienced between the stacks of second-hand bookshops.

Orwell says that the tops of books in such bookshops are the place 'where every bluebottle prefers to die', and this preference, being biological in origin, has not changed in the meantime. The dust of old books, and 'the sweet smell of decaying paper', still have a peculiarly choking quality that catch one in the back of the throat. And second-hand bookshops are still one of the few indoor public places where a person may loiter for hours without being suspected of any serious ulterior motive.

Orwell did not have a high regard for the customers, who struck him as awkward and mainly suffering from psychological problems. As a long-time *habitué* of second-hand bookshops, I should say that this is a fairly typical attitude of booksellers to buyers, whom they regard largely with contempt. This contempt arises not only from the character of book-buyers, but from their tastes. I knew a bookseller, a communist of the Enver Hoxha faction, who was constantly frustrated and irritated that the elderly black ladies of the area in which he had his shop were always asking for Bibles rather than for revolutionary literature that he thought that they, as the most downtrodden of the downtrodden, ought to have been reading. Another bookshop owner of my acquaintance so hated his customers that he would sometimes play Schoenberg very loudly to clear the shop of them. It was a very effective technique.

Not everything has remained the same since Orwell's day, however. He says that anyone ought to be able to make a go of a second-hand bookshop, but this is no longer the case. Such bookshops are declining fast in number – recently I was in a coastal town in England that a decade ago had ten of them, and now the last of them was about to close in a week's time.

Two developments have led to the decline of the second-hand bookshop. The first, of course, is the internet. The internet is both wonderful and terrible. For instance, it enables patients to learn a lot about their own diseases, and if they are discriminating, sometimes even to save their own lives. But medical information, or opinion, on the internet has probably already killed far more people than it has saved: the fact that Thabo Mbeki, the recently deposed president of South Africa, found a site on the internet while browsing that convinced him that AIDS was not caused by a virus, and that therefore treatment of HIV with drugs was harmful, resulted in untold premature loss of life that it will take many years for the internet to balance by lives it has saved.

With regard to books, the internet is a wonderful instrument for finding a book that you particularly need or want: if, for example (and for some obscure reason), you are searching for the 1490 edition of Pietro D'Abano's *Tractatus de Venenis*, then you can find it on a site that claims to list 110,000,000 books. Suffice it to say that you could spend several lifetimes scouring the bookshops of the world in the old-fashioned way without finding it.

But the pleasure of second-hand bookshops is not only in finding what you want: it is in leafing through many volumes and alighting upon something that you never knew existed, that fascinates you and therefore widens your horizons in a completely unanticipated way, helping you to make the most unexpected connections.

According to the owner of a bookshop that I have now been patronising for forty years (and who seemed to me to be of the older generation when I first met him, but now seems, mysteriously, to be precisely the same age as I), browsing in the fashion and for the purpose that I have just described is a thing of the past. Young people do not do it any more, as they still did when he started his life in the trade. Instead, they have a purely instrumental or utilitarian attitude to bookshops: they come in, ask whether he has such-and-such a title, and if he does not they leave at once, usually with visible disgruntlement: for what is the point of a bookshop that does not have the very title that *they* want here and now?

There are other pleasures of the imagination that those who do not browse forgo. When first I bought books from second-hand bookshops I eschewed those with inscriptions, and to this day there are buyers who regard any mark on a book as a defect. (Orwell tells us that working in a bookshop taught him how few really bookish people there were, and how 'first edition snobs' are much more common than lovers of literature. I suppose that first edition snobs are to literature what hi-fi addicts are to music.) But I have changed my mind over the years, and now even prefer books to be inscribed in some way.

I like copies of books inscribed by the author, particularly when dedicated with a message, and association copies: that is to say, copies that are inscribed by a known personage who has some intellectual or other connection with the book's contents. My rationalist friends find this taste of mine odd and surprising: after all, the value of a book, they tell me, is overwhelmingly in its content, and secondarily (perhaps) in its aesthetic appeal as a physical artefact. There is no rational reason why a book should be more valuable, interesting or beautiful merely because it has the name of a well-known, or at any rate traceable, person inscribed in it, any more than there is rational reason to suppose that by eating the flesh of a slain enemy you absorb some of his power.

This may be so in some abstract philosophical sense, but generations of bibliophiles have not believed it. To take one minor example from my own small and insignificant collection: a third edition of De Quincey's *Confessions of an English Opium Eater* (when it was still published anonymously in 1823) that was once owned by Edgell Rickword.

Rickword (1898 – 1982) was a *littérateur* who wrote books about Rimbaud and Gillray, and was an influential critic in his time who turned communist in the 1930s. He served in the First World War, during which he lost an eye, was highly decorated and became a war poet of the second rank. Some of his lines were memorable and moving:

I knew a man, he was my chum,
but he grew blacker every day,
and would not brush the flies away,
nor blanch however fierce the hum
of passing shells; I used to read,
to rouse him, random things from Donne –

Or:

In sodden trenches I have heard men speak,
Though numb and wretched, wise and witty things;
And loved them for the stubbornness that clings
Longest to laughter when Death's pulleys creak...

I am not at all in sympathy with Rickword's later political beliefs, to put it mildly; but a man who had suffered as he had suffered, and yet had gone on to a long and varied literary career, and who wrote the lines I have quoted, could hardly be contemptible. Therefore to treasure the treasured possessions of such a man is to do honour to the human spirit.

Books, even without association with anyone known, have an almost sacred quality in any case: it is necessary only to imagine someone ripping the pages out of a cheap and trashy airport novel one by one to prove to oneself that this is so. If we saw someone doing it, we should shudder, and think him a barbarian, no matter the nature of the book. The horror aroused by book burnings is independent of the quality of the books actually burnt.

One of my treasured books is a little classic of which I should never even have heard had I not browsed in so many bookshops. It is William Blades' *The Enemies of Books*, first published in 1880. The frontispiece is an engraving of John Bagford, described as 'shoemaker and biblioclast', and another of the delightful pictures is of a furtive charwoman feeding pages of a Caxton Bible to feed a fire. The enemies of books are ranged in chapters in a great chain of being: first come inanimate forces such as fire and water, rising to the lower animals such as bookworms and other vermin, and finally rising to the pinnacle of biblioclasm, that is to say the conscious book-destroyers, the bookbinders and book collectors. (John Bagford tore out the first pages of hundreds of rare volumes and bound them into a single folio volume, which is now in the British Library.)

Now William Blades was a civilised man who loved books and knew that one never really owned books: one was their trustee. He was a printer who waxed eloquent on the subject:

> Looked at rightly, the possession of any old book is a sacred trust, which a conscientious owner or guardian would as soon think of ignoring as a parent would of neglecting his child. An old book, whatever its subject or internal merits, is truly a portion of the national history...

One might add, 'And not of the national history alone, but of all mankind's history.' As Blades puts it, 'I do not envy any man that absence of sentiment which makes some people careless of the memorials of their ancestors...'

Inscriptions in books, even by the unknown, have the effect of reminding us that we are necessarily part of something bigger, and altogether grander, than ourselves. Inscriptions are, of course, intimations of mortality, for they are mostly by people who are dead but who wrote them with all the same disregard of death with which we pursue our own present moments. But they also give rise to other thoughts and feelings.

In my copy of *The Condemned Playground* by the critic, Cyril Connolly, published in 1945, is a short inscription. It is in the cultivated hand that one very rarely sees nowadays: a comparison of inscriptions shows how coarse handwriting has become in the last half-century or so. My guess is that the inscription was written by a young woman, no more than thirty years old when she wrote it. Her words were few and to me of a great poignancy: To my beloved husband, Christmas 1945.

Why should these words have struck me as so poignant? Because I think that, though they are simple and could hardly be more direct, no one would use them to inscribe a book now. At any rate, I have not found so vulnerably tender an inscription in any book since. It is not so much that our use of language has changed, as that our feelings have changed. For all our resort to psychobabble and endless talk about ourselves, we are less inclined to lay ourselves open to others, even those closest to us. Power is more important to us than love.

I recently found another poignant inscription in a novel by Rex Warner, entitled *Why Was I Killed?* Warner was a classicist and novelist most famous for his dystopian fantasy, *The Aerodrome*. My copy of *Why Was I Killed?*, printed in 1946, three years after the first edition, contains the following inscription, also in a cultivated hand:

Bought at Portmadoc and read while on holiday at Portmeirion
10.x.1947

Below it is another inscription, in a completely unchanged hand, dated thirty years and nine days later:

The last book read by Barbara during the illness which ended
in her death. She liked the book enormously. 19.x.1977

I read the book in October 2007, thirty years later still. For the last twelve months or so, I have taken to inscribing all the books I read, in a bid no doubt to outlast my own death.

THE PLEASURES OF PERFIDY

NO FEUDAL LORD EVER demanded more of his serf's time or product than the British state now demands of its subjects: indeed, if he did, he would have provoked an immediate peasants' revolt. Just as in the overpopulated parts of Nigeria the rule is 'If it moves, eat it,' such that there is hardly any bushmeat left, so in Britain the rule is, 'If it moves, tax it.' Even if you are not directly employed by the state in Britain, you spend almost half your working time working for it. This is what the French newspapers, as lazily incurious and ill-informed about Britain as the British newspapers are about France, call 'savage liberalism.'

And just as under feudalism the feudal lord was supposed to provide protection to his vassals as a *quid pro quo* for their labour or the product of their labour, so the state is supposed to protect (and educate, cure, insure and amuse, among other things) its dependants. Other countries, of course, are not very dissimilar in principle from Britain, though their feudal states may in practice be somewhat more efficient, and less morally and intellectually corrupt, than Britain's.

It is hardly surprising that so great a change in the organisation of society should have produced a great change in the manners and general culture of society (though of course it is possible that the causative relationship, if any, runs also in the other direction, in what one might call a dialectical fashion). Just how great that change has been is detectable in small things as in great.

Recently, I happened on a slim volume in a charity thrift shop (in England, even the organisation of these shops is morally and intellectually corrupt, but that is another story) entitled, *How Shall I Word It? – a Letter Writer for Men and Women on Domestic and Business Subjects*. This edition was published in August, 1943, at the height of the war, when extermination was under full swing. It is curious to think that, while people were being gassed at one end of Europe, other people were fretting about how to address a letter correctly to a Dowager Duchess. Since then, of course (and not unconnectedly), vulgarity, being democratically achievable by all, has become a virtue, and daintiness a kind of treason to the self.

This little volume was written by Ronald M Pelham. It was not the first edition: that had appeared in 1901, when the author was described as 'One of the Aristocracy.' From this I deduce (perhaps wrongly, and it isn't sufficiently important to confirm) that the author was a member of the family of the Earls of Chichester. The Eighth Earl was killed on active service in 1944 at the age of 22.

The subtitle of the first edition was slightly shorter and more elegant than the second: *A Letter Writer for Men and Women on All Subjects.* As befits an optimistic era when civilisation appeared to be advancing, the first edition was rather elegantly-produced, with a green cover on which was imprinted, in red and black, the picture of a beautiful young lady sitting at a desk, holding a pen lightly to her lower lip and looking into the distance for inspiration as to what to say. The price was the nominal equivalent of 20 pence.

The 1943 edition, again not surprisingly, was sadly utilitarian in design and production, with a plain yellow cover and inferior paper. I believe there was to be a further edition after the war, in 1949. In all, the book sold many tens of thousands of copies; it was much more popular than many tracts claiming the sympathies of the masses.

Between 1901 and 1943 the content varied little. The opening lines of the first edition were cut in the second:

> To know what to say and how to say it are two very important points in the art of writing letters, the two most important, in fact. But there are many others to be observed also, and by the observance or the neglect of them an opinion is often formed of the writer, and of his or her mind, and tastes, and training.

The 1943 edition begins with the second paragraph of the earlier edition:

> Everything about a letter should be as neat, simple, and dainty as possible. Use good plain note-paper – white or cream is always in good taste – and black ink.

Then follows advice about the handwriting:

> All flourishes and twirls should be rigidly avoided; they are vulgar and pointless.

Somewhat ironically, the words 'flourishes and twirls' are printed in bold in the earlier, but not the later edition; perhaps, though, emphasis in books of instruction by use of bold type is not vulgar and pointless.

What is interesting about this opening is that it is addressed to people who wish to create a good impression on others, a wish that has its good and bad sides, as most human wishes do. On the one hand it can lead to over-refinement, snobbery as to mere etiquette and social anxiety; it can be so overwhelming as to smother other human qualities and *desiderata*.

On the other hand, it requires effort, discipline and self-control in its fulfilment; it does not suggest that you should just do the easiest thing, take the line of least resistance, on all possible occasions. It is a stimulus to self-respect and is other-regarding; for to make a good impression, you have to put yourself in the position of others.

An early piece of advice in the book concerns how one should write to one's social superiors and one's social inferiors. The very fact that people can be written about in such a way gives one a jolt. But I wonder whether, in fact, this way of speaking, writing and thinking is more honest (and in some ways civilised and psychologically balanced) than our pretence that there are no such creatures as our superiors and inferiors? For it has been my observation that, in practice, the most fervent egalitarians are often egalitarian mainly about the people above them in the social scale; no one is above them, but their conduct often leads one to suppose that they have no difficulty in conceiving of and treating people as their inferiors. With the destruction of the notion of *noblesse oblige*, behaviour towards inferiors becomes more raw and unpleasant. The pretence that one believes in equality in any other sense than the religious or the abstraction of equality before the law leads directly to cognitive dissonance.

Be that as it may, it is interesting from the social history point of view that as late as 1943, and perhaps 1949, a popular book, read and probably consulted by thousands, could be published that unselfconsciously, and as a matter of course, uses the concept of social superiority and inferiority, without (I assume) resulting in howls of outraged derision.

If there is a certain honesty to this – a recognition, in softened form, of what the early political scientist, Robert Michels, called 'the iron law of oligarchy' – it must not be imagined that the author of this guide recommends total frankness in letter-writing. On the contrary: he might almost be taken as the very embodiment of *la perfide Albion*. At all times, even in conveying unpleasant or unwanted replies, he never raises his voice, he always considers feeling so as to word things in the most emollient possible fashion.

The author guides men and women through the tricky shoals of long, short and broken engagements, for example. From the standpoint of 2011, there is something almost quaint – the smell of patchouli, perhaps, or the presence of lace-fringed antimacassars on armchairs – about all this. Men and women perform an elaborate dance around one another (the subject of an awful lot of literature); who nowadays would not smile at instruction on how a gentleman should write a letter 'reproaching his fiancée with being a flirt':

> I feel sure that in your case it simply arose from a love of enjoyment, and the exuberance of our spirits, but if it gives you pleasure to amuse yourself by coquetting with other men at the expense of my feelings, I am deeply disappointed in you.

The book also advises as to how to reply to such a reproach (which it assumes is justified):

> Your words have stung me deeply, for, as you say, no self-respecting woman likes to be called a flirt, and I am not one.

She finishes:

> Having made my apology, I am desirous of making you withdraw your harsh words.

Much as we may smile at the naivety of all this, there is an underlying sophistication to it. She is in the wrong, but by characterising his justified reproach as harsh, she is giving him the chance to participate in guilt so that a certain equality is restored. It isn't logical, but it is sound, because, as La Rochefoucauld says, we never forgive those whom we have wronged.

It might be said that there is a tepidity, a milk-and-water quality, to human relations that are carried on in so polite a fashion. Writing to her dear Horace 'declaring her change of feelings,' Jessica Weir says:

> Week after week I have put off writing this letter to you partly because of the pain I know it will inflict on you, and partly in the hope that time might do away with the necessity for writing it, for it is to tell you that I do not and cannot feel for you that deep love which a woman should feel for the man she intends to marry.

Horace Masterson writes back:

> It was honest and brave of you to write to me so straightforwardly, and at the back of my mind I know you have done what is best... I give you back your freedom only at your own desire.

I do not think it an exaggeration to say that the sensibility here is at some distance from that expressed by (for example) most rap music. It is in some respects less honest than, say, the declaration that Jessica Weir is a two-timing bitch typical of her type, but it seems to me more, not less, civilised.

There is also a law of the conservation of dishonesty. If men are not dishonest in one way, they will be dishonest in another. We are faced, overall, not with a choice between lying and truthfulness, but between dishonesty about different things. Here, for example, is a 'proposal from a widower to a widow':

> Since my friendship with you and the great pleasure I have had in it, the loneliness of my life, and the anticipation of an even more lonely future has seemed to me unendurable.

This is not Romeo and Juliet redux, perhaps, but it is sensible. One senses that the widower, Mr Robert Rodd (such is our modern corruption that one immediately thinks of sado-masochism), might not be the most physically attractive person in the world, but maybe Mrs Barbara Marlowe is not either.

The reply favourable is not a paean to romantic bliss:

> That I can do something to brighten your life, and make your home a real home, is a great happiness to me, and it shall not be my fault if I fail.
> Believe me,
> Ever yours sincerely.

The reply unfavourable is polite yet manages to be firm and clear, without appeal:

> Though I value highly your devotion and the compliment you pay me, I must tell you frankly that, though valuing you and our friendship so highly, I do not feel the depth of affection which you desire...

I must say I would not like to be Mr Rodd meeting Mrs Marlowe for the first time after the receipt of that letter of refusal; I blush to think about it.

All in all, *How Shall I Word It?* reflects a social world that in some ways is more sophisticated than our own, and in some ways more interesting also. The way never to be bored is to know how to make fine distinctions, and the book, unconsciously no doubt, does that. Indeed, it assumes the need to do so:

> To persons with whom you are on terms of friendship, the word 'My' may be used as 'My dear Mrs –'

IT'S ALL YOUR FAULT

AS A MAN, OF COURSE, I do not gossip: but, now retired, I do sometimes discuss my erstwhile colleagues with others of my erstwhile colleagues, out of purely scientific interest.

Now it so happens that the other day I was having a scientific discussion of precisely this nature when the name of a mutual acquaintance came up. My interlocutor said that he did not like him, in fact he would not speak to him. I asked him why not.

'A few years ago,' he said, 'I had a run-in with him.'

'What about?' I asked.

My interlocutor frowned. He thought for a while, and then admitted that he couldn't any longer remember. But this did not seem to him a sufficient reason to resume relations. He had kept his resentment nice and warm, without rehearsing in his mind the reasons for it. It was like the grin of the Cheshire cat, that remained when the rest of the cat had disappeared.

One way and another, I have spent a lot of my life in the study of resentment, my own and that of others. I doubt whether there is any human being who has passed his life totally without feeling it; I know of many who, on the contrary, have spent their whole lives nourishing it.

I have been no personal exemplar in this matter, and perhaps am not still. For much of my early life I thought that an unhappy childhood, such as I had had, was both a licence to fail and to excuse myself for all of my manifold types of failing and personal incompetence. And even now, my first thought when confronted with such a failing or incompetence is to blame my childhood, and therefore my parents. I have then to remind myself that something like 85 per cent of my biblical span is now over, and that it is not seemly (among other things) to go on referring to what happened, or did not happen, more than half a century ago - and always to do so in the spirit of self-exculpation, never in any other spirit.

Doctor Johnson uses a phrase that I think is important in the context: 'He who would attend to the motions of his own mind...' And to do this honestly, without special pleading, and without a conceptual apparatus that obscures the clarity of any possible conclusion, can tell one a great deal not only about oneself but - assuming that others are not completely different from oneself - a great deal about the human world.

I have found it worthwhile to examine the advantages and disadvantages that accrued to me by the exercise of my resentment, and why it should be necessary to guard against it, for like some epidemic disease to which one has never developed immunity, it is likely to recur at any time.

It is first necessary to state that, for practical purposes, reasons are not causes and causes are not reasons. I know that there is a large philosophical literature devoted to the partial identity or otherwise of reasons and causes, but I have neither the time, nor the ability, nor the patience (because of the character my parents left me with) to review it. Besides, for my purposes the conclusion doesn't really matter.

When I review my failings and incompetence, of a kind that I am too ashamed or embarrassed to admit in public, but which life itself often forced me to do, I explain them by reference to my childhood - parental neglect, for example. As an initial explanation, this was indeed correct: a small child cannot be expected by himself to know what he should learn and what he should suppress in himself.

But it is one of the joys as well as the sorrows of being a man, as against being, say, an amoeba, that one creates oneself. A shortcoming seen and understood can almost always be overcome, in part if not in whole, by conscious effort. It is no excuse for a man to be violent to a woman that he saw his father behaving thus, if he also knows that it is wrong for him to hit a woman (this, you will be no doubt relieved to hear, is not one of my failings).

Therefore, I could have learned many of the things that my parents did not teach me but should have taught me. I have had time enough, but alas not inclination or persistence enough. The initial fault was perhaps theirs, but the subsequent fault was undoubtedly mine.

Anyhow, I did waste many years, whole decades in fact, in resentment. No man is so much a determinist that he fails to place moral blame upon his parents; and such was I. It never really occurred to me, I can honestly say not for a second in all those years, that my poor late mother had experienced hardships in her life a thousand times harder to contend with than my own, and that therefore, if anyone were to be excused, it was she. Resentment is fundamentally egotistical.

But it does have its compensations of a kind. They are sour, but just like the taste in fruit, so the taste in compensations can run to the sour end of the sweet-and-sour spectrum.

The first thing to remark about resentment is that it never lets you down, because it is powerful in its capacity to stimulate the imagination (in a similarly sour way). For example, if someone points out to a resentful person reasons why he should not be resentful, he will immediately come up with reasons why he should be. I have observed that when someone says 'Yes, but...' there is little purpose in continuing by providing reasons, evidence or arguments as to why that person should change his mind about the thing in question. Deeply unimaginative as that person might be in all other circumstances, when it comes to preserving his original standpoint from attack by people who want to argue him out of it, his imagination is infinitely fertile. It acts instantaneously, at the speed of light. 'Yes, but...' and its subsequent rationalisation emerges from the mouth of the resentful faster than a driver in Mexico City can apply himself to the horn when the traffic lights change from red.

So the sustainability, and therefore predictability, of resentment is established. When you are resentful, change does not frighten you because there will be none. No need, either, to fear or face up to the unknown, because everything has been decided in advance. You do not risk, for example, finding out that your incapacity is not caused by what you think it was, but rather by - your incapacity. So resentment allows you to dream on about all you would have achieved if things had been different (better, of course, for no one dreams of how little they would have achieved had things been worse).

But the real reward of resentment is that it changes the polarities of success and failure, or at least of the worth of success and failure. The fact that I am a failure in a certain regard shows that I am not only more sensitive than a vulgar success in that same regard, but really I am morally superior to him. To become a success, he has not had to contend with all that I have had to contend with to become a failure. Really, I am better than he, if only the world would recognise it.

Of course, the world does not recognise it, in fact stubbornly refuses to take any notice of it. But this does not really matter because it is grounds for - yes, further resentment. You see, the dirty trick that has been done me that makes me like I am, that is to say a failure, is only part of a persistent and recurring pattern. My original resentment can become a meta-resentment when the world refuses to recognise the justice of my complaints.

I hope by now that it is clear that I know all this by acquaintance rather than by mere report. This means that many of the failures and failings that I once attributed to my parents were really attributable to my resentment. When I say this, of course, I do not want to make my resentment into an entity that exists independently of my own conscious behaviour, otherwise I shall start resenting my resentment, and looking for the causes of why I should be so resentful: my genes for example, or something else to resent.

Resentment, therefore, is a labyrinth, and if I may be excused a mixed classical metaphor, it is necessary to cut its Gordian knot. This can only be done by a person consciously deciding to do so, and realising that his resentment is not only useless (if pleasurable) but harmful. And this is true even if some of the things that he is resentful of or about have or had an objective existence, and are rightfully to be regarded as injustices.

Now it is my belief, in part deriving from attending to the motions of my own mind, that resentment is pre-eminently the emotion or mode of feeling and thought of our time. When the social historians of the future, if there are any, come to characterise our era they will not call it the age of the atomic bomb, or the financial derivative age, or even that of the 100 per cent mortgage, they will call it the Age of Resentment. For everyone is on the *qui vive* for the supposed causes of his victim status that are deep-seated, beyond not only his control but beyond repair, at least without a total revolution in human affairs.

Whether increasing resentment led to the conferral of hero status on victimhood, or whether it was the other way round, I am not sure; probably the relationship was what we whose fathers were communist call dialectical.

But another cause of resentment, I feel sure (though I cannot prove, again because of the deficiencies of character bequeathed me by my parents) is the spread of tertiary education, especially in such subjects as sociology, psychology, and anything to which the word 'studies' may be attached. Indeed, it seems to me that they might all usefully be joined in one great faculty, to be called the Faculty of Resentment Studies. It would undoubtedly be the largest faculty in any self-respecting university, and would easily pay for itself. Professors of Resentment could teach such subdivisions of their subject as the art of rationalisation, rhetorical exaggeration, preservation of a lack of perspective, suppression of a sense of irony or humour, and so on and so forth. Of course, entry requirements would be minimal. All you would have to do to gain entry is to denigrate your parents at a public examination, and there could hardly be found a child nowadays not able to do that.

Over the entrance to the faculty will be written not the motto of the Academy, 'Know thyself,' but rather 'Talk about thyself,' 'Reveal nothing,' 'Remember that there is always someone better off than you' and, above all, 'Distinguish not between unfairness and injustice.'

What of the graduates of this institution? What happens to them afterwards? The best is for them to sink into outright unemployment; but if they find a job, it should be well below their capacities which, of course, it will be if they have studied diligently. They will then be safely launched on a career of joyful, or perhaps I should say satisfying, misery.

The other great thing about resentment is that there is a potentially infinite supply of it. Resentment is not a zero-sum game. Because A resents B does not mean that B cannot resent A, just as much or even more. Nor can objective conditions ever affect the supply. A billionaire can resent just as well as a pauper: and, of course, vice versa.

Attend to the motions of your own mind, and you will see that this is so.

OF EVIL AND EMPATHY

THE CLINICAL DIAGNOSIS of hysteria has long been attacked by doctors and others who believe that it has no explanatory or even descriptive value. They suggest that the word be abandoned; but, as others have pointed out, it has a tendency to outlive its obituarists. Somehow we cannot now do without it; although allegedly meaningless, it is useful.

So it is with the term 'evil'. However much philosophers and others tell us that it is without meaning when you examine it closely and therefore should not be used, we find that we cannot expunge it from our thoughts or vocabulary.

Of course, this difficulty does not in itself prove its validity; until about 1700, people might have said the same about the word 'witchcraft'. The indispensability of the word 'evil' might therefore be historically contingent, and not a reflection of the nature of the world. And I have some sympathy with those who find the word useless and even harmful because it is used as if it were an explanation of what we strongly disapproved of when it is merely a shorthand re-description of it. The following reasoning is not by any means uncommon: we know that John is evil because he behaves in such-and-such a way, and he behaves in such-and-such a way because he is evil.

We have a simulacrum of an explanation which satisfies us, but which in fact explains nothing; but, being satisfied, we look no further.

Having had much to do in my life, both as a doctor and journalist, with the darker side of life, evil – both the concept and the acts to which it is applied – has much interested me. Perhaps my interest has even been morbid, but if so, it is a morbid condition that I share with much of humanity, as a quick survey of the contents of a newspaper or a bookshop will demonstrate. Books and newspapers (I am told) are dying media among the young, but a survey of computer games will suggest a continuation of the fascination with evil. A high per centage of them have an implicitly Manichaean understanding of the world.

Explanations of evil, or attempts to do away with it (the word and concept, I mean, the underlying reality is, alas, even more intractable) therefore interest me, and I often buy books that claim to do so. My latest purchase to have failed to clarify my thoughts on the issue is *Zero Degrees of Empathy* by Simon Baron-Cohen.

Baron-Cohen is a famous psychologist, one of the greatest experts in the world on autism, a developmental condition in which children fail to learn how to interact socially in a normal fashion because (in the most extreme form) they lack the capacity to distinguish between objects and conscious beings. I mean no disrespect to him when I say that his effort at abolishing the term and concept of 'evil' from our thoughts does not convince me: a man is not to be blamed for failing to solve satisfactorily what others have failed to solve.

Let me give his theory as succinctly, and I hope fairly, as I can. We should, he says, replace the word 'evil' with 'lacking in empathy'. People who behave evilly lack empathy for those to whom they do it. Either they fail to understand the effects on others of what they do, or, if they do understand it, they don't care.

From where does this lack of empathy come? Professor Baron-Cohen tells us that, like many another human characteristic, the capacity to empathise varies along a normal distribution, at the tail ends of which are people with exceptional powers of empathy – I do not much care for the psychotherapist he describes as being of this ilk, in fact she makes me feel rather queasy – or of none. The people with no capacity for empathy are at best utter narcissists and at worst psychopaths. (For the sake of brevity, I here leave out his account of people with autism or Asperger's syndrome.) Most people, of course, fall between extremes, so that, in certain circumstances, and for varying lengths of time, they may show a lack of empathy. I doubt that many readers would disagree with this.

Baron-Cohen goes on to tell us that empathy has, or is caused by, certain pathways in the brain, and that these may be defective for various reasons: genetic or environmental. A lack of empathy runs in families, as demonstrated by the concordance rates among twins, identical and non-identical, as well as by adoption studies, where adopted children come to resemble their biological parents more than their adoptive ones; but also certain experiences, particularly early life experiences, may do permanent damage to the parts of the brain responsible for empathy, as well, of course, as pathological processes such as injury and disease (brain tumour, front-temporal dementia etc.).

I think his theory might very well be grist to the mill of anti-feminists, for he is very keen on the idea that the early experiences of love and security are vital in the development of empathic responses to others. By far the easiest way of giving children that vital early experience of love and security is to ensure that mothers devote a great deal of attention to their children, most other ways having failed miserably, *en masse* if not in every case. But that is by the by.

Now Baron-Cohen thinks that he has more or less solved the problem. There are, of course, details to be filled in; not everything is understood about the neural circuits of empathy, not every gene that contributes to the expression of empathy has been found. Environmental factors leading to psychopathy remain to be elucidated, though some are known; but, *grosso modo*, or in outline, we now understand evil, which is a neuropsychological state or trait of lack of empathy. Evil has been removed, one might say elevated, from the murky realm of metaphysics into the sunny uplands of science, where all is progress and light.

I am not so sure. In the first place, Baron-Cohen sometimes makes precisely the mistake that he accuses the users of the term 'evil' of making, namely of rendering the *explanandum* identical with the *explanans*. For example, he describes his discussion with a psychiatrist of the case of a woman who stabbed her two children to death as a way of getting back at her estranged husband, of whose new girlfriend she was jealous. The psychiatrist had found her to be normal, to be not suffering from any identifiable medical condition; but Baron-Cohen thought this ridiculous. At the time of her crime, he said, by definition she must have been suffering from a lack of empathy, even if she had now recovered it: for if she had not, she would not have committed the act.

Now what is being said here is quite obviously open to the objection that he has made to the concept of evil: we know the woman lacked empathy because of what she did, and she did what she did because of lack of empathy. If the concept of evil explains nothing, here (at any rate) the concept of lack of empathy stands in the same case.

Does Baron-Cohen's theory illuminate mass outbreaks of evil, such as in Lenin's Russia, Hitler's Germany, Pol Pot's Cambodia, or post-Habyarimana's Rwanda, for example? I think the answer is no.

In Rwanda, for example, if accounts are to be believed, thousands of perfectly ordinary people, of no apparently psychopathic tendencies, took up machetes and other instruments and killed their neighbours, then, enjoying their goods and feasting on their food, celebrated what they had done.

What would Baron-Cohen say about this (he does not use this example in his book)? Well, he would say, in certain circumstances – fear, mass hysteria, or whatever – some circuits in the brain overwhelm other circuits in the brain, those for example that are necessary for the expression of empathy. Remember that people are on a continuum of empathy: as circumstances grow more and more dire, so a bigger and bigger per centage of the population loses its capacity for empathy.

But we already know this from raw observation of the events: so when we read Baron-Cohen, we experience no thrill of enlightenment, no eureka moment in which we feel that we now understand what previously was opaque to us. He is, in fact, merely re-describing in slightly different terms what we already knew.

There is a deeper metaphysical problem that won't go away. It was the problem that William James dealt with so brilliantly in the first of his Gifford Lectures at Edinburgh University, published as *The Varieties of Religious Experience*, entitled 'Religion and Neurology'.

In a discussion of people with an abnormally high degree of empathy, Baron-Cohen mentions the case of a Buddhist monk who 'had spent his adult life learning to control both his reaction to his own pain and to that of others.' This monk had a brain scan while sitting in uncomfortable positions, his reaction to which he controlled by meditation. The brain scan suggested that his 'empathy circuits' were then 'overactive' – I assume this means more active than average.

Now Baron-Cohen is doubtful – I think rightly – that this state of mind can be described as being super-empathic. Here is what he says (he is not an elegant stylist, but his meaning is always clear):

> First, if someone can suppress their own pain sensations, while that might be a useful skill on the battlefield or in competitive sports, it is not clear that this is required for super-empathy. Secondly, if you suppress your *appropriate* [italics in original]

emotional response to another person's pain, how is that empathic? Whatever the monk was doing, and it was clearly abnormal, it doesn't fit my definition of empathy.

There are two points here. The first, and lesser, one is that the alleged empathic circuits are activated by a condition other than empathy. The neurology is thus rather more complex than we have hitherto been led to believe. But this is not fatal to Baron-Cohen, because he would not be foolish enough to suggest that just because certain areas of the brain light up in certain scanners during certain tasks, such as imagining an injured person, we now know all there is to be known about the neurology of compassion or empathy. There is always further research to be done.

But the italicised word 'appropriate' in the above passage *is* fatal: for who or what is to decide what constitutes an appropriate emotional response? Will further inspection of brain scans tell us? Will any natural fact tell us? I think we could contemplate brain scans until we are red, blue or green in the face and still not discern an answer. What we deem appropriate will be antecedent to anything that we find. True enough, we could, if we so wish, replace the term evil by that of lack of appropriate emotional response, but we have not thereby increased our level of understanding.

Whenever I read of scientists who claim to have furthered human self-understanding overall, on a metaphysical plane and not just in individual cases, I think of Hamlet's words to Guildernstern:

Why, look you now, how unworthy a thing you make of me! You would play upon me. You would seem to know my stops. You would pluck out the heart of my mystery. You would sound me from my lowest note to the top of my compass. And there is much music, excellent voice, in this little organ, yet cannot you make it speak? 'Sblood, do you think I am easier to be played on than a pipe? Call me what instrument you will, though you can fret me, yet you cannot play upon me.

Baron-Cohen is certainly not the first to think that he has plucked out the heart of Man's metaphysical mystery (for why should empathy be any different from any other quality?). Moleschott, for example, told us a long time ago that the brain secretes thought as the liver secretes bile. (Actually, the brain also secretes quite a lot of bile, metaphorically speaking of course.) I am afraid I think there is a lot of plucking still to be done: in fact, I think it will never be done. That is the heart of our mystery.

MURDER MOST ACADEMIC

IN SOME MODERN SOCIETIES – and certainly Britain is one of them – satire is prophecy. This makes effective satire difficult because reality so soon catches up with it. Satire is also dangerous and perhaps even irresponsible, for no idea is too absurd, it seems, for our political masters and bureaucratic elite to take seriously and put into practice – at public expense, of course, never their own.

Sometimes reality is far in advance of satire when it comes to absurdity. The results, however, are not always funny. If a satirist had come up with the idea of a violent criminal who had spent time in an asylum being admitted by a university to its doctoral programme in 'homicide studies', thereafter turning into a serial killer, that satirist would have been denounced for poor taste. But this is precisely what the University of Bradford did recently. A man with a long history of criminal violence became a serial killer while working on a PhD thesis at the university, the subject of his thesis being the methods of homicide used in the city during the nineteenth century. He himself used methods more reminiscent of the fourteenth.

Stephen Griffiths was 40. He had never worked and always lived at taxpayers' expense. At 17, he was sentenced to three years' imprisonment for cutting the throat (not fatally) of a supermarket security guard who tried to arrest him for shoplifting. In prison, doctors reported, Griffiths had a 'preoccupation with murder – particularly multiple murder'. They diagnosed him as a violent psychopath; that is, he had an intractable personality development that made him likely to commit new violent offences.

The doctors were right. Shortly after his release from prison, Griffiths committed more violent acts, including holding a knife to a woman's throat, and wound up imprisoned once more. He was then sent from prison to Rampton, the high-security mental hospital; but again, the doctors diagnosed him as a psychopath for whom they could do nothing, and after two months they returned him to prison, from which he was soon – much too soon, as it turned out – released.

He remained violent toward women. He managed to convince a jury that he was innocent of the charge of pouring boiling water on, and badly scalding, a sleeping girlfriend who had decided to leave him. Other girlfriends went to the police but were too terrified to testify in court, knowing that he would receive a short sentence at most. One girlfriend – whose legs he had cut with broken glass, whose nose he had broken, and whom he had knocked out – later told a reporter that he would attack her if she so much as looked at another man. When she left him, he hunted her down (despite court orders to stay away from her), slashed the tyres of her car, and daubed the wall outside her flat with the word 'slag'. He was convicted of harassment in 2009.

Such was the man whom the University of Bradford selected to pursue a doctorate in homicide studies, a subdivision of the Department of Criminal Justice Studies, with fees and living expenses paid by the government. Though computer checks on the criminal records of prospective employees are now routine in Britain, and medical students are checked, applicants for doctorates in homicide studies apparently are not; or if they are, no notice is taken of what is found. Griffiths did not hide his propensities with any great cunning; why should he have bothered, in these non-judgmental times of peace and tolerance toward all men? He kept hundreds of books about serial killers in his flat, disclosed to his psychiatrists his intention to become a serial killer, and told girlfriends that he skinned and ate rats alive, adding that his ambition was to become even more notorious than the Yorkshire Ripper. Nor did Griffiths hesitate to proclaim his oddity to the public; he used to take his pet lizards, which he also fed with live rats, for walks on a leash.

In 2009 and 2010, while pursuing his doctorate in the programme, Griffiths killed and ate three women, two cooked and one raw, according to his own account. He later told the police that he had killed other women.

He committed his last murder in front of closed-circuit video cameras installed in his apartment building. According to the building's caretaker, who saw the video and called the police, the victim, Suzanne Blamires, ran from Griffiths's flat with Griffiths, wielding a crossbow, in pursuit. She fell or was pushed, and he fired a bolt into her. Fully aware, even triumphant, that he was being recorded, Griffiths extended his finger to the camera and then dragged the lifeless body by the leg back into his apartment. There, he later claimed, he ate some of her. When asked for his name in court after his arrest, he identified himself as 'The Crossbow Cannibal'. That reply alone assured him the notoriety that he had made no secret of craving. He was convicted of the three murders in December 2010 and received a life sentence. Early reports suggest that Griffiths may be permitted to complete his doctorate – still at public expense, of course – while in prison.

His three known victims were prostitutes, as is often the case with such killers (a truck driver in Ipswich, Steven Wright, was convicted in 2008 of murdering five). This is said to indicate a hatred of women caused by sexual difficulties with them; psychologists will no doubt be interested in the fact that Griffiths hated his mother, who separated from his father when Griffiths was young and was reputed by neighbours to be a prostitute herself. Certainly she behaved in a sexually uninhibited way: she would go naked into the yard of their house in the town of Wakefield and have sex with a variety of men in full view of the neighbours. But the relation between early life and subsequent conduct is never fixed; many men have had mothers as irresponsible as Griffiths's without becoming serial killers. Indeed, he himself had a younger brother who did not; there is always something incalculable about human conduct.

Nevertheless, there are certain regularities, and one of them is the way in which the *victims* of men such as Griffiths are described in *The Guardian*, the house journal of the British intelligentsia and its bureaucratic hangers-on. This is important because it illustrates the way in which a dominant elite – dominant *de facto* if not always *de jure* – thinks about social problems.

An article describing the victims of Wright, the Ipswich murderer, was entitled 'The women put into harm's way by drugs'. A similar article about Griffiths's victims was headed '"Crossbow cannibal" victims' drug habits made them vulnerable to violence'. In other words, these women became prostitutes by *force majeure*, on the streets not because of choices they had made but because of chemical substances that controlled them without any conscious intervention on their part – no more than if, say, an abyss caused by an earthquake had suddenly opened up and swallowed them.

Now either we are all like this – no different from inanimate objects, which act and react mechanically, as Descartes supposed that dogs and cats did – or we are not. The view that we are brings with it certain difficulties. No one could live as if it were true; no one thinks of himself, or of those about him, as automatons; we are all faced with the need to make conscious decisions, to weigh alternatives in our minds, every waking hour of every day. Human life would be impossible, literally inconceivable, without consciousness and conscious decision-making. It is true that certain medical conditions, such as temporal-lobe epilepsy during fits, deprive people of normal consciousness and that they nevertheless continue to behave in a recognisably human way; but if all, or even most, of humanity suffered from those conditions, human life would soon be at an end.

Assuming, then, that not everyone is driven to what he does by his own equivalent of drug addiction, *The Guardian* must assume that Wright's and Griffiths's victims were fundamentally different from you and me. Unlike us, they were not responsible for their actions; they did not make choices; they were not human in the fullest sense. Not only is this a view unlikely to find much favour with women who resemble the victims in some way, it also has potentially the most illiberal consequences. For it would justify us, the full human beings, in depriving such women of liberty. If 'their hopeless addiction to heroin, alcohol or crack cocaine led them to sell their bodies in the red light district on the edge of Bradford city centre and made them vulnerable to violence', as the newspaper tells us, surely we should force our help on them to recover their full humanity, or, if that proves impossible, take them into preventive detention to protect them? They are the sheep, we the shepherds.

One problem of liberal social thought is that it consigns a larger and larger proportion of the human race to the category of people driven into trouble. But there are other difficulties, too. Precisely because it is impossible to think of human life in consistently mechanistic terms, the liberal is soon led into contradictions. Moral evaluations are inseparable from thought about human existence, even if the metaphysical foundations of such judgments remain contentious; so it is not surprising that the article about Griffiths's victims fairly oozes with morality, albeit of a saccharine and self-regarding kind, while at the same time pretending to avoid judgment.

For example, it refuses to use the word 'prostitute', replacing it with 'sex worker' and 'street worker'. The reason is clear enough: 'prostitute' has negative moral connotations. The word 'prostitution' suffers the same fate: it becomes 'sex work'. This seems to have the corollary that both the work and the worker are perfectly respectable, the work having a social status, perhaps, somewhere between supermarket shelf-stacking and neurosurgery. But if sex work is work like any other, are those who patronise sex workers 'customers' or 'clients' who ought to have the same protections that other consumers enjoy (such as 'money back if not satisfied')? Alas for them, no; the newspaper refers to them as 'punters', a term with connotations of vulgarity, dishonesty, and moral turpitude. But can a service be respectable whose clientele are scoundrels merely by the fact of availing themselves of it?

One of the three victims of Griffiths was 43-year-old Susan Rushworth. Her 'marriage had imploded as a result of domestic violence and she became addicted to heroin', the *Guardian* says. 'Her 21-year-old daughter began working the streets at 18 due to her crack cocaine and heroin addictions... They eventually worked together, looking for punters.' The article ends with the moral reflections of a friend of another victim – reflections that, given their position in the article and the complete absence of irony in it heretofore, one may assume that the newspaper more or less endorses: 'These women don't deserve to die. They're all somebody's daughter, yet they're described as prostitutes and it makes it so sleazy.'

No one, outside perhaps the Islamic Republic of Iran, would suggest that these women did deserve to die, of course. The friend's statement also seems, astonishingly, to imply that it would be all right – that is, not 'sleazy' – for women to sell sex to strangers on the streets of Bradford to pay for heroin, provided they were not called 'prostitutes'. It is the naming that is the shaming. Change the name, and you change the thing, or at any rate the moral significance of the thing. Language is a powerful instrument, but not as powerful as that.

What lies behind these mental contortions? It is a form of sentimentality, a mask for a deeper indifference, according to which people who suffer or have led unhappy lives must be transformed into blameless victims so that we can pity them. It is as if, were they to have contributed in any way to their own situation, all sympathy for them would have to be withdrawn or abandoned. And since the liberal wants to be seen, particularly by his peers, as a man superior in compassion to everyone else, he uses all his powers of rationalisation, generally increased by many years of education, to establish that such-and-such a group of people is without blame and thus suitably – indeed, necessarily – an object of his moral generosity. If, in the process, he comes to conclusions repugnant to common sense, so much the worse for common sense.

All this demonstrates the inferiority of a liberal secular, compared with a liberal religious, understanding of social problems. (I say this as someone without a religious axe to grind, and I exclude the more theocratic and intolerant end of the religious spectrum.) The liberal religious understanding is that men are sinners, including the men who do the understanding. This does not, or should not, preclude sympathy with sinners; for if it did, we should never show any sympathy at all. Use every man after his desert, and who shall 'scape whipping? Of course, some people – like Stephen Griffiths – are so repellent in their actions that it is impossible to sympathise with them to any extent (despite the fact that such people frequently receive declarations of love from foolish self-dramatisers), though doctors and others have the duty to treat them with due consideration. But the liberal religious understanding means that there is no need to deny the sin itself, and consequently no need for the religious liberal to twist his mind into knots in an attempt to deny the obvious. He can therefore afford to look social reality in the face, and not indulge in mental Houdini tactics to escape its supposed chains in order to preserve his self-image as a compassionate and generous person.

For myself, I never had much difficulty in recognising bad behaviour for what it was without withdrawing my sympathy from the person who, I thought, had behaved badly. During my medical career, I had many prostitutes among my patients (incidentally, they never described themselves as anything but prostitutes, though they would sometimes say that they were 'on the game'). It never occurred to me that they did not lead sordid lives, even those of the professional elite. One, for example, was a dominatrix with a website who, when not flying around the world humiliating judges and captains of industry for large sums of money, lived in a prosperous middle class neighbourhood. She did not tell her neighbours what she did for a living, and not only because she feared disapproval. She was not proud of it, even though we could laugh about it together.

In fact, I found prostitutes far more intellectually honest than the writers of such articles as those I have quoted. I recall a former prostitute who during her period of prostitution had struggled to raise her daughter well. She had succeeded, and her daughter now had a good job and a steady boyfriend. I could not help but recognise her struggle as heroic, even if she had created the need for such heroism in the first place. Neither she nor any other prostitute whom I met claimed to have been driven onto the streets by anything other than their own mistakes and cupidity. It is true that the cupidity of prostitutes was sometimes occasioned by a desire for drugs, but they did not attribute that desire for drugs to anything other than their desire for immediate gratification. As far as they were concerned, their behaviour was always explained by decisions that they had made.

The secular liberal, however, would like to convert them – religiously, as it were – to his own view of the matter: to convince them that it is (for example) the hopelessness of their addiction that accounts for their choices. Only in that way can the desire of the secular liberal for a providential role in the world be justified, though of course never fulfilled, which is just as well: for its fulfilment would destroy its justification.

THE WELSH CHEKHOV

WHEN I WAS YOUNG my father owned a factory in Tonypandy, a town in the Rhondda Valley of South Wales. He always disparaged the character of the Welsh, for whom I therefore conceived an affection that has remained with me ever since. You may be said truly to like a people when you are aware of their imperfections and are fond of them still. If one can be a patriot of a country not one's own, I am a Welsh patriot.

My memories of Tonypandy are hazy, for I was younger than ten when my father took me there. In those days, coal mining, not the administration of unemployment and its attendant social problems, was the Rhondda Valley's major industry. Our civilisation at the time was founded, as George Orwell once remarked, on coal, without which we would have lived in unlit and unheated houses. The miners were like Atlases; upon their shoulders a whole world rested. My visual recollection of Tonypandy is monochromatic – of everything begrimed with coal dust; of the slate roofs of tiny terraced houses dull in the perpetual, dirty rain; of black slag heaps lowering over the town. Whether this is a true memory or a reconstruction based on what I subsequently learned, I could not swear in a court of law.

Half a century later, while scouring the second-hand bookshops during a sojourn in Wales, I discovered a writer who came from Tonypandy: Rhys Davies, who published 20 novels and about 160 short stories before he died in 1978. Some critics of his day esteemed him highly, calling him the Welsh Chekhov. At least four books have appeared about him and his work, the first published in 1932, when he was only 31, and the most recent in 2009. And yet his name rings only the faintest of bells in the memory of even the best-informed about modern literature. Except by specialists, he is – unjustly – all but forgotten.

The book that I happened on was a slim volume of Davies's stories called *The Trip to London*, published in 1946. As soon as I read the opening sentence of the first story, 'The Benefit Concert', I knew that I had to read more, not just of this story but of this writer:

When it was decided to give a Benefit Concert for Jenkin, so
that he could buy an artificial leg, no one thought this ordinary
event would lead to such strife.

What follows draws the reader irresistibly on:

> But then no one suspected that the loss of his proper leg –
> it had gone gangrenous through neglect – had turned Jenkin
> into a megalomaniac. The affair not only divided the valley
> into bitterly opposed camps but it nearly caused a strike in the
> colliery. Imperfect mankind is addicted to warfare and a false
> leg is as good a pretext for liberating smouldering passions as
> greed for a continent.

Here, in euphonious and unhectoring prose, is the declaration
of a vindication of literature: that from the small change of life,
properly attended to, one can extract the wisdom that is the true
end of philosophy. The events may be small, but their meaning is
large.

The benefit concert takes place in the local chapel, called Horeb,
in the little town of Twlldu. The conflict arises after the concert
raises considerably more money than needed for the leg, and opinion
divides as to whether Jenkin or the chapel should get the extra funds.
The dispute is at once ludicrous and intractable; Jenkin refuses to
wear his leg until it is resolved, hobbling around town on crutches
to keep his supporters inflamed. For a time, passions run high; the
dispute gives life meaning. It is settled not by appeal to principle but
by boredom, the passage of time, and the distraction of a fire at the
house of one Mrs Roberts, who requires the help of another benefit
concert. In the end, Jenkin dons his leg, and the wily Horeb deacons,
who had lain low while the dispute persisted, have their chapel quietly
redecorated.

In a few pages, Davies conjures up for the reader not only
the atmosphere of a South Wales mining town or village, but its
human warmth and small-mindedness. The warmth and the small-
mindedness are two sides of the same coin – you can't have one
without the other. By implication, human life remains imperfectible
and always incomplete; there can be no gain without loss.

Davies has a sheer delight in detail that teaches us (if we are attentive) to look around with a fresh eye. For example, Jenkin's benefit concert is such a financial success because one of the Horeb deacons has persuaded Madame Sarah Watkins, an opera singer who hails originally from Twlldu and now lives 20 miles away, to come out of retirement and sing at the concert. (It is securing her participation that makes the deacons feel entitled to the extra money.) Under her name on the concert posters appear the words 'London, Milan, and Twlldu'. But on the night of the concert, the car that had been hired to fetch her was an old decrepit one driven by the fishmonger's lout of a son. And he had taken it into his head to kill two birds on this trip by collecting a small cask of herrings from the coast; it was already beside him on the front seat when he called for Madame Watkins, who brought with her a large suitcase. Secondly, no one had remembered to welcome her arrival with flowers. Thirdly, no one had thought that she would need, for changing into a concert dress, something more private than a vestry filled with coming and going persons connected with tonight's affair.

Madame Watkins, however, is a true professional:

Yet no one would have guessed the diva's fury when at last she mounted the platform and, amid thunderous applause, gave a superb bow. She advanced like an old ruined queen majestically unaware of new fashions and systems, giving an expert kick to the billowing train of her dragon-coloured but tattered dress. At sight of her, and perhaps the train, a little hiss of awe seemed to come from the goggling women in the audience.

That Madame Watkins may never have been an international success, except by Twlldu standards, is suggested by the fact that, according to local newspaper reports noted at the end of the story, she is sued by her grocer for unpaid bills and tells the court that 'she had been too good-hearted and lately had sung everywhere for nothing, in aid of this and that charity.'

The story takes a generous and uncondescending delight in the comedy, all the more remarkable in that it was published soon after the conclusion of one of the most catastrophic wars in world history; a delight in the foibles of mankind, its petty vanities, evasions, snobberies, and small lies, which, though not admirable in themselves, give interest, savour, and meaning to our existence. What a wealth of social meaning and personal history Davies conveys by the closely observed detail of Madame Watkins's 'expert kick to the billowing train of her dragon-coloured but tattered dress', a gesture that only she, out of thousands of women for miles around, could have made!

Davies's vision of life was not always so benignant; but over a writing career that spanned half a century, during which his subject matter included thwarted passion and murder, he never displayed disdain for those about whom he wrote. His compassion was clear-eyed and unsentimental. Mankind's feet of clay never made him cynical.

Davies's is a remarkable story, but it is typical of his reticence that biographical detail about him is not easy to come by, for he believed that the business of a writer was to write, not to become a self-publicist and obtrude himself on the world. He was born Rees Vivian Davies into the tiny petty *bourgeoisie* of the coal mining valleys, surrounded by, thoroughly conversant with, but not of the proletarian world. His father, who, like Chekhov's, ran a grocery store, extended credit to the miners during hard times. From an early age, Davies knew that he was different: his leanings in the macho world of Tonypandy were literary and aesthetic, and he was homosexual. Without going in for the excesses of political correctness, I think it reasonable to say that the Tonypandy of Davies's youth was no place to be homosexual. Davies's marginality, as to both class and sex, doubtless gave him special insight into the lies and evasions of mankind, having had to practice many himself.

After only a secondary education – which, however, was clearly a good one – Davies escaped South Wales in 1919 for the bohemian and relatively tolerant world of London, determined to become a writer. He found a congenial spiritual world in Charles Lahr's left-wing Progressive Bookshop, as much a club for *avant-garde* writers as a commercial enterprise. Lahr, a friend of D. H. Lawrence, clandestinely published the first English edition of *Lady Chatterley's Lover*, as well as Lawrence's banned book of poems, *Pansies*.

In those days of limited consumption, scarce comforts, and relatively few necessities, it was easier to live on next to nothing, which is what Davies did for long periods. His earliest published stories appeared individually in slim, often well-produced booklets. Then came his first collection in 1927: *The Song of Songs and Other Stories*, with a tiny print run of about 100 copies. The sureness of touch of these first stories is astonishing.

They are already infused with the compassionate and non-ideological tolerance that Davies retained to his dying day. 'A Gift of Death' begins:

> Maria came downstairs from her father's bedroom and in her usual quiet and melancholy way said to her aunt: 'He's gone.'
>
> Aunt Ann looked up from her Bible and opened her mouth wide in excitement. Then she searched for her handkerchief and wiped her tearless old eyes.
>
> 'Going before me they all are,' she moaned in Welsh.

It soon emerges that the dead man, whose wife died before him, was a religious bigot, for whom 'every day was a Sunday' and who made life in his house 'like a Sunday school'. He has turned his daughter Maria, now 33, into an old maid; she is ugly and stout, and the women who live nearby expect her to remain unmarried, though her father has left her with what, for the coal mining valleys, is a small fortune. But Maria has a plan. Scandalously, she has her father's funeral conducted by the less expensive of the town's two undertakers, not only to save money but because he is a bachelor, if an unattractive one: 'a little man, fussy and nervous, bird-like.' They agree to marry, he for her money and she to prove the neighbours wrong and to be respected in the town. Strangely enough, the unromantic nature of this doesn't appal. Instead, one respects the couple's clear-sighted appreciation of their situation and their determination to make the best of it. And almost every line of the story contains a telling detail that reveals something about a whole way of life. The reader enters an alien world as if it surrounds him: surely a sign of literary skill.

Having received a small advance for his first novel, *The Withered Root*, Davies travelled to the south of France. There, armed with an introduction from Lahr, he became friends with Lawrence, whom he accompanied from Bandol to Paris for medical tests on the elder writer's tuberculosis. (Davies smuggled the manuscript of *Pansies* back into England.) Davies, in his quiet way, was always his own man, and he had a subtler mind and sensibility than Lawrence did, but not surprisingly Lawrence would influence him. Both writers came from mining communities in which a sectarian Protestantism, highly suspicious of any pleasures of the flesh, especially sexual, held sway, and in which respectability in the eyes of the ever-vigilant neighbours was the ruling *desideratum*. In one of Davies's early stories, 'Revelation', we meet a married miner who has never seen his own wife naked.

Frustration, furtiveness, illicit liaisons, and hypocrisy proliferated in these circumstances. Protestant chapels, often lumpenly neoclassical and grandiose in form, and with names such as Bethel, Zion, and Pisgah, loomed over the rows of small, working men's houses in Welsh towns. (They remain to this day, though now they are often closed or converted to uses that are the very reverse of religious, such as nightclubs.) They were as much observation towers and centres of intelligence-gathering as places of worship; they were the symbols of a society rigidly policing itself.

Again, it is no surprise that Davies portrayed this religiosity as oppressive; how would it have portrayed *him*, had it known his nature? But he was an artist and not an ideologist; and so what comes across in his depiction of this society is that it was extraordinarily rich in human types, that its working men and their wives possessed deep and individual characters – not unrelated to their immersion in the Bible – and that, notwithstanding all the pressure on its people to conform, it was tolerant of true eccentricity (the unselfconscious kind that does not arise from an egotistical need to distinguish oneself from others). It is as though the strong but not impregnable boundaries freed people as much as they imprisoned them and gave to their lives an intensity that they would not otherwise have had. I am not convinced that life in the region has become richer for the abolition of the boundaries, or that any literature as fine-grained and sensitive will emerge from it again.

Nor did Davies ever suggest that sensual liberation, desirable as he no doubt thought it, would spell an end to human woes: he was never utopian. In a late novel, *Nobody Answered the Bell*, published in 1971, he depicted a lesbian relationship, in a port city on the south coast of England, in which the two women are as free, apart from the need to observe slight public discretion, as it is possible to be. They have enough money to live without working; they suffer no oppression from society. And yet their relationship slides downward, by a process that Davies describes with brilliant subtlety, into paranoia and hostility, and ends in murder and suicide.

Davies had a tragic but not dismal view of life, as a short story published in *The New Yorker* in January 1964, 'I Will Keep Her Company', illustrates to perfection. He must have been a quick worker, for the events in the story clearly took place during that exceptionally harsh winter, when snow thickly blanketed Britain. The story concerns a couple in their eighties, living in an isolated farmhouse in the Welsh hills and snowed in. Even today, bad weather can easily cut off such places; in 1963, the isolation would have been total.

The old woman in the story, Maria Evans, has recently died after a short illness and lies on the old four-poster bed. Her husband, John, both knows and refuses fully to acknowledge that she is dead. He goes downstairs from the bedroom with great difficulty, the house being so cold and his joints so arthritic, to continue the routine that his wife established. He knows that the district nurse is on her way:

> 'They'll be here today,' he said aloud... The sound of his voice was strange to him, like an echo of it coming back from a chasm. His head turning automatically toward the open door leading to the hallway, he broke the silence again, unwilling to let it settle. 'Been snowing again all night, Maria. But it's stopping now. They'll come today. The roads have been blocked. Hasn't been a fall like it for years.'

This is not only very moving – the old man's bewilderment at and refusal to accept the loss, the intensity of his underlying grief, is conveyed with wonderful economy – but very accurate. Every doctor has encountered something similar in his patients' families.

Evans tries to make the kitchen look cared for, so that when the district nurse arrives she will think that he is managing well and abandon her suggestion that he move into an old people's home. He tries to imitate his wife's way of doing things; she had supervised him while she was still capable of lying on the sofa downstairs, before her terminal illness forced her to take to bed. But he is clumsy. He breaks the clock, excusing himself to her. Then he gives up and returns to the bedroom, where he sits on a chair beside the bed where his dead wife lies. There he dozes as he slips down into death himself, his mind wandering to pleasant scenes of the past – also an accurate depiction of death from cold.

Meanwhile, Nurse Baldock has geared up a rescue operation involving a snowplough, a van, and a helicopter. She is, as her name seems to suggest, conscientious and bossy and, having completed a diploma in social studies in her spare time, believes herself entitled to a promotion. She had visited Evans a few days previously, when his wife had just died, and was prevented from removing the body by the snow. Now she is returning, determined to get his agreement to leave for the old people's home. When she finds him dead, she utters a bitter yet self-satisfied recrimination:

> This needn't have happened if he had come with me, as I wanted six days ago! Did he sit there all night deliberately? … Old people won't *listen*. When I said to him, 'Come with me, there's nothing you can do for her now,' he answered, 'Not yet. I will keep her company.' I could have taken him at once to Pistyll Manor Home. It was plain he couldn't look after himself. One of those unwise men who let themselves be spoilt by their wives.

In a few pages, with a highly sophisticated simplicity, Davies arouses emotions and thoughts as impossible to resolve into full coherence as life itself. John Evans's death is both tragic and a triumphant final expression of the love that gave his life meaning; we oscillate between sorrow and joy, between discomfiture and reassurance, as we read. As for Nurse Baldock, she encapsulates the mixture of good intentions, condescension, and careerism that is the modern welfare state. Rationally, we cannot refuse to endorse the efforts to rescue Evans; it would be a terrible world in which his predicament evoked no response. At the same time, we know that these efforts are not only beside the point but, at the deepest level, incapable of being other than beside the point.

Davies died of lung cancer in 1978, modest, tolerant, and unassuming to the end. He said that he had always had a taste for 'cultivating ruined characters'. His reticent but charming autobiography, *Print of a Hare's Foot*, suggests what he thought of his own life and work –that they would leave little trace, like a hare's footprint in the snow. In a world of publicity seekers, this became a self-fulfilling prophecy.

Without making exaggerated claims on Davies's behalf, one can see the parallel with Chekhov in the similarity of the two writers' intellectual outlooks. Both abominated cruelty but depicted human frailty without censoriousness or expressions of hatred. Both valued truth above convenience. The following words of Davies's, about the reaction of some of the Welsh to his work, have a Chekhovian ring:

> If... the author is one of those peculiar people with a liking for things that are best forgotten, then howls go up. Columns of correspondence appear... Warm letters protest that Welsh people *do not* do this, that, or the other; do not speak this way *nor* that way; do not go to bed in their day shirts; are not immoral and drunkards; do not eat peas with a knife; this is not a *true* mirror of Welsh life, but a lot of perverted trash, etc.

Above all, both writers steered clear of the low and dishonest ideological temptations of their age, which so often deformed the minds, work, and conduct of their contemporaries. In 1888, Chekhov wrote to the poet A. N. Pleshcheyev:

> I am afraid of those who look for a tendency between the lines, and who are determined to regard me either as a liberal or as a conservative. I am not a liberal, not a conservative, not a believer in gradual progress, not a monk, not an indifferentist. I should like to be a free artist and nothing more... I hate lying and violence in all their forms... Pharisaism, stupidity and despotism reign not in merchants' houses and prisons alone. I see them in science, in literature, in the younger generation... My holy of holies is the human body, health, intelligence, talent, inspiration, love, and the most absolute freedom – freedom from violence and lying, whatever forms they may take.

It is worth comparing this with a few of Davies's utterances. In an interview in a Welsh magazine, he said that of course Welsh writers wrote about Welsh subjects, but he added, 'No flag waving. A curse on flag waving.' During the war – which he detested, though he hated Nazism more – he wrote to his friend Raymond Marriott, 'When the great bestial War Machine is in action writers are of no use whatsoever, its activities, which are destructive, are in complete opposition to them.' And he wrote to a policeman friend, Louis Quinain, 'I'm one of those who believe that nothing on earth can impair one's own interior liberty – unless you allow it to. Though outwardly bothered and vexed, I have reached a certain calm.'

These are Chekhovian thoughts. Davies was a good writer and (not at all the same thing) a good man.

THE VANDALS IN RETREAT

DURING MY CHILDHOOD, WE still had pea soup fogs in London, so thick that you couldn't see your hand when you held it more than a few inches from your face. The fogs were exclusive to November, so that I imagined that they were simply features of the climate, like snow in winter. I longed for them to come. They were exciting, these fogs. They were just as described at the beginning of *Bleak House*: 'Fog everywhere... Gas looming through the fog in divers places in the streets... Most of the shops lighted two hours before their time – as the gas seems to know, for it has a haggard and unwilling look.'

Of course, it wasn't gaslight that loomed through the fogs of my childhood, but electric light. The shape of a double-decker bus would slowly transform from the merest blur into something more definite only a few feet away, its headlights like the malign yellow eyes of some devouring beast. Before the bus, a man would walk, guiding the driver through a gloom far more impenetrable than the darkest night. The fog was not merely an absence of light; it was the opponent and scatterer of light, locked in mortal battle with it and almost triumphing. The fogs killed thousands, mainly old people with lungs weakened from decades of smoking. I didn't know this at the time, and I don't suppose it would have worried me much if I had known it. Childhood is not an age of enlarged views and philanthropic feeling.

The decline of smokestack industries, the abandonment of domestic coal fires, and the passing of a Clean Air Act soon made the fogs as remote in memory as manual typewriters are now. Within less than a decade, they came to be associated more with the London of Sherlock Holmes than with the city of a few years before. No child would again experience the excitement that I had felt because of them.

But this was genuine progress. The fogs were a manifestation of the pollution that did terrible damage not only to people's lungs but to the buildings of the past, and therefore to something more intangible: people's view of the past. Soot and grime covered almost every building in every British city; one looked at a building and thought, 'How grim.' The country was like a vast Victorian funeral. This was one reason, no doubt, that Britain then undertook an orgy of urban destruction unparalleled in peacetime. The Luftwaffe had been bungling amateurs, it turned out, compared with the town and city fathers of Britain. The Germans managed to destroy a few cities – though none utterly beyond repair, if a will to repair had existed – but the local authorities ruined practically everything, with a thoroughness that would have been admirable in a good cause.

When they looked at a grimy building, the authorities, armed with new legal powers to plan and reconstruct towns and cities, saw only the grime and not the magnificence beneath. The authorities were not, on the whole, imaginative men, except when it came to imagining the fortunes that one could make from demolition and redevelopment. Advising them were architects and engineers who had converted *en masse* to modernism and who, even before the destruction brought by the war (which many of them welcomed), were groping toward Gropius. They agreed with Gropius's view that 'a breach has been made with the past, which allows us to envisage a new aspect of architecture corresponding to the technical civilisation of the age we live in; the morphology of dead styles has been destroyed; and we are returning to honesty of thought and feeling.' On this understanding, any thought of preservation, of harmonising the new with the old, let alone of new building in old styles, was a perversion.

The grime had become the sign of a past now hated with a lack of moral discrimination comparable to that once displayed by the jingoists, who had assumed that all was for the best in this, the best of all possible islands. Postwar Britain was a defeated power in everything but the military sense; its old industries, which had caused the grime, could not return it to prosperity; much better, then, to pull everything down and start again. The grime symbolised Gradgrind and Bounderby, and nothing else.

That the Soviet Union emerged triumphant from World War II would also prove a catastrophe for the British urban environment, for it supposedly showed the superiority of central planning over its absence. Intellectuals viewed British towns and cities as the antithesis of planning: like Topsy, they just growed. It didn't occur to the intellectuals that these were places where successive generations, over many centuries, had produced an urban environment that had charm and was intensely social and liveable, largely because those who built it had to live in what they built; or that where planning had taken place – in Bath, for example, or in the New Town section of Edinburgh – it was carried out by men of the highest possible calibre, for a population of refined and elegant taste. In fact, refinement and elegance were now ideologically suspect. To live in elegance in a civilisation (at least as it then was) which rested on the labours of others in horrible industries that maimed people, blighted lives, and blotted landscapes was like living in peace with an art collection stolen from Jewish families during the war. Thus the towns and cities of Britain needed a new moral and physical beginning. And as rational men, the planners knew what people needed: roads and car parks, so that they might conveniently get to and make use of their shopping and cultural centres. Many mediaeval lanes, and entire Georgian streets, were destroyed in the name of driving and parking – the appetite for which seemed only to grow with the feeding, and now less than ever has been met.

The planners and city fathers saw attachment to the city of the past as politically sinister. In 1947, the Labour-led city council of Bristol, which had been severely bombed during the war, laid plans to redevelop the city rather than restore it. When the local shopkeepers' association polled 13,000 people to see whether they liked the council's plans, and only 400 answered affirmatively, the council denounced the poll: 'The so-called poll is without any official sanction and can carry no weight. The slipshod, inefficient and utterly undemocratic methods by which it is being conducted are reminiscent of Hitler's early efforts in political demagoguery.'

Of course, the poll was probably not scientific, according to the canons of academic political research; but the results were surely startling enough to merit serious consideration by the city council. The notion that one could disregard the poll because it lacked 'official sanction' offers insight into where the councillors believed both power and wisdom properly lay: with themselves. The reference to Hitler was peculiar, for it suggested that the preservation of buildings was somehow a harbinger of Nazi revolution. It was ironic as well, for the councillors failed to see that their own desire to organise the old, higgledy-piggledy city into a 'rational' plan that fulfilled an ideological ideal was very much like the Nazis' radical architectural ambitions for German towns and cities.

But throughout Britain, many city engineers and architects proved only too willing to engage in that project. For instance, it was the hope of Sir Herbert Manzoni, the city engineer of Birmingham, to pull down every non-modernist building in the city centre. Luckily, he died in 1963 before achieving his ambition, but he got quite far, and his spirit sputtered on after him, with the magnificent Victorian library of 1866 pulled down in 1974 and replaced with an inverted concrete ziggurat of such ugliness and (now) dilapidation that it defies description, at least by me. Its environs serve now as a giant *pissoir* and, at night, as a safe haven for drunks and rapists; and thus the Albert Speers of Britain have converted the Victorian dream of municipal munificence into the nightmare of administered *anomie*.

I find it difficult to write temperately on this subject. I have only to see an example of the mass desecration of Britain's architectural heritage to start trembling with rage. No town or city in Britain has inherited so little in the way of beauty that officials did not think it worth destroying. Recently in Rotherham I saw the historic environs of a magnificent fifteenth-century church falling into ruins, while all around there was a concrete mess, aesthetically worthy of being the administrative capital of an autonomous region of Soviet Central Asia at the height, or the depth, of the Brezhnev era.

My wife tells me to calm down; as she rightly notes, I can do nothing about this disaster now. But it is not merely the physical ugliness of what has been done that affects me; it is the ugliness of soul that was necessary for it to be done. The men entrusted with planning and rebuilding Britain's towns and cities, one cannot help but think, must have suffered from a deep sense of humiliation, an awareness that, in an age of the most startling technical progress, they were not equal to the most jobbing of jobbing provincial builders of two and a half centuries earlier. Destruction of the heritage was all that was open to them, then, and in this, at least, they excelled. They were like Satan, who, expelled from heaven, exclaimed:

Me miserable! which way shall I fly Infinite wrath, and infinite despair? Which way I fly is Hell; myself am Hell.

They certainly produced a visual hell, all the more hellish because they allowed elements of what existed before to remain, so that the contrast was inescapable. In what was once the beautiful small city of Worcester, to take one more example, part of the graceful complex of ecclesiastical buildings next to the cathedral was destroyed in order to erect the Giffard Hotel, a concrete building in the style of Le Corbusier that would have gladdened the hearts of Nicolae and Elena Ceauşescu. The hotel now vies with the cathedral for one's visual attention: it is impossible to screen it out.

Yet matters have improved greatly in the last few years. Acts of official vandalism are rarer, and when attempted cause a public outcry. Citizens have formed groups to protect what remains of their heritage and no longer stand by watching the destruction of whole townscapes. Old buildings are routinely adapted to new purposes (as civilised people have known how to do for centuries) instead of being treated as impediments to progress or to traffic. Victorian buildings are cleaned up instead of demolished, and the architectural detail beneath the grime has come as a revelation to many who previously might have held the Victorians in contempt. London's remaining Victorian railway stations have been modernised, keeping their basic features, so that the elegance and beauty of the ironwork is obvious to all. St. Pancras station, a masterpiece of Victorian Gothic architecture, has been lovingly (and, admittedly, expensively) restored and made the terminus of the train to Paris. Fittingly, the concourse has a statue of the poet Sir John Betjeman, whose protests helped save the station from demolition and replacement – perhaps by something as ugly as the new Euston station, a few hundred yards up the road, which took the place of the magnificently neoclassical original Euston station. The open space around Euston, probably not coincidentally, is as dirty as anywhere in London: people vote with their litter.

Not only has the official vandalism been much reduced; architecture and urbanisation have considerably improved. Cities such as Birmingham, Leeds, and Manchester have undergone something of a revival, though it is too late to save the parts of them destroyed in the frenzy of self-hatred, utopianism, social engineering, and financial corruption that I have described.

Among other discoveries made by the town planners, architects, and the general public is that cities with central residential districts are better places to live than those that relegate all domiciles to the outer fringes and leave the centres as ghost towns every evening.

Birmingham and Manchester have also belatedly discovered an unsuspected asset that the late eighteenth and nineteenth centuries bequeathed: they have more canals than Venice. Before the advent of railways, the portage of goods in industrial Britain was largely by canal, and Birmingham and Manchester were at the centre of canal networks. The canals were beautifully constructed, but they were then left derelict for more than a century and became ditches where thistles grew and rubbish was dumped. The brick or iron bridges that span them are, despite the utilitarianism of their construction, of a surprising and moving elegance. The early industrialists were not quite as impervious to aesthetic considerations as Gradgrind and Bounderby might have led one to suppose.

These canals criss-crossed the cities' hearts. As if by some operation of the *zeitgeist*, houses and flats began to rise in large numbers along the canals during the 1990s, and, in some cases, they were elegant places in which someone with an aesthetic sense might actually like to live. The raw concrete that during the worst years of destruction became a kind of phallic symbol for British architects was nowhere to be seen; walls were made of brick, or at least received a brick veneer. Many details could have been done better, doubtless, but one's first impression was not horror.

The repeopling of city centres, largely with the young and educated middle class, brought other advantages. For many, cultural activities were now within easy reach – indeed, walking distance – rather than a tedious drive or ride away. Such cultural amenities as already existed (and Birmingham and Manchester always had good orchestras) expanded, and new ones arrived. It astonishes me how well one can now eat in these cities, given their long, dismal record of bad food. In other words, the civilised pleasures and advantages of living in a city began to make themselves felt.

But to this I must now enter several caveats. The first is that much of the building, though more attractive than anything erected for many years, is not of high quality. With few exceptions, no contemporary British architect believes that he builds *sub specie aeternitatis*; on the contrary, he expects what he constructs to be pulled down soon and replaced. That a building should be sound enough to last perhaps 30 years is the city council's main demand, which is conducive neither to solidity nor to fine workmanship. This explains why builders have used methods and materials that look well enough when new but will soon look tawdry.

The second caveat is that far more houses and flats were built than demand could absorb. This didn't seem to matter much while prices were rising: a house by a canal, bought new in Birmingham for £200,000, was, within a few years, worth upward of £600,000. But, as we have since seen, the whole British economy was like Ophelia after she had fallen into the brook:

> Her clothes spread wide, And mermaid-like a while they bore her up Which time she chanted snatches of old tunes, As one incapable of her own distress, Or like a creature native and endued Unto that element; but long it could not be Till that her garments, heavy with their drink, Pulled the poor wretch from her melodious lay To muddy death.

This is the fate, it seems, of economies that base their prosperity upon asset inflation – often a deliberate government policy. When blocks of flats remain empty, as they now do, can dereliction be far behind?

The third, and potentially most serious, caveat relates to the behaviour of the British population. Every Friday and Saturday night (and often other nights as well), thousands of young adults invade Britain's towns and cities, intent on getting publicly drunk and making a nuisance of themselves in the name of self-expression. No one, apparently, has ever asked them not to, let alone told them; and by now, such activities as screaming at 2am, hair pulling, vomiting in the gutter, smashing glasses, and climbing at random into passing vehicles are seen as inalienable rights – perhaps because they have yet to be alienated. Menace is never far away.

People have sometimes accused me of exaggerating the chaos of these street scenes, to which I can reply that one American journalist who harboured such a suspicion came to investigate for himself. I took him to central Birmingham at 10pm one Saturday night, before the fun really began; in less than five minutes, he was convinced that I had not exaggerated.

No doubt some people exist who do not mind this behaviour, but few will tolerate it for long, especially as they get older. It will surely alienate the old from the young and drive them away; and if civilisation requires at least some understanding and sympathy between generations, and an ability to live together, this will ultimately prevent a lasting renaissance of the cities.

Still, Rome wasn't built in a day, and it is a considerable relief that the worst of the architectural vandalism and brutalism is now behind us. It was a nightmare, but we have almost woken up.

MODERNITY'S UNINVITED GUEST

IT IS AN UNENVIABLE FATE for an author to be remembered, if at all, for a devastating review of his principal work by a much greater writer; but such was the fate that befell Soame Jenyns at the pen of Doctor Johnson.

The book that occasioned Johnson's scorn was *A Free Enquiry into the Nature and Origin of Evil*, which Jenyns first published anonymously in 1756. Johnson's review brings to mind Truman Capote's famous remark about Jack Kerouac's autobiographical novel, *On the Road*: that it was not writing, it was typing. For Johnson said of Jenyns: 'When this [author] finds himself prompted to another performance, let him consider, whether he is about to disburden his mind, or employ his fingers; and, if I might venture to offer him a subject, I should wish, that he would solve this question: Why he, that has nothing to write, should desire to be a writer?'

In this case, however, the criticism was rather unfair; and Jenyns, by all accounts an amiable man, was mortified and harboured a deep but concealed resentment against Johnson for the rest of his life. After Johnson died, Jenyns published some vengefully scurrilous verses about the great man:

> Here lies poor Johnson. Reader, have a care, Tread lightly, lest you rouse a sleeping bear; Religious, moral, generous, and humane He was – but self-sufficient, rude, and vain; Ill-bred and over-bearing in dispute, A scholar and a Christian – yet a brute.

Another of the scholar and Christian's objections to Jenyns's book was its inadequacy to treat its subject. Johnson granted that the nature and origin of evil were a 'very difficult and important question'. But they were also one, he added, that 'this author's endeavours will not free from the perplexity which has entangled the speculatists of all ages.'

For Jenyns, as for all writers of his time, the word 'evil' conveyed something much wider than it does today. It meant all that caused mankind suffering. It included 'moral evil' – extreme human wickedness – but also 'natural evil', the suffering brought about by epidemics, earthquakes, droughts, floods, and the like. It is not surprising that the word should have undergone a change of meaning, for in the intervening period the proportion of human suffering caused by moral, as against natural, evil has increased dramatically, thanks to our growing mastery of nature. When Jenyns wrote, for example, half of all children died, principally from infectious disease, before they reached the age of five; the causes of every known disease remained utterly mysterious, notwithstanding the pedantic flummery of the epoch's physicians.

A Free Enquiry appeared the year after the Lisbon earthquake, which killed some 30,000 people and destroyed in five minutes what it had taken centuries to build. The earthquake caused a philosophical crisis throughout Europe, for it was difficult to see the divine justice in this catastrophe, visited alike upon the virtuous and the vicious, the provident and the improvident, the humble and the proud. Earthquakes still happen, of course, but their effects have become attenuated in countries where many people are rich, educated, or leisured enough to worry about the origin of evil. The recent Chilean earthquake, many times more severe than its predecessor in Haiti, killed under half of one per cent as many people because of Chile's far-sighted precautions against earthquakes. We have reached the stage when the harm done by what once would have been called acts of God seems as much the effect of moral as of natural evil.

To explain natural evil, Jenyns had, like many believers before him, to reconcile the presence of terrible human suffering in the world with the existence of an omnipotent and wholly beneficent deity. His answer was optimistic, his theodicy derived, as Johnson pointed out, from Alexander Pope's attempt in his long poem *An Essay on Man* to 'vindicate the ways of God to Man'. Jenyns came to the same conclusion as Pope (though it is more likely that his conclusion determined his reasoning than the reverse): namely, that whatever is, is right. In short, the sum of happiness in the universe was, is, and will always be the greatest possible.

How did Jenyns (and others before him) arrive at this remarkable conclusion? It is impossible to conceive of any system such as a universe without subordination of parts to a whole, Jenyns said. This means that there must be beings of different capacities and advantages, 'to the comparative want of which advantages we give the names of folly, weakness, deformity, and imperfection, and very unjustly repute them Evils.' But they are not really evils, for the whole system of super- and subordination could not exist without them. The positive advantages that we do enjoy, meanwhile, are the free gift of a benevolent God, who could, after all, have refrained from creating anything at all.

Jenyns goes on to say that such supposed evils as poverty, 'inquietudes of mind' and pain are necessary to the operation of the universal system. Without poverty, 'none could have submitted to... the drudgeries of life', which would make for even greater poverty; 'inquietudes of mind' could have been avoided only by depriving man of the very inclinations and passions that make him the creature he is, between beast and angel; and as for pain, 'what numberless lives would be lost in every trifling pursuit, or flung away in ill humour, was the piercing of a sword no more painful than the tickling of a feather?' The evils of existence are necessary to prevent even greater evils; and therefore we cannot really count them as evils at all.

Doctor Johnson finds this unctuously complacent, the opinion of a man who, born into the gentry, has never known the pangs of want or poverty. It is not true that the poorest or hungriest man is the most active in improving his situation, for extreme poverty and hunger often depress the spirit rather than stimulate it. Besides, the question is not whether poverty, misery, and pain are required for the operation of the system as a whole – Johnson is willing to admit that perhaps they are – but whether the quantity of these evils currently experienced is necessary and inevitable. Of course, the distinction between avoidable and unavoidable suffering requires judgment and often cannot be made with absolute certainty. 'To these meditations,' as Johnson puts it, 'humanity is unequal.'

The free market is sometimes said to work in much the way that Jenyns said that the universe worked: the evil that it sometimes brings – increases in unemployment during recessions, for example – is unavoidable, except by embracing an even greater evil, such as general impoverishment. This does not mean that unemployment is not an evil but only that, to quote Jenyns, 'there is no more pain in it, than what is necessary to the production of happiness.' But it seems indecent for a man beyond the reach of destitution to preach to a man whose house is about to be repossessed that all is for the best in this, the best of all possible worlds – just as Jenyns's privileged, healthy, and prosperous preaching about evil seemed indecent to Doctor Johnson.

Nevertheless, it was not quite fair to Jenyns to say that his optimistic theodicy was only the complacent consequence of his good fortune. Alexander Pope, from whom he took it, was much less fortunate. Not only was Pope born Catholic in a country in which it was difficult for Catholics to make their way; he suffered immensely throughout his life – or what he once called 'this long disease, my life' – from Pott's disease, a tubercular infection of the spine that turned him into, in his own words, 'a spider'. Johnson, in his life of Pope, movingly describes the effects of Pope's illness:

> He was then so weak as to stand in perpetual need of female attendance… When he rose, he was invested in bodice made of stiff canvas, being scarce able to hold himself erect till they were laced, and he then put on a flannel waistcoat. One side was contracted. His legs were so slender, that he enlarged their bulk with three pair of stockings, which were drawn on and off by the maid; for he was not able to dress or undress himself, and neither went to bed nor rose without help. His weakness made it very difficult for him to be clean.

That such a man, labouring under so many disadvantages, became a wit, a *bon viveur*, and the foremost literary figure of his day, acclaimed in France as in England, seemed an illustration of the truth that out of evil good may come. In fact, one could believe (as Johnson hints) that Pope's misfortunes were the source of his greatness, for they imposed single-mindedness upon him. Literature was one of the few fields in which his disabilities did not preclude a triumphant career.

So perhaps Pope, unlike Jenyns, had earned the right to declare that 'whatever is, is right'. Still, the genius required for Pope to overcome the natural evil was exceptional; and though good may come of evil, it does not invariably, or even often, do so. To think otherwise is – as Johnson wrote of Jenyns – to decide 'too easily, upon questions out of the reach of human determination, with too little consideration of mortal weakness, and with too much vivacity for the necessary caution.'

Jenyns's explanation of natural evil, flawed though it may be, underlies his subsequent explanation of moral evil. Since natural evil is inevitable, he explains, man had to be created not only capable of evil but willing to commit it, so that the natural evil should not be unjustly visited on the innocent. Evil in man is the counterpart of evil in nature. And since no man is perfectly good, he has no right to complain if evil should befall him.

The superficiality of this argument requires, from a modern standpoint, little commentary. But even Doctor Johnson – a man with a delicate sense of personal imperfection who once stood for several hours bareheaded in the rain in the Uttoxeter marketplace, in penance for having been disrespectful a half-century earlier to his father, who had run a bookstall there – did not criticise it strongly. Both he and Jenyns were a world away from our modern concerns about evil. Accustomed to our comforts and our delicate sensibilities, we would find their world unbelievably harsh; yet their notion of evil strikes us as naive and almost innocent. Despite the violence of Johnson's review of Jenyns, the two men agreed more than they differed. They lived on the cusp of the Enlightenment but were both, at least in their treatment of evil, pre-Enlightenment in outlook. The burning question for them was not 'Why do men behave evilly?' but 'Why is there evil at all?'

The distinction between the pre-Enlightenment and Enlightenment attitudes toward evil was illustrated the year after Jenyns published his book, when a man named Robert-François Damiens tried to stab Louis XV with a knife. The king was hurt but not severely. (It is one of the ironies of history that in the Age of Despotism, the autocrat moved unguardedly among his subjects, while today, guards surround the elected head of even a small democracy as if he were a jewel above price.) Damiens was publicly executed in the Place de la Grève after enduring prolonged torture. For most of the population, this was only as it should and had to be; it was the natural fate of all regicides or attempted regicides. As it was for Ravaillac, the assassin of Henri IV a century and a half earlier, so it must be with Damiens. Precedent was indistinguishable from natural law.

A few *philosophes* (Louis XV among them) were horrified, however, by the brutality of Damiens's execution and by the suffering he was made to undergo. This suffering was neither natural nor inevitable, the *philosophes* maintained; it was not inscribed in the constitution of the universe but undergone because men chose to inflict it. That regicides had 'always' met this fate was not sufficient grounds; the question had to be examined in the light of reason. In other words, the *philosophes* diverted attention away from theodicy – the explanation for the existence of evil in a world created by a perfectly benevolent deity – to the behaviour of men. As Pope, half a harbinger and half an opponent of the Enlightenment, put it: 'Know then thyself, presume not God to scan; / The proper study of mankind is Man.'

The Enlightenment held out the hope that with enough of this 'proper study', man would come to know himself sufficiently to eliminate the evil and suffering that had always beset his existence. Man would obtain something like a Newtonian knowledge not only of the universe but of himself, with all the predictive and mechanical advantages that such understanding had brought in the study of inanimate nature.

And in a certain sense, the promise of the Enlightenment has been triumphantly fulfilled in our modern societies – surely as regards natural evil. Thanks to rational inquiry, to take but one instance, the infant mortality rate since Jenyns wrote has fallen 98 per cent. We live lives cleaner, more comfortable, and freer from pain than those of any people who have ever existed. Nobody today has to endure one-hundredth of the physical tortures, brought by illness and the efforts to treat it, that Philip II of Spain and Charles II of England had to endure.

Nor can one say that no moral advance occurred because of the Enlightenment. Just as we are freer from disease, so, too, our mental lives are freer. Of course, dictatorships over thought still exist in the world, but they are on the defensive and have come to seem somehow unnatural. Freedom is now the default setting of human thought. No one can tell us what to think, say, or write, at least not without our consent.

But an uninvited guest has arrived at this banquet of human advancement: evil. Whether men behave better or worse, individually or in the aggregate, than they did before the Enlightenment, is probably a question that we cannot answer approximately, let alone definitively. But what is certain is that moral evil has not only failed to disappear but has taken on a more deliberate, calculated character.

Whereas the torturers of Damiens did their evil unselfconsciously because it was the natural or preordained thing to do, modern evil is done after intellectual reflection, divorced from any tradition that might guide conduct.

The two greatest moral catastrophes of the twentieth century, wrought by Lenin and Hitler, were perverse effects of the Enlightenment. Lenin and Hitler were creatures of the Enlightenment not in the sense that they were enlightened, of course, but in the sense that they believed they had the right and the duty to act in accordance with their own unaided deductions from their own first principles. Everything else they regarded as sentimentality. Lenin preached no mercy to the non-proletarian, Hitler none to the Jew. The truth of their theories, supposedly rational and indubitable, was more evident to them, more real in their minds, than the millions killed as a consequence of those theories. If a syllogism ended in a command to commit unspeakable evil, you did not doubt the premises or the argument but obeyed the command.

This post-Enlightenment way of thinking continues to have its defenders. The celebrated British historian Eric Hobsbawm, a lifelong Marxist, said not long ago that had the Soviet Union turned out much better than it did, the deaths of 20 million to achieve it would have been a worthwhile price to pay. One cannot accuse Hobsbawm of thinking small.

That evil has not disappeared *pari passu* with German measles puzzles and troubles us. Evil remains a conundrum, as evidenced by Marxist literary theorist Terry Eagleton's recently published book *On Evil*. Eagleton is not one of those Marxists for whom, like the late historian and Stalin apologist Edward Hallett Carr, the problem of evil does not exist. 'I don't think there are such things as bad people,' Carr once said. 'To us Hitler, at the moment, seems a bad man, but will they think Hitler a bad man in a hundred years' time, or will they think the German society of the thirties bad?'

Eagleton sees clearly that this will not do. Helping him in this recognition is that he is a Christian as well as a Marxist, and no Christian can believe wholly in social determinism. The problem of the human heart is real, not just a remediable social artefact. The relationship between society and human behaviour is dialectical, Eagleton believes. Society has its effect, but it is acting on an already imperfect nature, which in turn is bound to produce an imperfect society.

Significantly, Eagleton begins his book by citing (as have others) the case of James Bulger. Here is the opposite of childhood innocence, for the two boys knew that what they were doing was deeply wrong but went ahead and did it anyway. The human mystery is that neither their environment nor their nature can fully explain them. Man is not only wolf to man; he is mystery to man.

So the Enlightenment project has failed, at least in explaining man fully to himself. However successful it has been in other regards – and we are all, even its bitterest enemies, children of the Enlightenment – we do not know ourselves any better than we did in Jenyns's and Johnson's day. Self-understanding may even have regressed since Johnson, for no man was better at self-examination than he. If more people proved adept at it, perhaps the prevalence of evil would decline. Johnson was highly imperfect, knew himself to be so, and always struggled against his imperfections without expecting more than partial victory. He did not approve of Pope's theodicy, but he could agree with the famous lines summing up the human predicament:

> Created half to rise, and half to fall;
> Great lord of all things, yet a prey to all;
> Sole judge of truth, in endless error hurl'd;
> The glory, jest, and riddle of the world!

SYMPATHY DEFORMED

TO SYMPATHISE WITH THOSE who are less fortunate is honourable and decent. A man able to commiserate only with himself would surely be neither admirable nor attractive. But every virtue can become deformed by excess, insincerity, or loose thinking into an opposing vice. Sympathy, when excessive, moves toward sentimental condescension and eventually disdain; when insincere, it becomes unctuously hypocritical; and when associated with loose thinking, it is a bad guide to policy and frequently has disastrous results. It is possible, of course, to combine all three errors.

No subject provokes the deformations of sympathy more than poverty. I recalled this recently when asked to speak on a panel about child poverty in Britain in the wake of the economic and financial crisis. I said that the crisis had not affected the problem of child poverty in any fundamental way. Britain remained what it had long been – one of the worst countries in the Western world in which to grow up (see 'Childhood's End'). This was not the consequence of poverty in any raw economic sense; it resulted from the various kinds of squalor – moral, familial, psychological, social, educational, and cultural – that were particularly prevalent in the country.

My remarks were poorly received by the audience, which consisted of professional alleviators of the effects of social pathology, such as social workers and child psychologists. One fellow panellist was the chief of a charity devoted to the abolition of child poverty (whose largest source of funds, like that of most important charities in Britain's increasingly corporatist society, was the government). She dismissed my comments as nonsense. For her, poverty was simply the 'maldistribution of resources'; we could thus distribute it away. And in her own terms, she was right, for her charity stipulated that one was poor if one had an income of less than 60 per cent of the median national income.

This definition, of course, has odd logical consequences: for example, that in a society of billionaires, multimillionaires would be poor. A society in which every single person grew richer could also be one in which poverty became more widespread than before; and one in which everybody grew poorer might be one in which

213

there was less poverty than before. More important, however, is that the redistributionist way of thinking denies agency to the poor. By destroying people's self-reliance, it encourages dependency and corruption – not only in Britain, but everywhere in the world where it is held.

I first started thinking about poverty when I worked as a doctor during the early eighties in the Gilbert Islands, a group of low coral atolls in an immensity of the Central Pacific. Much of the population still lived outside the money economy, and the per capita GDP was therefore extremely low. It did not seem to me, however, that the people were very poor. Their traditional way of life afforded them what anthropologists call a generous subsistence; their coconuts, fish, and taros gave them an adequate – and, in some respects, elegant – living. They lived in an almost invariant climate, with the temperature rarely departing more than a few degrees from 85. Their problems were illness and boredom, which left them avid for new possibilities when they came into contact with the outside world.

Life in the islands taught me a lively disrespect for per capita GDP as an accurate measure of poverty. I read recently in a prominent liberal newspaper that 'the majority of Nigerians live on less than $1 a day'. This statement is clearly designed less to convey an economic truth than to provoke sympathy, evoke guilt, and drum up support for foreign aid in the West, where an income of less than $1 a day would not keep body and soul together for long; whereas it is frequently said that one of Nigeria's problems is the rapid increase in its population.

I spent the years 1983 to 1986 in Tanzania, a country that presented an experiment in treating poverty as a matter of maldistribution. Julius Nyerere, the first – and, until then, the only – president, had been in charge for more than 20 years. His honorific, *Mwalimu* – Teacher – symbolised his relation to his country and his people. He had become a Fabian socialist at the University of Edinburgh, and a more red-blooded one (according to his former ally and foreign minister, Oscar Kambona, who fell out with him over the imposition of a one-party socialist state) after receiving a delirious, orchestrated reception in Mao's China.

One can say a number of things in Nyerere's favour, at least by the standards of post-independence African leaders. He was not a tribalist who awarded all the plum jobs to his own kind. He was not a particularly sanguinary dictator, though he did not hesitate to imprison his opponents. Nor was he spectacularly corrupt in the manner of, say, Bongo of Gabon or Moi of Kenya. He was outwardly charming and modest and must have been one of very few people to have had good personal relations with both Queen Elizabeth II and Kim Il-sung.

Nyerere wished the poor well; he was full of sympathy and good intentions. He thought that, being so uneducated, ignorant, and lacking in resources, the poor could not spare the time and energy – and were, in any case, unqualified – to make decisions for themselves. They were also lazy: Nyerere at one point complained about the millions of his fellow countrymen who spent half their time drinking, gossiping, and dancing (which suggested to me that their lives were not altogether intolerable).

But Nyerere knew what to do for them. In 1967, he issued his famous Arusha Declaration, named for the town where he made it, committing Tanzania to socialism and vowing to end the exploitation of man by man that made some people rich and others poor. On this view of things, the greater accumulation of wealth, either by some individuals or by some nations, could be explained only by exploitation, a morally illicit process. The explanation for poverty was simple: some people or nations appropriated the natural wealth of mankind for themselves. It was therefore a necessary condition of improvement, as well as a form of restitution, that they no longer be allowed to do so and that their wealth be redistributed. So Tanzania nationalised the banks, appropriated commercial farms, took over all major industry, controlled prices, and put all export trade under the control of para-governmental organisations.

There followed the forced collectivisation of the rural population – which is to say, the majority of the population – into *Ujamaa* villages. *Ujamaa* is Swahili for 'extended family'; as Nyerere insisted, all men were brothers. By herding the people into collectivised villages, Nyerere thought, the government could provide services, such as schools and clinics. After all, rich countries had educated and healthy populations; was it not evident that if the Tanzanian people were educated and healthy, wealth would result? Besides, collectively the villagers could buy fertiliser, perhaps even tractors, which they never could have done as individuals (assuming, as Nyerere did, that without government action there would be no economic growth). Unfortunately, the people did not want to herd fraternally into villages; they wanted to stay put on their scattered ancestral lands. Several thousand were arrested and imprisoned.

The predictable result of these efforts at preventing the exploitation of man by man was the collapse of production, pauperising an already poor country. Tanzania went from being a significant exporter of agricultural produce to being utterly dependent on food imports, even for subsistence, in just a few years. Peasants who had once grown coffee and sold it to Indian merchants for soap, salt, and other goods uprooted their bushes and started growing meagre amounts of corn for their own consumption. No reason existed for doing anything else because growers now had to sell their produce to para-governmental procurement agencies, which paid them later, if at all, at derisory prices in a worthless currency that peasants called 'pictures of Nyerere'.

Nyerere blamed shortages of such commonplaces as soap and salt on speculators and exploiters, rather than on his own economic policies. He made the shortages the pretext for so-called crackdowns, often directed at Indian traders, which eventually drove them from the country. Nyerere's policies were no more soundly based than those of Idi Amin, who drove out the Indians more brutally. Anti-Semitism, it has often been said, is the socialism of fools. I would put things another way: socialism is the anti-Semitism of intellectuals.

With foreign exchange exhausted, only the funds that the honey-tongued Nyerere continued to obtain from the World Bank and foreign donors enabled the country to avoid mass starvation. By the time I reached Tanzania, the country had become completely dependent on handouts. Aid represented two-thirds of Tanzania's foreign exchange earnings; one might say that its largest export was requests for such aid. In the rural area where I lived, the people dressed in hand-me-downs sent by European charities. A single egg was a luxury. One of the goals that had induced Nyerere to move to socialism, ironically, was national 'self-reliance'.

The foreign aid that allowed Nyerere's policies to continue well after the economic disaster was evident had precisely the baleful effects that Peter Bauer, the development economist who contradicted the professional orthodoxies of his time, predicted. The aid immensely increased the power of the sole political party by giving its officials control over scarce goods. When I was in Tanzania, you needed political connections to buy even a bottle of beer – the famous local monopoly brand, Safari, which, the saying went, caused you to pass directly from sobriety to hangover without passing through drunkenness. The regime provided ample opportunities for corruption. Most Tanzanians were slender; you could recognise a party man by his girth.

Thanks to foreign aid, a large bureaucracy grew up in Tanzania whose power, influence, and relative prosperity depended on its keeping the economy a genuine zero-sum game. A vicious circle had been created: the more impoverished the country, the greater the need for foreign aid; the greater the foreign aid, the more privileged the elite; the more privileged the elite, the greater the adherence to policies that resulted in poverty. Nyerere himself made the connection between privilege and ruinous policies perfectly clear after the International Monetary Fund suggested that Tanzania float its currency, the Tanzanian shilling, rather than maintain it at a ridiculously overvalued rate. 'There would be rioting in the streets, and I would lose everything I have,' Nyerere said.

Long years of living under this perverse regime encouraged economically destructive attitudes among the general population. While I was impressed by the sacrifices that Tanzanian parents were willing to make to educate their children (for a child to attain a certain stage of education, for example, a party official had to certify the parents' political reliability), it alarmed me to discover that the only goal of education was a government job, from which a child could then extort a living from people like his parents – though not actually from his parents, for he would share his good fortune with them. In Tanzania, producing anything, despite the prevailing scarcity of almost everything, became foolish, for it brought no reward.

When I returned to practice among the poor in England, I found my Tanzanian experiences illuminating. The situation was not so extreme in England, of course, where the poor enjoyed luxuries that in Tanzania were available only to the elite. But the arguments for the expansive British welfare state had much in common with those that Nyerere had used to bring about his economic disaster. The poor, helpless victims of economic and social forces, were, like Ophelia in the river, 'incapable of their own distress'. Therefore, they needed outside assistance in the form of subsidies and state-directed organisations, paid for with the income of the rich. One could not expect them to make serious decisions for themselves.

This attitude has worked destruction in Britain as surely as it has in Tanzania. The British state is today as much a monopoly provider of education to the population as it is of healthcare. The monopoly is maintained because the government and the bureaucratic caste believe, first, that parents would otherwise be too feckless or impoverished to educate their children from their own means; and second, that public education equalises the chances of children in an otherwise unequal society and is thus a means of engineering social justice.

The state started to take over education in 1870, largely because the government saw a national competitor, Prussia, employing state power to educate its children. But practically all British children went to school already: according to the calculations of economist and historian E. G. West, 93 per cent of the population was by then literate. It is true that the British state had started providing support to schools long before, but in 1870 67 per cent of school income still came from the fees that parents paid.

Not all British children received a good education before the state intervened: that was as vanishingly unlikely then as it is today. But it is clear that poor people – incomparably poorer than anyone in Britain today – were nonetheless capable of making sacrifices to carry out their highly responsible decisions. They did not need the state to tell them that their children should learn to read, write, and reckon. There is no reason to suppose that, left alone, the astonishing progress in the education of the population during the first three-quarters of the nineteenth century would not have continued. The 'problem' that the state was solving in its destruction of the voluntary system was its own lack of power over the population.

As in Tanzania, the state-dominated system became self-reinforcing. Because of the high taxation necessary to run it, it reduced the capacity and inclination of people to pay for their own choices – and eventually the habit of making such choices. The British state now decides the important things for British citizens when it comes to education and much else. It is no coincidence that British advocates of the cradle-to-grave welfare state were great admirers of Julius Nyerere – who, incidentally, has been proposed for Roman Catholic canonisation, thus bringing close to reality Bauer's ironic reference to him as Saint Julius.

The only time I ever saw Nyerere in person was in Dodoma, the dusty town designated to become Tanzania's new capital. He was expected to drive by, and by the side of the road sat a praise singer – a woman employed to sing the praises of important people. She was singing songs in praise of Nyerere, of which there were many, with words such as: 'Father Nyerere, build and spread socialism throughout the country and eliminate all parasites.'

The great man drove past in a yellow Mercedes. The praise singer was covered in dust and started to cough.

CHILDHOOD'S END

BRITAIN IS THE WORST country in the Western world in which to be a child, according to a recent UNICEF report. Ordinarily, I would not set much store by such a report; but in this case, I think it must be right – not because I know so much about childhood in all the other 20 countries examined but because the childhood that many British parents give to their offspring is so awful that it is hard to conceive of worse, at least on a mass scale. The two poles of contemporary British child rearing are neglect and overindulgence.

Consider one British parent, Fiona MacKeown, who in November 2007 went on a six-month vacation to Goa, India, with her boyfriend and eight of her nine children by five different fathers, none of whom ever contributed financially for long to the children's upkeep. (The child left behind – her eldest, at 19 – was a drug addict.) She received about £30,000 in welfare benefits a year (and in 2011 was convicted of fraudulently claiming a further £19,000 of income support between February 2005 and March 2008), and doubtless decided – quite rationally, under the circumstances – that the money would go further, and that life would thus be more agreeable, in Goa than in her native Devon.

Reaching Goa, MacKeown soon decided to travel with seven of her children to Kerala, leaving behind one of them, 15-year-old Scarlett Keeling, to live with a tour guide ten years her elder, whom the mother had known for only a short time. Scarlett reportedly claimed to have had sex with this man only because she needed a roof over her head. According to a witness, she was constantly on drugs; and one night, she went to a bar where she drank a lot and took several different illicit drugs, including LSD, cocaine, and pot. She was seen leaving the bar late, almost certainly intoxicated.

The next morning, her body turned up on a beach. At first, the local police maintained that she had drowned while high, but further examination proved that someone had raped and then forcibly drowned her. So far, three people have been arrested in the investigation, which is continuing.

About a month later, Scarlett's mother, interviewed by *The Observer*, expressed surprise at the level of public vituperation aimed at her and her lifestyle in the aftermath of the murder. She agreed that she and her children lived on welfare, but 'not by conscious choice', and she couldn't see anything wrong with her actions in India apart from a certain naivety in trusting the man in whose care she had left her daughter. Scarlett was always an independent girl, and if she, the mother, could turn the clock back, she would behave exactly the same way again.

It is not surprising that someone in Fiona MacKeown's position would deny negligence; to acknowledge it would be too painful. But – and this is what is truly disturbing – when the newspaper asked four supposed child-rearing experts for their opinions, only one saw anything wrong with the mother's behaviour, and even she offered only muted criticism. It was always difficult to know how much independence to grant an adolescent, the expert said; but in her view, the mother had granted too much too quickly to Scarlett.

Even that seemed excessively harsh to *The Observer*'s Barbara Ellen. We should not criticise the mother's way of life, she wrote, since it had nothing to do with her daughter's death: 'Scarlett died for the simple fact that she was in the wrong place at the wrong time with the wrong people, as well as being blitzed with drugs, late at night, in a foreign country.' On this view, being in the wrong place at the wrong time with the wrong people is a raw fact of nature, not the result of human agency, decision, education, or taste. It could happen to anybody, and it just happened to happen to Scarlett. As for drugs, they emerge from the ether and blitz people completely at random. It all seems very unfair.

A columnist for *The Guardian* took a similarly exculpatory line:

Anyone taking even a fleeting glance at recent news will have picked up a crucial message: women with children by more than one partner are apparently hussies, who deserve everything they get. The opprobrium... served up to Fiona MacKeown, mother of murdered 15-year-old, Scarlett Keeling... has been hideous to behold. The spitting criticism is particularly interesting when you compare it to attitudes to men in the public eye. Rod Stewart (seven children by five women), Jack Nicholson (five children by four women), and Mick Jagger (seven children by four women) are painted as great, swinging studs. Anyone else smell a vile double standard?

No one criticises Rod Stewart, Jack Nicholson, or Mick Jagger for how they behave; therefore, apparently, there was nothing wrong with how Fiona MacKeown behaved.

It is worth remembering that *The Observer* and *The Guardian* are not the publications of a lunatic fringe but the preferred newspapers of those who work in the educational and social services, and of broadcasting elites (the BBC advertises vacancies almost exclusively in *The Guardian*). Not every person who reads these newspapers agrees with everything written in them – and both, commendably, offer a little space to writers whose worldview differs from their own – but the general moral tone must be one with which most readers agree. In other words, it is likely that a large part of the educated elite sees nothing wrong, or at least affects to see nothing wrong, with MacKeown's conduct.

This non-judgmentalism surely helps explain why British youth are among the Western world's leaders in such indicators of social pathology as teenage pregnancy, violence, criminality, underage drinking, and consumption of illicit drugs. Britain has the third-highest rate of teenage pregnancy in the industrialised world, according to the UNICEF report (only the United States and New Zealand are higher) – a startling case recently made headlines of 16-, 14-, and 12-year-old sisters, all of whom gave birth within a year of one another. British children have the earliest and highest consumption of cocaine of any young people in Europe, are ten times more likely to sniff solvents than are Greek children, and are six to seven times more likely to smoke pot than are Swedish children. Almost a third of British young people aged 11, 13, and 15 say they have been drunk at least twice.

What explains the non-judgmental attitude among elites? The reluctance to criticise Fiona MacKeown might be an expression of sympathy for someone in the throes of grief: however foolishly (or worse) she behaved, she certainly did not deserve the murder of her daughter. Furthermore, the *Guardian* and *Observer* journalists might argue, we do not know enough about the details of her life to criticise her fairly. Perhaps she is a good mother in most respects; perhaps her children, apart from the drug addict and the murdered Scarlett, are happy, and will lead lives of fulfilment and achievement. After all, no style of upbringing guarantees success or, for that matter, failure; and therefore we should suspend judgment about her.

I suspect, however, that the main consideration inhibiting elite criticism of MacKeown is that passing judgment would call into question the shibboleths of liberal social policy for the last 50 or 60 years – beliefs that give their proponents a strong sense of moral superiority. It would be to entertain the heretical thought that family structure might matter after all, along with such qualities as self-restraint and self-respect; and that welfare dependency is unjust to those who pay for it and disastrous for those who wind up trapped in it.

One day after Scarlett Keeling's murder, a nine-year-old girl, Shannon Matthews, went missing from her home in Dewsbury. Twenty-four days later, after an extensive police search, she was found alive, locked in a drawer under a bed in her stepfather's uncle's house. Police soon arrested the stepfather, 22-year-old Craig Meehan, for possession of 140 pornographic pictures of children, and charged the uncle, Michael Donovan, with kidnapping. Shannon's mother, Karen Matthews, 32, was also arrested, for child cruelty, neglect, and obstructing the police by lying during the search for her daughter.

Karen Matthews, who received welfare payments of £400 a week, had borne seven children to five different men. She called two of her children with the same father 'the twins', thus transferring the meaning of 'twin' from the relatively unusual biological occurrence of double birth to what she clearly thought the equally unusual social circumstance of full siblinghood. Three of her children lived with their fathers, and four lived with her and Meehan, whom Shannon reportedly regarded as her father. Shannon's true father – one Leon Rose, who has since 'moved on' to live with another 'partner' – apparently was happy to find himself usurped by the young Meehan; but Karen Matthews's brother reported that Shannon often spoke of Meehan's violence to her and of her deep unhappiness at home.

The reasons for Shannon's abduction have not yet emerged, but again *The Guardian* managed to distract the reader's attention from less than optimal family arrangements. Instead, it ran an upbeat story on the housing project where the Matthews family lived; that way, the obvious could be ignored rather than denied. *The Sun*, whose readership is virtually entirely working class, had described the project as 'like Beirut – only worse'. But *The Guardian*, whose readership is largely middle class and employed in the public sector, drew attention to the improvements that had taken place in the project, thanks to the local council's having spent several million pounds on it over the previous three years – supplying traffic bollards shaped like penguins, for example. Before the improvements, one resident said, 'We'd houses burgled, sheds burned, caravans blown up.' Now, only one house in 90 is robbed per year; and, thanks to the penguins, joyriding by youths in stolen cars is presumably much reduced. The implication is clear: with more public spending of this kind everywhere in the country, administered by *Guardian* readers and their peers, everything will be all right. It won't matter in the slightest if children either have no fathers, or different fathers every few years.

One might dismiss the stories of Scarlett Keeling and Shannon Matthews as the kind of horrific things that can take place in any society from time to time. But I think that they are the tip of an iceberg. As the liberal newspapers' response shows, the problem with British childhood is by no means confined to the underclass. Our society has lost the most elementary common sense about what children need.

Almost half of British children are born out of wedlock; the unions of which they are the issue are notoriously unstable. Even marriage has lost much of its meaning. In a post-religious society, it is no longer a sacrament. The government has ensured that marriage brings no fiscal advantages and, indeed, for those at the lower end of the social scale, that it has only disadvantages. Easy divorce means that a quarter of all marriages break up within a decade.

The results of this social dysfunction are grim for children. Eighty per cent of British children have televisions in their bedrooms, more than have their biological fathers at home. Fifty-eight per cent of British children eat their evening meal in front of the television (a British child spends more than five hours per day watching a screen); 36 per cent never eat any meals together with other family members; and 34 per cent of households do not even own dining tables. In the prison where I once worked, I discovered that many inmates had never eaten at a table together with someone else.

Let me speculate briefly on the implications of these startling facts. They mean that children never learn, from a sense of social obligation, to eat when not hungry, or not to eat when they are. Appetite is all they need consult in deciding whether to eat – a purely egotistical outlook. Hence anything that interferes with the satisfaction of appetite will seem oppressive. They do not learn such elementary social practices as sharing or letting others go first. Since mealtimes are usually when families get to converse, the children do not learn the art of conversation, either; listening to what others say becomes a challenge. There is a time and place for everything: if I feel like it, the time is now, and the place is here.

If children are not taught self-control, they do not learn it. Violence against teachers is increasing: injuries suffered by teachers at the hands of pupils rose 20 per cent between 2000 and 2006, and in one survey, which may or may not be representative, 53 per cent of teachers had objects thrown at them, 26 per cent had been attacked with furniture or equipment, two per cent had been threatened with a knife, and one per cent with a gun. Nearly 40 per cent of teachers have taken time off to recover from violent incidents at students' hands. About a quarter of British teachers have been assaulted by their students over the last year.

The British, never fond of children, have lost all knowledge or intuition about how to raise them; as a consequence, they now fear them, perhaps the most terrible augury possible for a society. The signs of this fear are unmistakable on the faces of the elderly in public places. An involuntary look of distaste, even barely-controlled terror, crosses their faces if a group of young teens approaches; then they try to look as if they are not really there, hoping to avoid trouble. And the children themselves are afraid. The police say that many children as young as eight are carrying knives for protection. Violent attacks by the young between ten and 17, usually on other children, have risen by 35 per cent in the last four years.

The police, assuming that badly behaved children will become future criminals, have established probably the largest database of DNA profiles in the world: 1.1 million samples from children aged ten to 18, taken over the last decade, and at an accelerating rate (some law enforcement officials have advocated that every child should have a DNA profile on record). Since the criminal justice system reacts to the commission of serious crimes hardly at all, however, British youth do not object to the gathering of the samples: they know that they largely act with impunity, profiles or no profiles.

The British may have always inclined toward harshness or neglect (or both) in dealing with children; but never before have they combined such attitudes with an undiscriminating material indulgence. My patients would sometimes ask me how it was that their children had turned out so bad when they had done everything for them. When I asked them what they meant by 'everything', it invariably meant the latest televisions in their bedrooms or the latest fashionable footwear – to which modern British youth attaches far more importance than Imelda Marcos ever did.

Needless to say, the British state's response to the situation that it has in part created is simultaneously authoritarian and counterproductive. The government pretends, for example, that the problem of child welfare is one of raw poverty. Britain does have the highest rate of child poverty, bar the United States, in the West, as defined (as it usually is) by the per centage of children living in households with an income of less than 60 per cent of the median. (Whether this is a sensible definition of poverty is a subject rarely broached.) But after many years of various redistributive measures and billions spent to reduce it, child poverty is, if anything, more widespread.

The British government thus pursues social welfare policies that encourage the creation of households like the Matthews', and then seeks, via yet more welfare spending, to reduce the harm done to children in them. But was the Matthews household poor, in any but an artificial sense? At the time of Shannon's current stepfather's arrest, the household income was around £50,000; it lived free of rent and local taxes, and it boasted three computers and a large plasma-screen television. Would another £3,000 or £5,000 or £10,000 have made any difference?

A system of perverse incentives in a culture of undiscriminating materialism, where the main freedom is freedom from legal, financial, ethical, or social consequences, makes childhood in Britain a torment both for many of those who live it and those who observe it. Yet the British government will do anything but address the problem, or that part of the problem that is its duty to address: the state-encouraged breakdown of the family. If one were a Marxist, one might see in this refusal the self-interest of the state-employee class: social problems, after all, are their *raison d'être*.

THE PERSISTENCE
OF IDEOLOGY

IN 1960, THE SOCIOLOGIST Daniel Bell published *The End of Ideology*, in which he argued that ideology – understood in the sense of a coherent, single-minded philosophical outlook or system of abstractions intended as much as a lever to change society as a description to explain it – was dead, at least in the West, and in the United States in particular. A combination of democracy and mass prosperity had 'solved' the political questions that had agitated humanity since the time of Plato.

There were to be no more grand and transformative, if woefully erroneous, ideas; all that remained was public administration, with, at most, squabbles over small details of policy. The new version of the old saw, *mens sana in corpore sano*, a sound mind in a sound body, was a capitalist economy in a liberal democratic polity. That was the lesson of history.

In 1989, as the Soviet Union and Eastern Europe were reforming – indeed collapsing – so rapidly that it became clear that Communism could not long survive anywhere in Europe, Francis Fukuyama went one step beyond Bell and wrote an essay for *The National Interest* titled 'The End of History?' In this soon-to-be-famous article, later expanded into a book, Fukuyama suggested that the end of ideology that Bell saw in the West was now global. By 'the end of history', he did not mean the end of events, of course; one team or another would continue to win the FA Cup, and there might yet be wars between national rivals. But broadly, history had given its lesson and mankind had taken it. Henceforth, those who resisted the march of liberal democracy were like the Luddites, those workers at the beginning of the Industrial Revolution who smashed machines, blaming them for destroying the independent livelihoods of workers at home.

At the end of his essay, however, Fukuyama – more concerned to understand the world than to change it, by contrast with Marx – implicitly raised the question of the role of ideology in the world's moral economy. With no ideological struggles to occupy their minds, what will intellectuals have to do or think about? Virtually by definition, they like to address themselves to large and general questions, not small and particular ones: as Isaiah Berlin would say, by temperament, they are hedgehogs, who know one large thing, not foxes, who know many small things. Fukuyama admitted that he would miss ideology, if only as something to oppose. 'I have ambivalent feelings for the civilisation that has been created in Europe since 1945, with its North Atlantic and Asian offshoots,' he wrote. 'Perhaps this very prospect of centuries of boredom at the end of history will serve to get history started once again.'

As it turned out, of course, we did not have long (let alone centuries) to suffer existential boredom. Our dogmatic slumbers – to use Kant's phrase for the philosophic state from which reading David Hume roused him – had barely begun when a group of young fanatics flew commercial airliners into the Twin Towers and the Pentagon, thus demonstrating that pronouncements of the death of both ideology and history were somewhat premature.

In truth, we should have known it, or at least guessed it, without needing to be reminded. Fukuyama's concluding sentences contain a hint of the psychological function that ideology plays. It is not just disgruntlement with the state of the world that stimulates the development and adoption of ideologies. After all, disgruntlement with society there has always been and always will be. Dissatisfaction is the permanent state of mankind, at least of civilised mankind. Not every dissatisfied man is an ideologist, however: for if he were, there would hardly be anyone who was not. Yet ideology, at least as a mass phenomenon, is a comparatively recent development in human history.

Who, then, are ideologists? They are people needy of purpose in life, not in a mundane sense (earning enough to eat or to pay the mortgage, for example) but in the sense of transcendence of the personal, of reassurance that there is something more to existence than existence itself. The desire for transcendence does not occur to many people struggling for a livelihood. Avoiding material failure gives quite sufficient meaning to their lives. By contrast, ideologists have few fears about finding their daily bread. Their difficulty with life is less concrete. Their security gives them the leisure, their education the need, and no doubt their temperament the inclination, to find something above and beyond the flux of daily life.

If this is true, then ideology should flourish where education is widespread, and especially where opportunities are limited for the educated to lose themselves in grand projects, or to take leadership roles to which they believe that their education entitles them. The attractions of ideology are not so much to be found in the state of the world – always lamentable, but sometimes improving, at least in certain respects – but in states of mind. And in many parts of the world, the number of educated people has risen far faster than the capacity of economies to reward them with positions they believe commensurate with their attainments. Even in the most advanced economies, one will always find unhappy educated people searching for the reason that they are not as important as they should be.

One of the first to notice the politicisation of intellectuals was the French writer Julien Benda, whose 1927 *La trahison des clercs* – 'the treason of the clerks', with 'clerk' understood in its mediaeval sense as an educated person distinct from the uneducated laity – gave a phrase to educated discourse. Today, people most frequently use the phrase to signify the allegiance that intellectuals gave to Communism, despite the evident fact that the establishment of Communist regimes led everywhere and always to a decrease in the kind of intellectual freedom and respect for individual rights that intellectuals claimed to defend.

Benda meant something much wider by it, though support for Communism would have come under his rubric: the increasing tendency of intellectuals to pursue lines of thought not for the sake of truth, or for guiding humanity *sub specie aeternitatis*, but for the sake of attaining power by adopting, justifying, and manipulating the current political passions of sections of humanity, whether national, racial, religious, or economic. The political passions that Benda most feared when he wrote his book were nationalism, xenophobia, and anti-Semitism, which then had plenty of intellectual apologists, and which indeed soon proved cataclysmic in their effects; but really he was defending the autonomy of intellectual and artistic life from political imperatives.

That ideological ways of thinking have survived the collapse of Communism in Eastern Europe and the Soviet Union would not have surprised Benda. The collapse did severely reduce Marxism's attractiveness, and despite decades of attempts by intellectuals to dissociate the doctrine's supposed merits from the horrors of the Soviet system, it was only natural that many people believed that the death of Marxism meant the death of ideology itself. But as Benda might have predicted, what resulted instead was the balkanisation of ideology – the emergence of a wider choice of ideologies for adoption by those so inclined.

The most obvious example of an ideology that came into prominence – or better, prominently into our consciousness – after Communism's fall was Islamism. Because of its emphasis on returning to Islamic purity, and its apparent – indeed noisy – rejection of modernity, most people failed to notice how modern a phenomenon Islamism was, not just in time but in spirit. This is evident from reading just one of Islamism's foundational texts: Sayyid Qutb's *Milestones*, first published in 1964. The imprint of Marxism-Leninism is deep upon it, especially the Leninist component.

Qutb starts with cultural criticism that some might find eerily prescient. 'The leadership of mankind by Western man is now on the decline, not because Western culture has become poor materially or because its economic and military power has become weak,' he writes. 'The period of the Western system has come to an end primarily because it is deprived of those life-giving values which enabled it to be the leader of mankind.' Since, according to Qutb, those 'life-giving values' cannot come from the Eastern Bloc, he thinks (like Juan Domingo Perón, the Argentinean dictator, and Tony Blair, the former British Prime Minister) that a Third Way must exist: which, he says, can only be Islam.

Just as in Marx only the proletariat bears the whole of humanity's interests, so in Qutb only Muslims (true ones, that is) do. Everyone else is a factionalist. In Qutb's conception, the state withers away under Islam, just as it does – according to Marx – under Communism, once the true form is established. In Marx, the withering away comes about because there are no sectional material interests left that require a state to enforce them; in Qutb, there is no sectional interest left once true Islam is established because everyone obeys God's law without the need for interpretation and therefore for interpreters. And when all obey God's law, no conflict can arise because the law is perfect; therefore there is no need for a state apparatus.

One finds a unity of theory and praxis in both Qutb's Islamism and Marxism-Leninism. 'Philosophy and revolution are inseparable,' said Raya Dunayevskaya, once Trotsky's secretary and a prominent American Marxist (insofar as such can be said to have existed). And here is Qutb: 'Thus these two – preaching and the movement – united, confront 'the human situation' with all the necessary methods. For the achievement of freedom of man on earth – of all mankind throughout the earth – it is necessary that these methods should work side by side.'

Like Lenin, Qutb thought that violence would be necessary against the ruling class (of bourgeois in Lenin's case, unbelievers in Qutb's): 'Those who have usurped the authority of God and are oppressing God's creatures are not going to give up their power merely through preaching.' Again like Lenin, Qutb believed that until human authority disappeared, the leader's authority must be complete. Referring to 'the Arab' of the Meccan period – an age whose moral qualities he wants to restore – Qutb says: 'He was to be trained to follow the discipline of a community which is under the direction of a leader, and to refer to this leader in every matter and to obey his injunctions, even though they might be against his habit or taste.' Not much there with which Lenin could have disagreed. The British Stalinist historian Eric Hobsbawm wrote of himself: 'The Party had the first, or more precisely, the only real claim on our lives… Whatever it had ordered, we would have obeyed.'

Qutb is as explicit as Lenin that his party should be a vanguard and not a mass party, for only a vanguard will prove sufficiently dedicated to bring about the revolution. And like Leninism, Qutb's Islamism is dialectical:

> [Islam] does not face practical problems with abstract theories, nor does it confront various stages with unchangeable means. Those who talk about Jihaad in Islam and quote Qur'anic verses do not take into account this aspect, nor do they understand the nature of the various stages through which the movement develops, or the relationship of the verses revealed at various occasions with each stage.

Compare this with Lenin's *Left-Wing Communism, an Infantile Disorder*:

Right doctrinairism persisted in recognising only the old forms, and became utterly bankrupt, for it did not notice the new content. Left doctrinairism persists in the unconditional repudiation of certain old forms, failing to see that the new content is forcing its way through all and sundry forms, that it is our duty as Communists to master all forms, to learn how, with the maximum rapidity, to supplement one form with another, to substitute one for another, and to adapt our tactics to any such change that does not come from our class or from our efforts.

There are many other parallels between Leninism and Qutb's Islamism, among them the incompatibility of each with anything else, entailing a fight to the finish supposedly followed by permanent bliss for the whole of mankind; a tension between complete determinism (by history and by God, respectively) and the call to intense activism; and the view that only with the installation of their systems does Man become truly himself. For Qutb's worldview, therefore, the term Islamo-Leninism would be a more accurate description than Islamofascism.

Qutb was a strange man: he never married, for example, because (so he claimed) he found no woman of sufficient purity for him. You wouldn't need to be Freud to find the explanation suspect, or to find his reaction to Greeley, Colorado, in 1950, where he spent time on a scholarship – he saw it as a hotbed of unrestrained vice – somewhat hysterical, a cover for something seething deeply and disturbingly inside him. Devotion to an ideology can provide an answer of sorts to personal problems, and since personal problems are common, it isn't surprising that a number of people choose ideology as the solution.

Ideological thinking is not confined to the Islamists in our midst. The need for a simplifying lens that can screen out the intractabilities of life, and of our own lives in particular, springs eternal; and with the demise of Marxism in the West, at least in its most economistic form, a variety of substitute ideologies have arisen from which the disgruntled may choose.

Most started life as legitimate complaints, but as political reforms dealt with reasonable demands, the demands transformed themselves into ideologies, thus illustrating a fact of human psychology: rage is not always proportionate to its occasion but can be a powerful reward in itself. Feminists continued to see every human problem as a manifestation of patriarchy, civil-rights activists as a manifestation of racism, homosexual-rights activists as a manifestation of homophobia, anti-globalists as a manifestation of globalisation, and radical libertarians as a manifestation of state regulation.

How delightful to have a key to all the miseries, both personal and societal, and to know personal happiness through the single-minded pursuit of an end for the whole of humanity! At all costs, one must keep at bay the realisation that came early in life to John Stuart Mill, as he described it in his *Autobiography*. He asked himself:

> 'Suppose that all your objects in life were realised; that all the changes in institutions and opinions which you are looking forward to, could be effected at this very instant: would this be a great joy and happiness to you?' And an irrepressible self-consciousness distinctly answered, 'No!' At this my heart sank within me: the whole foundation on which my life was constructed fell down. All my happiness was to have been found in the continual pursuit of this end. The end had ceased to charm, and how could there ever again be any interest in the means? I seemed to have nothing left to live for.

This is the question that all ideologists fear, and it explains why reform, far from delighting them, only increases their anxiety and rage. It also explains why traditional religious belief is not an ideology in the sense in which I am using the term, for unlike ideology, it explicitly recognises the limitations of earthly existence, what we can expect of it, and what we can do by our own unaided efforts. Some ideologies have the flavour of religion; but the absolute certainty of, say, the Anabaptists of Münster, or of today's Islamists, is ultimately irreligious, since they claimed or claim to know in the very last detail what God requires of us.

The most popular and widest-ranging ideology in the West today is environmentalism, replacing not only Marxism but all the nationalist and xenophobic ideologies that Benda accused intellectuals of espousing in the 1920s. Now, no one who has suffered respiratory difficulties because of smog, or seen the effects of unrestrained industrial pollution, can be indifferent to the environmental consequences of man's activities; pure *laissez-faire* will not do. But it isn't difficult to spot in environmentalists' work something more than mere concern with a practical problem. Their writings often show themselves akin to the calls to repentance of seventeenth-century divines in the face of plague epidemics, but with the patina of rationality that every ideology needs to disguise its true source in existential angst.

For example, a recent column in *The Guardian*, by the environmental campaigner George Monbiot, carried the headline, 'The planet is now so vandalised that only total energy renewal can save us.' Monbiot, it is true, does not offer us heaven on earth if we follow his prescriptions; only the bare – and by no means certain, for 'we might have left it too late' – avoidance of total biological annihilation. But behind Monbiot's urgency, even hysteria, one senses a deep lust for power. He cannot really believe what he says, for starters. 'Do we want to be remembered,' he asks rhetorically, 'as the generation that saved the banks but let the biosphere collapse?' If it is really true that we must either have 'total energy renewal' or die, however, we cannot be remembered as the generation that let the biosphere collapse, for if we let it collapse, *ex hypothesi* no one will be around to remember us. This reminds me of patients I used to see who would threaten suicide, in the clear expectation of a long life ahead, unless someone did what they wanted. And though Monbiot says that it is uncertain that anything we do now will make any difference, he nevertheless proposes that every human being on the earth follow his prescriptions.

The environmentalist ideology threatens to make serious inroads into the rule of law in Britain. In 2008, six environmentalists were acquitted of having caused £35,000 worth of damage to a power station in Kent – not because they did not do it but because four witnesses, including a Greenlander, testified to the reality of global warming.

One recalls the disastrous 1878 jury acquittal in St. Petersburg of Vera Zasulich for the attempted assassination of General Trepov, on the grounds of the supposed purity of her motives. The acquittal destroyed all hope of establishing the rule of law in Russia and ushered in an age of terrorism that led directly to one of the greatest catastrophes in human history.

A GROSS DECEPTION

IN BRITAIN, GOVERNMENT SPENDING is now so high, accounting for more than half of the economy, that it is increasingly difficult to distinguish the private sector from the public. Many supposedly private companies are as dependent on government largesse as welfare recipients are, and much of the money with which the government pays them is borrowed. The nation's budget deficit in 2010, in the wake of the financial crisis, was 10.4 per cent of GDP, after being 12.5 per cent in 2009; even before the crisis, the country had managed to balance its budget for only three years out of the previous 30.

Deficits are like smoking: difficult to give up. They can be cut only at the cost of genuine hardship, for many people will have become dependent upon them for their livelihoods. Hence withdrawal symptoms are likely to be severe; and hardship is always politically hazardous to inflict, even when it is a necessary corrective to previous excess. This is what Britain faces.

For some politicians, running up deficits is not a problem but a benefit, since doing so creates a population permanently in thrall to them for the favours by which it lives. The politicians are thus like drug dealers, profiting from their clientele's dependence, yet on a scale incomparably larger. The Swedish Social Democrats understood long ago that if more than half of the population became economically dependent on government, either directly or indirectly, no government of any party could easily change the arrangement. It was not a crude one-party system that the Social Democrats sought, but a one-policy system, and they almost succeeded.

For countries that operate such a one-policy system, especially as badly as Britain does, economic reality is apt to administer nasty shocks from time to time, requiring action. When the new coalition government came into power last year, the economic situation was cataclysmic. The budget deficit was vast; the country had a large trade deficit; the population was among the most heavily indebted in the world; and the savings rate was nil. Room for manoeuvre was therefore extremely limited.

The previous years of fool's gold – asset inflation brought by easy credit – had allowed the Labour government to expand public spending enormously without damaging apparent prosperity. Gordon Brown, as Chancellor of the Exchequer and then Prime Minister, boasted that he had found the elixir of growth: his boom, unlike all others in history, would not be followed by bust. During Brown's years in office, however, three-quarters of Britain's new employment was in the public sector, a fifth of it in the National Health Service alone. Educational and healthcare spending skyrocketed. The economy of many areas of the country grew so dependent on public expenditure that they became like the Soviet Union with supermarkets.

Britain was living on borrowed money, consuming today what it would have to pay for tomorrow, the day after tomorrow, and the day after that; the national debt increased at a rate unmatched in peacetime; and when the music stopped, the state found itself holding unprecedented obligations, with no means of paying them. Without aggressive reforms, it was clear, Britain would soon have to default on its debt or debauch its currency. Both alternatives were fraught with dire consequences.

In the end, the new government chose to attack the deficit from both ends: by cutting spending and by increasing taxes. As many commentators noted, this approach risked a reduction of aggregate demand so great that short-term growth would be impossible and a prolonged recession, even depression, would be probable. Domestic demand would plummet, and export-led growth, many feared, would not be able to rescue the economy, for two reasons: first, Britain's industry was so debilitated that its competitiveness in sophisticated markets could not be restored from one day to the next by, say, a favourable change in the exchange rate; and second, the country's traditional export markets were experiencing difficulties of their own.

But the general economic argument was not what fueled the fierce intellectual and street protests that in recent months have opposed the government's efforts to reduce the deficit – efforts so far more symbolic than real, for state borrowing requirements have only increased since the coalition's arrival in power. Nor were the protests directed against the tax increases. Since the end of World War II, the British have grown accustomed to the idea that the money in their pockets is what the government graciously consents to leave them after it has taken its share. When (as rarely happens) the Chancellor of the Exchequer reduces a tax instead of increasing it, even conservative newspapers say that he has 'given money away', as if all money came from him in the first place. The wealth is the government's and the fullness thereof: where such a belief is prevalent, no tax increase will seem either illegitimate or oppressive.

What did provoke the furious opposition was the government's proposals to reduce spending in such areas as education and healthcare, as well as its plan to increase tuition at public universities. Hundreds of thousands of demonstrators, disproportionately consisting of public workers and students, gathered on London's streets. One demonstrator, Charlie Gilmour, became famous. The adopted son of the lead guitarist of Pink Floyd, with a personal fortune in the tens of millions of pounds, he was the very image of the caviar anarchist. Dressed expensively in black and booted to match, his dark locks flowing poetically behind him, he stomped the roofs of cars and stormed the Cenotaph, the most important war memorial in the country. Later, he claimed not to have realised what it was, though he was a student – of history, no less – at Cambridge, and you would need to be either illiterate or virtually blind to miss the words 'OUR GLORIOUS DEAD' inscribed on it. His contrition and appearance in court in a suit and tie, in an attempt to avoid a prison sentence, afforded the nation some light relief in these most difficult times.

The student demonstrators were right to be angry, but their anger was misdirected. They were merely protesting at the prospect of paying for their education, which would force upon them or their parents the difficult but important question of whether the university education that they received was worth the debt that they would incur to pay for it. How easy it is to proceed to college without having to consider such sordid matters, or make such difficult calculations, because the state – that is to say, the taxpayer – subsidises you!

In fact, British young people have been subjected to a gross deception, which, if they recognised it, would make them far angrier than the demonstrators were. The previous government decreed that 50 per cent of British youth should attend university, irrespective of students' educational attainment or of the economy's capacity to make use of so many graduates. In so doing, it doubled state expenditure on education in only eight years. This centralised planning had a predictable effect: the standard of university teaching and education fell significantly, as did the value of the average degree. While the number of graduates expanded, employers complained that young Britons were increasingly unable to write a simple sentence properly or do basic arithmetic.

For the students, however, the connotation of university education lagged behind its denotation: in other words, though education declined in quality, students felt entitled to the same advantages that had accrued to graduates back when education was better. Graduates grumbled about the lowly positions that they had to take after graduating, which people who had not gone to university would once have satisfactorily filled. It was perhaps unsurprising, then, that students, suddenly asked to fund their delayed maturation for themselves, should explode in wrath. They saw the reform not as an attempt to align education with the needs and capacities of the real economy – by making students question the value of education and by encouraging universities to offer something of real value – but as a means of restricting access to education to the rich; this despite the fact that the total loan necessary to obtain a university education, supposedly an advantage for life, would still be a fraction of an average mortgage.

The biggest demonstration against the government's proposals was on March 26. A quarter of a million people took to the streets – in solidarity with themselves. Many were teachers protesting the proposed cuts in education spending. Yet after a compulsory education lasting 11 years and costing, on average, £60,000 per pupil, about a fifth of British students who do not attend university after secondary school are barely able to read and write, according to a recent study from Sheffield University. Considering the disastrous personal consequences of being illiterate in a modern society, this is a gargantuan scandal, amounting to large-scale theft by the educational authorities. No anarchist ever smashed a window because of this scandal, however; and so it is impossible to resist the conclusion that the demonstration was in defence of unearned salaries, not (as alleged) of actual services worth defending.

Protesters were also agitating against proposed cuts to the National Health Service. The cumulative increase in spending on the NHS from 1997 to 2007 was equal to about a third of the national debt. After all this spending, Britain remains what it has long been: by far the most unpleasant country in Western Europe in which to be ill, especially if one is poor. Not coincidentally, Britain's healthcare system is still the most centralised, the most Soviet-like, in the Western world. Our rates of post-operative infection are the highest in Europe, our cancer survival rates the lowest; the neglect of elderly hospital patients is so common as to be practically routine. One has the impression that even if we devoted our entire GDP to the NHS, old people would still be left to dehydrate in the hospitals.

From 1997 to 2007, the number of people employed by the NHS rose by a third, with the number of doctors employed by it doubling and overall remuneration for personnel increasing by 50 per cent per head. Yet it became ever more difficult for patients to see the same doctor twice, even during a single hospital admission; the standard of medical training declined, according to 99 per cent of surgeons in training, while senior surgeons admitted that they wouldn't want their trainees operating on them; and a government inquiry found that productivity in the NHS – admittedly, not easy to measure – had declined markedly.

Wherever one looks into the expanded public sector, one finds the same thing: a tremendous rise in salaries, pensions, and perquisites for those working in it. In Manchester, for example, the number of council employees earning more than £50,000 a year rose from 68 to 1,746 between 1997 and 2007. In effect, a large public service *nomenklatura* was created, whose purpose, or at least effect, was to establish an immense network of patronage and reciprocal obligation: a network easy to install but hard to dislodge, since those charged with removing it would be the very people who benefited most from it.

One of the Labour government's gifts to public employees was overly generous pensions. While Gordon Brown raised taxes on pensions funded by private savings, he increased pensions for public sector workers. In many cases, these government pensions, if they had not been paid for with current tax receipts and (to a growing extent) borrowing, would have required funds of millions of dollars to support. In other words, Brown was Bernard Madoff with powers of taxation. I leave it to readers to decide whether that makes him better or worse than Madoff.

The press usually defends the public sector, viewing it as an expression of the general will and a manifestation of a rationally planned society, manned by selfless workers. It was thus quick to warn of the direst possible consequences of Cameron and Clegg's austerity measures: school overcrowding, unnecessary deaths in hospitals, fewer or no social services. The streets would run with blood; mass poverty would return.

Unfortunately, it does not follow from the existence of immense waste in the public sector that budget cuts will target that waste. After all, most of the excess is in wages, precisely the element of government spending that those in charge of proposed reductions will be most anxious to preserve. It is therefore in their interest that any budget reduction should affect disproportionately the service that it is their purpose to provide: cases of hardship will then result, the media will take them up, and the public will blame them on the spending cuts and force the government to return to the *status quo ante*. Another advantage of cutting services rather than waste, from the perspective of the public employee, is that it makes it appear that the budget was previously a model of economy, already pared to the bone.

I have seen it all before, whenever cuts became necessary in the NHS budget, as periodically they did. Wards closed, but the savings achieved were minimal because labour legislation required the staff – the major cost of the system – to be retained. Surgical operations were likewise cancelled, though again the staff was kept on. To effect any savings in this manner, it was necessary for the system to become more and more inefficient and unproductive. It was as if the bureaucracy had reversed the cry of the people at the beginning of Lewis Carroll's *Sylvie and Bruno*, 'More bread! Less taxes!', replacing it with 'More taxes! Less bread!'

So it is not surprising that *The Guardian*, which one could almost call the public sector workers' mouthpiece, has reported that hospital emergency departments are already feeling the budgetary pressure and risk being overwhelmed, even before the cuts have been implemented in full. Meanwhile, one can still find plenty of bureaucratic jobs advertised in the *Health Service Journal*, the publication for non-medical employees of the NHS. One hospital seeks an Associate Director of Equality, Diversity, and Human Rights; another is looking for an Interim Deputy Director of Operations and Transformation. Part of the 'transformation' in that case seems to be a reduction in the hospital's budget, and it is instructive that the person who will be second in command of that reduction will be paid between £600 and £800 per day.

The legacy of Britain's previous government, which expanded the public sector incontinently, is thus an almost Marxian conflict of classes, not between the haves and have-nots (for many of the people in the public service are now well-heeled indeed) but between those who pay taxes and those who consume them.

In this conflict, one side is bound to be more militant and ruthless than the other, since taxes are increased incrementally – and everyone is already accustomed to them, anyway – but jobs are lost instantaneously and catastrophically, with the direst personal consequences. Thus those who oppose tax increases and favour government retrenchment will seldom behave as aggressively as those who will suffer personally from budget reductions. Moreover, when, as in Britain, entire areas have lived on government charity for many years – with millions dependent on it for virtually every mouthful of food, every scrap of clothing, every moment of distraction by television – common humanity dictates care in altering the system. The extreme difficulty of reducing subventions once they have been granted should serve as a warning against instituting them in the first place, but in Britain, it appears, it never will. We seem caught in an eternal cycle, in which a period of government overspending and intervention leads to economic crisis and hence to a period of austerity, which, once it is over, is replaced by a new period of government overspending and intervention, promoted by politicians, half charlatan and half self-deluded, who promise the electorate the sun, moon, and stars.

When our new government came into power – after a period in opposition during which, fearing unpopularity, it failed to explain the real fiscal situation to the electorate – there was broad, if reluctant, acceptance that something unpleasant had to be done; otherwise, Britain would soon be like Greece without the sunshine. But the acceptance was on narrow grounds only, and this is worrying because it implies that we are far from liberating ourselves from the binge-followed-by-austerity cycle. A large part of the public still views the state as the provider of first resort, which means that the public will remain what it now is: the servant of its public servants.

As soon as the crisis is over, though this may not be for some time, the politicians are likely again to offer the public security and excitement, wealth and leisure, education and distraction, capital accumulation without the need to save, health and safety, happiness and antidepressants, and all the other *desiderata* of human existence. The public will believe the politicians because – to adapt slightly the great dictum of Louis Pasteur – impossible political promises are believed only by the prepared mind. And our minds have been prepared for a long time, since the time of the Fabians at least.

If you have enjoyed this book, please do mention it to your friends and family. As a small, independent publisher, Monday Books unfortunately lacks the resources for nationwide publicity campaigns, and so relies greatly on, and is very grateful for, word-of-mouth recommendation and support.

Our books are available in most good bookshops, from various online retailers and from our own website, www.mondaybooks.com (with free p&p through the UK on all titles, and worldwide on all paperbacks). Our titles are also available as eBooks at Amazon and iTunes.

Our blog, at www.mondaybooks.wordpress.com, carries information about forthcoming titles and the company generally.

Not With A Bang But A Whimper / **Theodore Dalrymple**
(hbk, £14.99)

IN A SERIES of penetrating and beautifully-written essays, Theodore Dalrymple explains his belief that a liberal intelligentsia is destroying Britain. Dalrymple writes for *The Spectator, The Times, The Daily Telegraph, New Statesman, The Times Literary Supplement* and the *British Medical Journal.*

'Theodore Dalrymple's clarity of thought, precision of expression and constant, terrible disappointment give his dispatches from the frontline a tone and a quality entirely their own... their rarity makes you sit up and take notice'
- *Marcus Berkmann, The Spectator*

'Dalrymple is a modern master'
- *The Guardian*

'Dalrymple is the George Orwell of our times... he is a writer of genius'
- *Dennis Dutton*

Second Opinion: A Doctor's Dispatches from the Inner City
Theodore Dalrymple (hdbk, £14.99)

THEODORE DALRYMPLE has spent much of his working life as a doctor in a grim inner city hospital and the nearby prison; his patients are drug addicts and drunks, violent men and battered women, suicidal teenagers and despairing elderly. For many years, Dalrymple - acknowledged as the world's leading doctor-writer - wrote a column in The Spectator in which he recounted his experiences. This collection of those shocking, amusing and elegant columns offers a window into a world many of us never see.

'**The harsh truths he tells are all the more shocking because the media, in general, is unwilling to tell them**' - *Daily Telegraph*

'**He actually cares about the people at the bottom of the social heap while public sector jobsworths and slimy politicians only pretend to**' - *Daily Express*

'**A rare voice of truth**' - *The Spectator*

'**He could not be further from the stereotype of the "little Englander" conservative... he is arguably our greatest living essayist**' - *Standpoint*

From all good bookshops, online from www.mondaybooks.com or via 01455 221752.
All of our titles are also available as eBooks from amazon.co.uk

Sick Notes / **Dr Tony Copperfield**

(ppbk, £8.99)

WELCOME TO the bizarre world of Tony Copperfield, family doctor. He spends his days fending off anxious mums, elderly sex maniacs and hopeless hypochondriacs (with his eyes peeled for the odd serious symptom). The rest of his time is taken up sparring with colleagues, battling bureaucrats and banging his head against the brick walls of the NHS.

If you've ever wondered what your GP is really thinking - and what's actually going on behind the scenes at your surgery - *SICK NOTES* is for you.

'A wonderful book, funny and insightful in equal measure'
– Dr Phil Hammond (Private Eye's 'MD')

'Copperfield is simply fantastic, unbelievably funny and improbably wise... everything he writes is truer than fact'
– British Medical Journal

'Original, funny and an incredible read' *– The Sun*

Tony Copperfield is a Medical Journalist of the Year, has been shortlisted for UK Columnist of the Year many times and writes regularly for *The Times* and other media.

***When Science Goes Wrong* / Simon LeVay**

(ppbk, £7.99)

WE LIVE in times of astonishing scientific progress. But for every stunning triumph there are hundreds of cock-ups, damp squibs and disasters. Escaped anthrax spores and nuclear explosions, tiny data errors which send a spacecraft hurtling to oblivion, innocent men jailed on 'infallible' DNA evidence…just some of the fascinating and disturbing tales from the dark side of discovery.

'Spine-tingling, occasionally gruesome accounts of well-meant but disastrous scientific bungling'
– The Los Angeles Times

'Entertaining and thought-provoking'
– Publisher's Weekly

'The dark – but fascinating – side of science… an absorbing read' *– GeoTimes*

**From all good bookshops, online from
www.mondaybooks.com or via 01455 221752.
All of our titles are also available as eBooks from amazon.co.uk**

A Paramedic's Diary / Stuart Gray
(ppbk, £7.99)

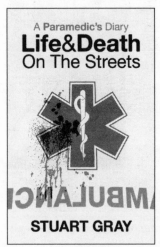

STUART GRAY is a paramedic dealing with the worst life can throw at him. *A Paramedic's Diary* is his gripping, blow-by-blow account of a year on the streets – 12 rollercoaster months of enormous highs and tragic lows. One day he'll save a young mother's life as she gives birth, the next he might watch a young girl die on the tarmac in front of him after a hit-and-run. A gripping, entertaining and often amusing read by a talented new writer.

As heard on BBC Radio 4's Saturday Live and BBC Radio 5 Live's Donal McIntyre Show and Simon Mayo

In April 2010, Stuart Gray was named one of the country's 'best 40 bloggers' by *The Times*

So That's Why They Call It Great Britain / Steve Pope
(ppbk, £7.99)

FROM THE steam engine to the jet engine to the engine of the world wide web, to vaccination and penicillin, to Viagra, chocolate bars, the flushing loo, the G&T, ibruprofen and the telephone... this is the truly astonishing story of one tiny country and its gifts to the world.

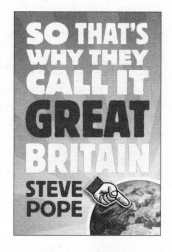

***Perverting The Course Of Justice* / Inspector Gadget**
(ppbk, £7.99)

A SENIOR serving policeman picks up where PC Copperfield left off and reveals how far the insanity extends – children arrested for stealing sweets from each other while serious criminals go about their business unmolested.

'**Exposes the reality of life at the sharp end**'
– *The Daily Telegraph*

'**No wonder they call us Plods... A frustrated inspector speaks out on the madness of modern policing**'
– *The Daily Mail*

'**Staggering... exposes the bloated bureaucracy that is crushing Britain**' – *The Daily Express*

'**You must buy this book... it is a fascinating insight**'
– *Kelvin MacKenzie, The Sun*

In April 2010, Inspector Gadget was named
one of the country's 'best 40 bloggers' by *The Times*.

**From all good bookshops, online from
www.mondaybooks.com or via 01455 221752.**
All of our titles are also available as eBooks from amazon.co.uk

Wasting Police Time / **PC David Copperfield** (ppbk, £7.99)

THE FASCINATING, hilarious and best-selling inside story of the madness of modern policing. A serving officer - writing deep under cover - reveals everything the government wants hushed up about life on the beat.

'**Very revealing**' – *The Daily Telegraph*
'**Passionate, important, interesting and genuinely revealing**' – *The Sunday Times*
'**Graphic, entertaining and sobering**' – *The Observer*
'**A huge hit... will make you laugh out loud**'
– *The Daily Mail*
'**Hilarious... should be compulsory reading for our political masters**' – *The Mail on Sunday*
'**More of a fiction than Dickens**'
– *Tony McNulty MP, former Police Minister*
(On a BBC *Panorama* programme about PC Copperfield, McNulty was later forced to admit that this statement, made in the House of Commons, was itself inaccurate)

Generation F / **Winston Smith**

(ppbk, £8.99)

YOUTH WORKER Winston Smith
- winner of the Orwell Prize for his
edgy, controversial and passionate
writing - opens a door on the murky,
tragic world of children's care homes
and supported housing schemes.
Frightening, revealing and sometimes
very funny, *Generation F* is his story.

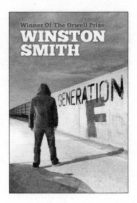

'Winston Smith paints a terrifying picture'
- *The Daily Mail*

'What carried the day was his passion and conviction
that we should know what wrongs had been done in our
names' - *Orwell Prize judges*

In Foreign Fields / **Dan Collins**

(ppbk, £7.99)

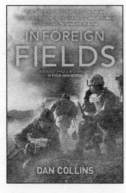

A STAGGERING collection of 25 true-life stories of astonishing battlefield bravery from Iraq and Afghanistan... medal-winning soldiers, Marines and RAF men, who stared death in the face, in their own words.

'**Enthralling and awe-inspiring untold stories**'
– *The Daily Mail*

'**Astonishing feats of bravery illustrated in laconic, first-person prose**' – *Independent on Sunday*

'**The book everyone's talking about... a gripping account of life on the frontlines of Iraq and Afghanistan**'
– *News of the World*

'**An outstanding read**' – *Soldier Magazine*

Kidnapped / **Colin Freeman**

(ppbk, £8.99)

WHAT'S IT like to be kidnapped by khat-chewing Somali pirates who are armed to the teeth and would kill you in a heartbeat? Colin Freeman, *Sunday Telegraph* foreign correspondent, found out the hard way. This is the story of his terrifying ordeal in captivity – an astonishing adventure told in a surprisingly funny and fond way.

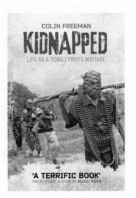

'More than simply a terrific book on the scourge of Somali piracy, Freeman's wry style and heartfelt candour raises *Kidnapped* to the highest rank'
– **Tim Butcher, author of *Blood River***

'A witty and admirable account... Self deprecating humour which makes you laugh out loud'
– ***The Daily Telegraph***

'Brings humour to otherwise serious proceedings, from the complexities of toilette in arid mountains to talking football with his abductors, and also gives a frank account of the nuts and bolts of foreign news reporting'
– ***The Independent***